THE
EVERYTHING.
GUIDE TO
INVESTING IN CRYPTOCURRENCY

Dear Reader,

After over a decade of covering investing topics as a journalist and writer, it's rare for me to see much excitement in the tools we invest in. Sure, everyone is out to get rich, but normally investors reserve their adrenaline for specific stocks while portfolio managers stick to whatever strategy they're pitching. Most veteran investors hardly allow a hint of emotion trickle as they lay out their thesis. Maybe that's why I found bitcoin so interesting when I got my first chance to write about it a few years ago. Supporters used emotional pleas to convince the world it wasn't just a currency or just an investment. It was a way of life. A philosophy.

Despite this enthusiasm, few could legitimately predict what would happen to bitcoin in 2017 when suddenly some of these advocates turned into millionaires. Discussing cryptos then turned into a much larger conversation as supporters were emboldened by the price appreciation. Expressing skepticism in the crypto discussion seemed on par with rejecting someone's religion or worldview. The problem? People weren't just investing in cryptos. They were placing their hopes and dreams on the rise and fall of a coin that had no long-term track record.

That's why I decided to write this book. It's a detailed introduction to what a new crypto investor should know about these coins, beyond the blind narrative that they're destined for growth. With this information and basic understanding in hand, you can form a calculated opinion of a coin and the risks involved, and determine for yourself just how much you're willing to put into either the future of currency or simply the next in a long line of investment fads.

It's up to you to decide.

Ryan Derousseau

Welcome to the EVERYTHING® Series!

These handy, accessible books give you all you need to tackle a difficult project, gain a new hobby, comprehend a fascinating topic, prepare for an exam, or even brush up on something you learned back in school but have since forgotten.

You can choose to read an Everything® book from cover to cover or just pick out the information you want from our four useful boxes: e-questions, e-facts, e-alerts, and e-ssentials.

We give you everything you need to know on the subject, but throw in a lot of fun stuff along the way too.

We now have more than 400 Everything® books in print, spanning such wide-ranging categories as weddings, pregnancy, cooking, music instruction, foreign language, crafts, pets, New Age, and so much more. When you're done reading them all, you can finally say you know Everything®!

QUESTION

Answers to
common questions

FACT

Important snippets
of information

ALERT

Urgent
warnings

ESSENTIAL

Quick
handy tips

PUBLISHER Karen Cooper

MANAGING EDITOR Lisa Laing

COPY CHIEF Casey Ebert

ASSOCIATE PRODUCTION EDITOR Jo-Anne Duhamel

ACQUISITIONS EDITOR Zander Hatch

DEVELOPMENT EDITOR Peter Archer

EVERYTHING® SERIES COVER DESIGNER Erin Alexander

Visit the entire Everything® series at www.everything.com

THE
EVERYTHING®
GUIDE TO
INVESTING IN
CRYPTO
CURRENCY

**From Bitcoin to Ripple, the Safe and Secure Way
to Buy, Trade, and Mine Digital Currencies**

Ryan Derousseau, Regular Contributor to *Fortune* and *Money*

Adams Media
New York   London   Toronto   Sydney   New Delhi

Adams Media
An Imprint of Simon & Schuster, Inc.
57 Littlefield Street
Avon, Massachusetts 02322

Copyright © 2019 by Simon & Schuster, Inc.

All rights reserved, including the right to reproduce this book or portions thereof in any form whatsoever. For information address Adams Media Subsidiary Rights Department, 1230 Avenue of the Americas, New York, NY 10020.

An Everything® Series Book.
Everything® and Everything.com® are registered trademarks of Simon & Schuster, Inc.

First Adams Media trade paperback edition March 2019

ADAMS MEDIA and colophon are trademarks of Simon & Schuster.

For information about special discounts for bulk purchases, please contact Simon & Schuster Special Sales at 1-866-506-1949 or business@simonandschuster.com.

The Simon & Schuster Speakers Bureau can bring authors to your live event. For more information or to book an event contact the Simon & Schuster Speakers Bureau at 1-866-248-3049 or visit our website at www.simonspeakers.com.

Manufactured in the United States of America

1 0 9 8 7 6 5 4 3 2 1

Library of Congress Cataloging-in-Publication Data
Names: Derousseau, Ryan, author.
Title: The everything® guide to investing in cryptocurrency / Ryan Derousseau, regular contributor to Fortune and Money.
Description: Avon, Massachusetts: Adams Media, 2019.
Series: Everything®.
Includes index.
Identifiers: LCCN 2018055599 | ISBN 9781507209325 (pb) | ISBN 9781507209332 (ebook)
Subjects: LCSH: Cryptocurrencies. | Bitcoin. | Electronic funds transfers. | Investments.
Classification: LCC HG1710 .D47 2019 | DDC 332.4--dc23
LC record available at https://lccn.loc.gov/2018055599

ISBN 978-1-5072-0932-5
ISBN 978-1-5072-0933-2 (ebook)

Many of the designations used by manufacturers and sellers to distinguish their products are claimed as trademarks. Where those designations appear in this book and Simon & Schuster, Inc., was aware of a trademark claim, the designations have been printed with initial capital letters.

This publication is designed to provide accurate and authoritative information with regard to the subject matter covered. It is sold with the understanding that the publisher is not engaged in rendering legal, accounting, or other professional advice. If legal advice or other expert assistance is required, the services of a competent professional person should be sought.
—From a *Declaration of Principles* jointly adopted by a Committee of the American Bar Association and a Committee of Publishers and Associations

Acknowledgments

To my parents, who sat me down at the table and drilled me on multiplication tables until it became second nature. (I also have to give a nod to the calculator I now use instead!) To my early editors and sources that taught me the tools to evaluate an investment, which has kept me safe professionally and financially. And to my wife and kid, who get to listen to me rant about these esoteric topics on a regular basis.

Contents

Introduction

IF YOU'VE BEEN FOLLOWING the news, you've probably heard about something called "cryptocurrencies." You've heard they can appreciate in value by hundreds of dollars. You've also heard that their value sometimes crashes overnight, never to recover. You've wondered if you should invest in them. But just what are cryptocurrencies?

This book answers that question for you. It tells you what cryptocurrencies are, why they're important, and why you may consider investing in them, if you like to gamble.

You'll also look at questions like:

- How is the value of cryptocurrency such as bitcoin determined?
- What's a blockchain, and why is it important to cryptocurrencies?
- What purpose do these things we call cryptocurrencies serve?
- How do you make money from cryptocurrencies?
- How life-changing will these currencies be in the next decade and beyond?

If you're thinking of investing in this new field, it's on you to conduct the research and delve into what makes a new cryptocurrency different, unique, or special. Since it's such a new market, the research you conduct will determine how much you believe in the future of cryptocurrencies. There's almost unanimous consensus about the potential of the blockchain. Some claim the blockchain is the most important invention since the Internet itself. Billions of dollars have flowed into it. Where cryptocurrencies fit in a future where the blockchain is ever-present will determine whether these coins can pay off big in your investment portfolio. No one wants to miss out on a big payday if cryptocurrency really takes off.

Investing in bitcoin or another cryptocurrency is like any other kind of investing: the more you know, the better and more intelligent your strategy will be. And the greater the chances are that it pays off. This book will give you the guidance and initial understanding of the concepts and strategies used to safely invest in cryptocurrencies. It's a resource to provide you with the tools so you can safely explore this new world. With *The Everything®* *Guide to Investing in Cryptocurrency* in your hand you can step confidently into this new world of investing and hope your money will grow.

This book tells you what cryptocurrencies are, why they're important, and why you may consider investing in them, if you like to gamble.

CHAPTER 1

Welcome to the Cryptocurrency Craze

In a matter of only a few years, bitcoin has transformed from a theory into one of the era's most closely watched and intriguing investment trends. Potential for the coin and other cryptocurrencies now run the gamut, depending on whom you talk to. Some prognosticators have argued that the price of bitcoin will reach beyond $100,000. Many others claim it's a bubble on the level of the largest market mirages in history. Such is the world of cryptocurrency investing where the truth likely lies somewhere in the middle. Now that you're thinking of entering the space, make sure to embrace some of that excitement, but also keep in mind what you're buying when you declare yourself a crypto investor. It's far more than purchasing a digital coin. This chapter offers an initial explanation of cryptocurrencies and will serve as a first step on your new journey.

What Are Cryptocurrencies?

At its basic level, cryptocurrencies are a very simple concept. They're digital coins, created online, and meant for online spending. Developed via software code, cryptos are a way to transfer value, most often via digital means, like when you're purchasing something online.

FACT

While the spending of bitcoins launched on the Internet has primarily been relegated to the online world, there are ways in which you can use them in your everyday shopping. The payment processor company Square gives its merchants the option to accept bitcoins. This allows any shop that uses Square's functionality, from the antique store to your local coffee shop, to accept bitcoins.

Take a very simple scenario, such as using a quarter to purchase a piece of gum. When you buy that gum, you're giving the quarter to a shopkeeper in order to pay for the slice of gum. The quarter is a tangible coin that a US shopkeeper trusts. He knows that if he takes the quarter, it will cover the cost of the gum and the profit that he expected to gain from the sale. It's a very predictable transaction. A quarter's value doesn't change all that dramatically in a short time. What will cost twenty-five cents today will likely run twenty-five cents tomorrow. (Over many years, that quarter won't buy you as much, due to inflation, but for the short term, it does, which is valuable for commerce.)

One bitcoin is essentially the same as a quarter except it's not tangible. It's a piece of code, and only you, as the owner, have the identifier, which is known as the coin's key. You can pass that identifier on to someone else, in order to purchase an item. That person then receives a new identifier for the bitcoin, and the old identifier becomes obsolete. You can't actually hold bitcoin. You can't feel it. But when someone accepts bitcoin, she is viewing it the same way as that quarter.

But one bitcoin has grown to become much more expensive than one slice of gum. That's because a whole community has grown around the cryptocurrency craze, willing to give bitcoin owners more and more for that one coin.

Why Would Anyone Want This Digital Coin?

If bitcoin and other cryptocurrencies function just like regular money, then why would anyone want to use them instead of the fiat currency (that is, the regular currency) that we all are used to? It's a fair question, one that the world has only begun to sort out. The answer depends greatly on who you are and why you're choosing to use the coin.

The Anti-Federal Reserve Crowd

Early adopters saw bitcoin as a tool to spend without requiring a central bank to dictate the terms of the currency. Regular currency, like the US dollar, is subject to inflation. This is, to an extent, controlled by the Federal Reserve. It increases or decreases the amount of money flowing through the world markets through its use of interest rates. On a very basic level, when there's more money flowing into the market, then the supply rises, decreasing the value of one dollar. When the Fed restricts dollars, then the value rises. The Federal Reserve does this to retain a consistent inflation rate, so the economy doesn't grow too fast. Hyper-growth can lead to an overvaluation of goods you purchase, which would hurt the currency. Hyperinflation leads to a devaluation of the currency altogether and the Federal Reserve is mandated to try and hold inflation in check.

ALERT

This is a very simplistic definition of inflation. Since the economy has become global in nature, there are a lot of factors that would increase demand in the US dollar, like a devaluation of a foreign currency. The Federal Reserve must account for all of those factors, as it sets interest rates.

Digital coin enthusiasts don't believe that government entities should have the power to dictate these fluctuations in the money supply. One of the original goals of a cryptocurrency is to avoid inflation altogether. That's why bitcoin has a maximum number of coins—21 million—it can ever have in circulation.

The Business Case for Cryptocurrencies

What started as a libertarian dream, however, actually has a legitimate business use. It costs money to spend money. As odd as that is, there's a reason banks and financial institutions have grown so large. It's because they can collect fees in countless number of ways as money moves through their systems. For businesses, this can become very costly.

One of the easiest ways to imagine this is when you're going on a trip to Europe and you have to exchange dollars for euros. When you go to the exchange counter at the airport, you not only receive less money back than you put in—because the dollar is worth less than a euro—but you also lose a large chunk to a fee that the exchange agency charges to give you the euro. Now imagine that on a wide scale, where a business is making exchanges in the millions of dollars every day. Clearly there is an incentive to reduce that cost.

FACT

The US Treasury handles the actual dollar development and distribution, but it's dictated by the interest rate determined by the Federal Reserve. If the Fed decreases the interest rate, then it encourages banks to borrow more funds since the cost has dropped. Rate increases discourage borrowing, since it's expensive, and therefore, less money flows through the financial system.

That's where a digital coin has an advantage, since it isn't tangible. It can serve as an independent third party. Instead of going to a teller, you could use bitcoin to exchange the dollars by buying bitcoin with US dollars then selling them for euros once in Europe. The transaction is processed on bitcoin's decentralized platform, leaving the transaction fee for processing the digital coin as the only fee the company has to pay. That saves you the cost of the much higher exchange fee created by the middleman. Financial institutions and other organizations are seeing the value of that, particularly in areas where the local currencies aren't as stable.

The Everyday Use of Cryptocurrencies

When evaluating why you and other regular spenders of currency would want to use cryptocurrencies, the discussion becomes a little more difficult.

While there are benefits to a digital coin that's un-hackable, lives online, and will transfer almost immediately to the retailer when you purchase an item, it hasn't outweighed the ease of use and trust in the American dollar. Whether cryptos become a more prominent tool for everyday purchases depends on the ease of use. Regular consumers are going to spend the currency that's safest and simplest for them to use. Right now, that's the US dollar. If there was a reason for bitcoin or another cryptocurrency to replace the US dollar, and it was as easy to use as dollars are today, then it could grow. But that reality hasn't presented itself yet.

It's, however, still early days in cryptocurrency usage. To get a sense of just how early, let's look at how the entire market began.

An Origin Story

Maybe you believe you already know how you feel about cryptocurrencies. Maybe you're reading this to get an understanding of what exactly cryptocurrencies are before rushing to judgment. Either way, you should know where they come from in order to theorize about their future. Their origin story also provides a backdrop on why the technology supporting cryptocurrencies has the potential to shift the way the world operates.

Satoshi Nakamoto and the Creation of Bitcoin

Bitcoin, the original cryptocurrency, has an origin story that contains a number of mysteries, mostly because the creator of the coin has never come forward and proven that he or she published the concepts that would launch the crypto craze and form what you now know as bitcoin.

In 2008, an author using the pseudonym Satoshi Nakamoto published a paper outlining a new structure to develop a decentralized, peer-to-peer currency. In the paper, Nakamoto explains the concept of the blockchain, which produces a decentralized digital ledger and will become the backbone to bitcoin. Many enthusiasts had attempted to launch a digital currency in the early 2000s, but it wasn't until this framework published—in which the notion of the blockchain was described—that the ability to structure a currency completely decentralized from any oversight was shown to be possible. The author of the paper remains a mystery to this day.

Nakamoto's vision worked because she or he conceptualized the notion of removing the requirement of trust in order to process a payment. For instance, when you pay by check, you're trusting that the bank will provide the funds to the vendor based on what's in your checking account. The vendor accepts the check, trusting that the bank will ensure you have the funds for the service provided. The concept Nakamoto described removed the notion that vendors and consumers needed a third party, such as a bank, to provide this trust. Instead, this blockchain, or digital ledger, would verify the information as the transaction unfolds. Therefore, if you were trying to spend all your bitcoins on a car, the blockchain would first double check all the transactions ever provided by you to ensure you have the funds to supply the car dealer with the amount of bitcoins required for the purchase. Trust is no longer a factor—the blockchain verifies that you have the funds. This opens up dramatic opportunities to bypass traditional financial systems.

To this day, despite many efforts to uncover the person or group behind the pseudonym, the identity of Nakamoto remains a mystery. Some have claimed that Craig Wright, an Australian entrepreneur, is Nakamoto. But efforts by Wright to prove this have fallen short.

FACT

Nakamoto has an estimated 980,000 bitcoins, based on analyses done in the early days of bitcoin's popularity. If this number holds true, then when bitcoin's price rises, Nakamoto's crypto wealth matches some of the richest people in the world. At bitcoin's peak, Nakamoto's paper wealth placed him just behind Paul Allen, the cofounder of Microsoft, on the *Forbes* 400: The Wealthiest in America list.

Bitcoin Changes Everything

Shortly after this concept paper was published, Nakamoto created the first bitcoin. This technological breakthrough—the blockchain—separated bitcoin from all other previous attempts to develop online or digital currency. From this code and concept, many other cryptocurrencies have been birthed in an effort to fix problems within bitcoin, improve upon what Nakamoto started, or to jump into the cryptocurrency craze in search of a quick buck.

All Cryptos Have Their Own Origin Story

While you won't find many cryptocurrencies' origins as unique as the patriarch coin, bitcoin, they all have their reasons for existence and a purpose for using them. The first piece of advice in investing in cryptocurrencies is to understand and recognize these origin stories. It's the first chance you have to see whether it's a legitimate tool or a scam. Who is behind the cryptocurrency? Does it seem to be a viable concept? Does it make sense to link a cryptocurrency to this concept?

Reading these narratives will be a first step in recognizing what's worth investing in and which cryptocurrencies have value.

The Blockchain

Without a computer science degree, it's not always easy to conceptualize the blockchain. It's essentially a digital ledger that tracks transactions within its code, providing a public, searchable, and infinite record of a cryptocurrency (or other item in which the chain was built to track). What's different about the blockchain, separating it from past attempts to develop a digital currency? It's important to at least tangentially understand the mechanics of the blockchain in order to grasp and differentiate between the various cryptocurrencies.

Nakamoto developed the blockchain as he searched for a cryptographic answer to the digital coin. Cryptography is often synonymous with encryption, or protecting data from outsiders. It's the effort to develop codes, systems, and mirages to protect data, scrambling it so no one can piece all the information together, unless they have a code that does it automatically. Often, this is done through encryption, which is a specific way to scramble the data so nothing can read it except the owner of the information. But in some ways, bitcoin's blockchain also uses complete transparency to accomplish its goal. Although there are plenty of touch points in the coin-purchasing process where encryption plays a major role, such as when you receive a private key to unlock your coins (lose the key and you lose the coins), the bitcoin's blockchain itself is completely open, since others can see where those coins move over time.

Each bitcoin has its own digital signature, and each owner of the coin has a mark that represents his or her ownership. It sits within the ledger. This means each coin is tracked through the entire lifetime of its use. This creates a level of historic transparency, both for good and ill. For instance, the IRS can go back and track every purchase ever made with bitcoins. It also means you don't need a third party—such as a bank—to process transactions, since the blockchain can do it automatically through this code, tracking every coin along the way.

Digital Contracts Unlock Blockchain Potential

Since blockchains don't necessarily require a third party, they have created a new type of "smart" contract, which offers even more uses for the blockchain, beyond cryptos. Ethereum, the company that developed the second most popular cryptocurrency, ether (which also goes by ethereum), created the digital or smart contracts first theorized by Nick Szabo, a sort of crypto-philosopher, in the late 1990s. Blockchains that have the ability to create smart contracts can approve agreements that two sides initiate. For instance, let's say Company A wants to send $10,000 worth of ether to Company B for coding services that Company B provides. Within the digital contract there can be certain benchmarks that Company A demands that Company B must live up to in order to receive payment. As Company B works its way through those requirements the project is tracked on the blockchain. It's like a digital project manager. At the end, no one needs to confirm that the requirements were reached because the blockchain has traced every step, sending Company B the coins once it fulfills all the benchmarks.

ALERT

Since Ethereum's breakthrough with smart contracts, a number of other companies have developed similar tools, trying to improve on the original concept. Part of your investment research is to ensure that there's an actual need for this improvement. One way to judge if another concept also has some legs is that there are companies putting money behind it, whether as an investor or as a client.

These contracts have a dramatic impact on business interest within the blockchain landscape. IBM, for instance, is using the blockchain tools developed by Stellar's contract technology to conduct transactions among some banks in the South Pacific. At the time of the announcement, IBM estimated it would help conduct $1 billion of cross-border payments in this manner.

The uses for these contracts go beyond international payments. Supply chain firms can incorporate such a contract to track movements of supplies, paying vendors once it receives shipments intact. It provides security in compliance-heavy arenas, since the rules around the compliance can be incorporated into the blockchain contract, ensuring business is conducted correctly from a legal standpoint. And it improves transparency, both internally and externally. Companies can use internal blockchains to track these movements and then can turn to them when needing an accounting of shipments.

The potential remains extremely significant. Some have likened the advent of the blockchain to the creation of the Internet, and businesses are only now beginning to figure out the various ways in which they can use the technology.

Where Do Cryptocurrencies Fit?

Cryptocurrencies are how the blockchain confirms these agreements or transactions, depending on the situation. It's why when businesses use the Stellar blockchain, they will conduct the transaction in its cryptocurrency, lumens. Then the businesses can sell the lumens to cash out and obtain the value in their local currency.

Imagine a currency exchange that was completely digital. This would be the blockchain where there are euros, dollars, and yen, along with lumens, bitcoins, and other digital coins available for transacting. A Japanese business could sell something in dollars, move the payment into lumens by adding it to the blockchain, and then send it to Japan, where it would cash out the lumens for yen. Instead of paying a huge fee on the transaction, they pay a very small price, due to the blockchain and the cryptocurrency, lumens. The whole thing, in this case, would be tracked on the blockchain via the use of the lumens.

Exchange of Value

There are blockchains that don't require cryptocurrencies, since there's no monetary transaction occurring. But in blockchains where there's an exchange of value, either through retail, services, contracts, investing, or lending, then the cryptocurrency is the token used to track the digital ledger. For instance, if Nakamoto sold his very first bitcoin, then as it moved around the bitcoin atmosphere, being bought and sold, there would be a stamp on the bitcoin blockchain providing a digital map to everyone who ever owned the coin.

QUESTION

Does this mean that everyone will see what I purchase and when? No. The blockchain tracks through a series of numeric key identifiers. You won't see your name on bitcoin's blockchain by simply buying a coin. But if someone had the resources—such as the IRS—they could find out by seeking information through the exchanges, which were built to more easily conduct crypto transactions.

Where Do Cryptocurrencies Live?

Understanding where cryptocurrencies live takes a little imagination. It means we'll have to get into the intricacies of the computer science and design.

Cryptocurrencies are decentralized, meaning the blockchain incorporates them to conduct business within its infrastructure. But the blockchain is a peer-to-peer network, so instead of living on one server, the blockchain's code lives on many different nodes. A node is a term used to describe the computers or electronic devices that have downloaded the blockchain's code. Imagine you created your own website on WordPress. In a non-blockchain world, it would live on WordPress's servers. In a blockchain design, your website wouldn't live on WordPress's servers, but on a series of computers that have opted in to run WordPress's code and store the various websites. This decentralization is a key aspect of crypto's design, since in many cases it allows a community of developers to determine the fate of the currency.

Of course, if a computer were to help WordPress host the code and, therefore, your website, you would expect them to receive some sort of payment to do so. We'll discuss this later in this chapter in the context of mining.

How Have They Become a Tool for Investment?

As more people or businesses use a specific cryptocurrency, it appreciates. Let's imagine the following scenario: let's take Nakamoto's very first bitcoin again and say it's early days in cryptos, when no business accepted them. The only other person in the world who knows about bitcoin is an owner of a sandwich shop. Now let's say Nakamoto, excited about going somewhere he can actually spend his new currency, buys a $5 sandwich with one bitcoin. Now the value of one bitcoin is $5.

As more people become aware of bitcoin, suddenly they're willing to sell far more for one coin. Now, the sandwich shop owner can pay his $2,000 rent using the bitcoin, since there's a larger community willing to spend that much for the single coin. That community's desire is tracked via the bitcoin spot prices on exchanges, which calculate the current value of the coin. It's basic supply and demand.

You invest in cryptocurrency because you're betting that the cryptocurrency you own will appreciate even further. Imagine that it's appreciated so far from its original value of $5 that now the sandwich shop owner could sell that original bitcoin for a luxury vacation or a car. It's this price appreciation that people invest in. That's why it's important to understand the technology behind the cryptocurrency, since you'll need to determine whether it has the chance of having far more users than just a single sandwich shop.

Who Has Joined In?

In the past few years, as the price of these tokens has gone to the moon and back, traditional investment firms and exchanges have embraced the currency as a legitimate form of investment. The Chicago Board Options Exchange and the Chicago Mercantile Exchange began offering the trading of future contracts in late 2017, which opened up the opportunity for at-home E*TRADE users to buy and sell futures. The best performing electronic trade fund in 2017 also invested in bitcoin.

More and more consumer-facing businesses have begun to accept bitcoin as a form of currency as well, including Overstock.com, PayPal, Playboy, Microsoft, and even Etsy vendors.

Individuals have also jumped into the bitcoin waters. Tim Draper, a famous venture capitalist known for his early investment in Skype, bought $19 million worth of bitcoins in 2014, which would be worth about $270 million if he held onto the entire amount, according to reports. The Winkle-voss twins, most notable for accusing CEO Mark Zuckerberg of stealing their idea for Facebook (and being played by the actor Armie Hammer in the movie *The Social Network*), have been early adopters of the tokens, amass-ing millions to billions, depending on the price of bitcoin.

You'll have good company, if you decide to move forward with your own plans to invest.

It's a Large Infant

While cryptocurrencies remain an infant market, you can tell by its dra-matic growth that it's larger than your average child. The market capitaliza-tion of the entire cryptocurrency space now surpasses $350 billion, with bitcoin accounting for about 40 percent of the space. There're more than 1,600 different cryptocurrencies tracked by CoinMarketCap.com, account-ing for billions in value beyond bitcoin.

Coins such as ethers, lumens, Ripple's XRP, Cardano's ADA, litecoin, and a number of others have come to the fore, claiming to solve parts of the cryp-tocurrency riddle that bitcoin can't. These coins provide diversity within the space, driving analysis and investment.

How Do People Spend Them?

What's unique about cryptocurrency investing, unlike most of your other investments, is that you have the choice to spend them as they're intended to be spent: as a currency. It's one thing you'll want to think about as you consider investments, since you'll need to determine whether users spend the tokens or just hoard them. A cryptocurrency's transaction rate indicates a demand, which will improve spending, grow the popularity of the coins, and, eventually, appreciate the value.

Bitcoin has the widest rate of adoption, which shouldn't surprise you, since it's the highest-appreciated coin. There's a plethora of ways that people spend them, from PayPal to buying flights on Expedia. If you need to cash out the bitcoins fast, you can buy gift cards and then spend the gift cards for everyday purchases. There are even some restaurants that accept the coin.

The most prominent way to spend many of the top cryptocurrencies is in the gaming industry, where the digital coins have long been embraced as an acceptable form of payment to buy upgrades within games or to purchase new titles.

The reason more retailers don't accept the coins is because they're afraid to be caught with a diminishing asset. Since bitcoin is volatile and can sometimes take up to a few days to sell, a coin can drop significantly in value after a purchase. This leaves restaurants and other outlets in a precarious situation, since they have fixed costs. They don't want to accept a lot of bitcoin, only to see the value fall shortly after you leave the eatery.

Transactions Remain a Thorn

Yet, despite all this growth, transaction volumes—or the amount of times these coins are used for purchasing products—remain at pre-hyped levels. Bitcoin, for instance, has a transaction rate that's similar to pre-2017 levels, when the price of the coin was less than $900. It's this lack of transaction volume growth that gives critics a rallying cry, comparing the coins to the infamous tulip mania that swept Holland into hysteria in 1593.

Cryptocurrencies have a few more benefits, however, than tulips can provide. That gives them some armor against this lack of spending.

The Mining Process

One separation from digital coins and, say, the US dollar, is that there's typically a set limit on the amount of coins that will exist when a new cryptocurrency pops up. For instance, bitcoin has 21 million coins that can be mined within its code, and it takes a tremendous amount of energy and computing power to mine these coins. In total, about 80 percent of those coins have been mined. Once the twenty-first millionth coin does get dragged out of the code, there will never be another bitcoin.

This adds an investing layer that you see often in commodities such as oil and gold. Since those natural resources are limited, there's a ceiling on the supply that reaches the market. When it comes to the dollar, that ceiling isn't there. The Federal Reserve can increase and decrease the amount of money within the economic system, which changes the supply, in hopes to control inflation or fight deflation. Many crypto-enthusiasts enjoy the fact that there's not a governmental stranglehold on the token supply.

What Is Mining?

Most of the blockchains that create and host cryptocurrencies are peer-to-peer networks, meaning they run with the aid of nodes, or a community of computers that all host the code that makes up the blockchain. In the digital world, this allows the code to exist. But the peer-to-peer network extends further, because these computers also help to approve transactions. For approving transactions, they're paid with user fees. They also receive the new coins that are unlocked by approving the transactions.

The reason the blockchain has its name is because within the code, the files look like a series of blocks. In fact, *block* is a term within the blockchain that essentially is a file that holds a specific number of transactions. Consider it one page on a ledger (and remember, since the blockchain is a digital ledger, it has an infinite number of pages). The miners approve transactions, and once they've approved enough transactions to fill up a block, it's confirmed on the chain of code. For doing so, the miner receives a Proof of Work problem, which is the blockchain's way of proving that the work the miner did resulted in enough energy (in this case computing power) to require payment. This Proof of Work is essentially an algorithmic riddle, which the miner's computers solve. Once it's solved, the miner receives a new coin.

ALERT

The process described using the Proof of Work setup was designed for bitcoin, and is used by many bitcoin offshoots. However, other coins encourage different ways to reward miners, while reducing the energy required to uncover new coins. These coins, such as Cardano's ADA and NEM, use tactics that encourage spending of the coins, as one mines, to reward miners and increase transaction rates.

Since miners are the first ones to hold new coins, they also want to sell bitcoins in order for the supply of the coins to reach the demand by regular users. You don't need to mine coins in order to own them, but it's an important concept to grasp to help you differentiate between the positives and negatives of each coin's mining tactics.

The Complexity in Bitcoin Mining

Since the most easily reached bitcoins have been mined to this point, it takes a massive enterprise to find new ones. Warehouses filled with computers running scripts to untangle another coin run twenty-four hours a day, seven days a week, in many cases. These mini-enterprises, often with a staff of one person, can sap a town's energy supply. Some small towns and cities have even banned the mining of coins because of the impact on their local energy capabilities. In 2018, it was expected that mining operations in Iceland would require more energy than the power it required to keep every home within the country, combined, lit.

As the mining becomes more profitable—if the price of a coin rises—then the supply has tightened. Theoretically, that should improve the appreciation of the coin.

FACT

As the price of cryptos rise, it becomes more profitable for mining operations to use more power and seek out new coins. In 2018, based on the price of bitcoin, cryptocurrency analyst Alex de Vries estimated that miners would find it profitable to use sixty-four terawatts of energy per year. That's more than the entire country of Switzerland.

Not All Mine

There are some cryptocurrencies—like Ripple's XRP—that originally controlled the supply of the coin in a way similar to the Federal Reserve. This means the company or the owners of the cryptocurrency determine when to release more coins into the market. In order to fend off criticism that Ripple was trying to tightly control XRP, potentially creating inflationary pressures, Ripple revamped its strategy, so 1 billion XRP will be released each month via an escrow account, until all coins have released to the public. This rubs some investors the wrong way, since it differs from the libertarian views that are prominent within the cryptocurrency space. You'll want to keep this in mind, as you do your research.

Ripple creators won't introduce coins to the market forever. There's still a cap of 100 billion XRPs that could ever come to market. It's just that the Ripple owners control when new coins are released. About 40 percent of the total XRPs created are in circulation.

Is It Like Gold? A Stock?

Since cryptocurrency investing is so new, everyone wants to find the proper comparison. Is it like buying gold? What about a stock? Maybe it's more like oil. "Sure" and "absolutely not" are reasonable responses to all of these analogies.

The Comparisons to Gold

There are two big reasons why cryptocurrencies, particularly bitcoin, are often compared to gold. First, there's a finite supply of both. Like gold, there's only a certain amount in existence, and once it's gone, there's no way to get more. The other reason is because of the lack of connection to federally controlled payment systems. The Federal Reserve can't determine inflation is a risk and increase the supply of gold. Bitcoin and gold live outside this control, which appeals to those who are skeptical of the larger institutions.

As an investor, you don't necessarily need to know much about mining, other than the limit that miners may reach. But understanding this process will also help explain your fees when you transact the coins. For instance, bitcoin miners approve the transactions, taking a fee for the service based on the price of the coin, which can rise dramatically when bitcoin appreciates. For XRP, on the other hand, there's no such requirement, which reduces the cost of the transaction.

Don't take these comparisons too far though. Despite gold's proclivity toward volatility, it's nothing compared to bitcoin. From late 2015 to late 2018, gold moved forward a total of 11 percent, while the price has ranged from just above $1,000 to nearly $1,400. That's a Steady Eddy compared to bitcoin, which saw lows of nearly $315 and highs well above $19,000.

Gold also has history on its side. When things go badly, gold investors realize they can sell gold to vendors, if needed. There are certain apocalyptic situations, such as if the electric grid was completely destroyed, in which bitcoins would cease to exist, and therefore hold no value. While these are minor concerns, it does impact the perception (and buyer) of bitcoin and other cryptos.

Comparisons to Stocks

When you get down to the basics of what exactly a cryptocurrency is, you've essentially bought into a startup. The currency's creator likely launched an initial coin offering to raise funds. You've invested because you think this technology will grow. It's a lot like buying stock in a company in that sense, except you don't actually own a share of the firm so there's no investor services or opportunity to vote on future plans.

This also means you're buying into a very early stage startup. While rates of startup failures range from 60 percent to 90 percent, depending on what survey you're looking at, the overall result is that most startups fail. Realize that failure remains a likely possibility in the case with your investment. We haven't seen a high-profile blockchain startup fail yet, since it's so new, but that will occur. What happens to the cryptocurrency after such a name goes under, particularly if it's an unexpected bankruptcy? It remains a mystery.

FACT

That isn't to say that the blockchain universe hasn't seen its fair share of failures. According to a Bitcoin.com study, 46 percent of the 2017 initial coin offerings—which blockchain startups use to raise money—have failed or never raised enough money to get off the ground. That number rises to 59 percent when you include companies that have gone dormant.

Its Own Type of Investment

The best way to view cryptocurrencies is like a commodity; however, it's a new type of commodity. Since there are typically restrictions on the supply limits of a cryptocurrency, it would be foolhardy not to at least recognize that there's a supply crunch that will play a role in a cryptocurrency's appreciation. How much of a crunch remains uncertain, since although bitcoin has 21 million coins available, there's the 1,600 other cryptocurrencies offering their services as well. Could that deplete the supply crunch? It's worth watching as more bitcoins are mined.

But the reason cryptocurrency stands on its own is because we've never seen a commodity in such infancy. It's something completely new. Gold was never like this, since it was a form of currency prior to becoming a commodity investment. Even the US used to be on the gold standard, which supported our fiat currency. The oil rush in the early 1900s didn't produce this level of "new." It just dramatically increased the supply of oil available, coinciding with an increase in demand as factories and industrial uses grew.

Understand that it's more like a commodity, as of now, and not a currency, since people aren't spending it. But realize that could change if acceptance of a crypto increases.

ESSENTIAL

While it's true cryptos currently look like a unique type of investment, since they're new, as the space matures expect cryptocurrency to begin to work similarly to another investment (whether it's gold or a currency remains to be seen). But as an investor today, you're betting on the appreciation it will experience during that maturation process.

I'm Investing in What Exactly?

What exactly are you buying? Well, by and large, you're purchasing the actual cryptocurrency itself, unless you decide to go the fund, futures, or trust route (we'll talk about this later). This means you can use it as an investment by hiding it from the outside world and not selling until you're ready. The other option is to actually spend it incrementally. That is open to you, because there's no difference in buying cryptocurrencies and holding cash (except for the expected returns). If you decide to spend it, then the shares you have in the currency will drop.

Beyond that, you're also linking your saddle to a startup. By purchasing the cryptocurrency, you're saying that you believe the technology behind the cryptocurrency—the company that created the blockchain in which the cryptocurrency resides—will grow, and therefore the currency used to transact will also appreciate. If it's simply a decentralized currency without a company supporting the coin, like bitcoin, then you're of the belief that this coin will become a more prominent way to process transactions, replacing cash or other currencies.

The "Store of Value" Complaint

One of the main arguments for crypto naysayers is the claim that bitcoin has no store of value. This means that if something were to happen to bitcoin's blockchain, making it completely obsolete, the bitcoins you own would become worthless or unusable.

That's not the case for other commodity investments such as gold. If the financial system were to be destroyed tomorrow, you would still be able to trade gold or oil or another commodity to buy goods, just like people did a thousand years ago. Since there's an agreed-upon belief that these commodities have value, no matter what, you don't need another currency, such as the US dollar, to quantify it.

The Lack of Trust

Part of this store of value conundrum is bitcoin hasn't reached a level where it's universally trusted. This leads to the massive price swings. In order to reduce the price swings, there needs to be more trust. It's a chicken-or-egg scenario. People will need to use bitcoin more often in order to improve trust, and the trust must grow in order to increase transactions. Both must occur.

Does It Matter to an Investor?

To a short-term investor of bitcoin, it doesn't matter that cryptocurrency doesn't have a store of value. You're hoping it increases its trust-level to reach a point where the perception of its inherent store of value improves. While bitcoin, or any cryptocurrency for that matter, will have difficulty crossing this barrier because it lacks durability (it requires electricity to function), that doesn't mean it can't become a more reliable store of value than today. With that, more trust will come. Long term, it's a narrative you'll hope plays out in your favor.

The Prototype of a Successful Investor

As you can tell in this chapter (as well as Chapter 2), there are a lot of unknowns in the world of cryptocurrency investing. This will make for sporadic and scary moves in the price, which can leave many people running for a safer asset. The investors who succeed believe deeply in the potential of cryptocurrencies. They believe deeply in the potential for the blockchain. And they believe that cryptocurrencies will eventually move beyond a very alternative asset, as they are now. In essence, this means they have patience. They're not looking for a quick buck, but instead are hoping to capitalize on the forward momentum that will come over the next few years, as cryptocurrency adoption builds, blockchain technology improves, and the opportunities to use e-currency increases.

If you're one of these people who believe in cryptocurrencies' future, then the next question you must answer is, do you have the funds to invest.

CHAPTER 2

Reality Check

When you hear that bitcoin's price jumped 1,166 percent in a single year, as it did in 2017, it's understandable you would dream about all the riches that could come your way by simply buying a few coins. But cryptocurrencies aren't a get-rich-quick scheme (except some that fail) and a whole bunch of risk accompanies them. This chapter discusses the mentality you need and the composure you must show in order to succeed at crypto investing. It's not just what you invest in, but how you fund your investment.

Why You Shouldn't Invest in Cryptocurrencies

With cryptos being a new asset class, they still have plenty to prove before the general public sees them as a viable bet. Coming up with a list of reasons not to invest in them doesn't take much time:

- It's a new market
- The technology changes daily
- The players change rapidly
- There are a number of scams
- There are new regulations
- There are limited ways to spend
- There are limited ways to sell
- It's easy to lose
- It's easy to steal
- No one knows what the future holds

All these reasons combined create a significant number of unknowns in the marketplace, which leads to dramatic falls and rises in the price of the coins. If you can't handle watching what you invested potentially disappear overnight, then this isn't the asset for you. Volatility has become the only true constant within the crypto investment market.

ALERT

Because of the questions in the market, particularly the one about whether this is a viable currency, bitcoin can move quickly on simple news items. In early 2018, a South Korean government official incorrectly stated that the country would ban crypto trading. The price of both bitcoin and ethereum fell by 14 percent shortly after the comments, since the country is a prominent crypto marketplace.

The Volatility Can Be Staggering

Imagine this: if you had bought one bitcoin on November 14, 2017, it would have cost about $6,500. Within just over a month, that investment would have risen nearly 200 percent to over $19,300, netting you about $13,000. Not a bad month. Of course, you can't possibly predict bitcoin's peaks and valleys. Within two months of that high, nearly all of those gains would have disappeared, leaving you with nothing but your initial investment.

That's the type of volatility you must expect before stepping into this market. This example uses bitcoin, which is among the most stable of all cryptocurrencies. The bucking bronco of an investment ride becomes even more precarious as you try to step into altcoins, which are cryptocurrencies that aren't bitcoin.

Rich One Day...

When prices rise or fall dramatically, the movements get covered by the press, which leads to the coverage of braggadocious investors coming out of the woodwork, espousing their belief that they've solved the riddle to making a fortune in the crypto market. This can lead to enthusiasm from regular investors who hope to have discovered a quick path to riches.

Australian journalist Derek Rose detailed his experience investing in bitcoin, and it turned out quite different. In mid-2017, he had about $70,000 to $100,000 invested into a few different coins, and then he saw IOTA and EOS (two types of altcoins) fall in price. He decided to buy on margin, which meant he was borrowing the funds to continue to invest further into the two names. By November, he had a few million in his account, which he used to buy bitcoin, right as the coin shot up well over $10,000. It's the best-case scenario for any investor, no matter if they're placing their money in cryptocurrencies or something more traditional, like Apple stock.

FACT

Despite the reports of bitcoin millionaires, the number of actual large investors in the coin remains small. Only 3 percent of bitcoin wallets hold more than one bitcoin. And only 10 percent of wallets hold more than $250 worth of bitcoin, according to BitcoinPrivacy.net.

While Rose had invested in bitcoin and other cryptos since 2013, he increased his exposure to the investment in a big way at the exact moment that prices started to rocket skyward. It's the dream that cryptocurrency backers want to sell. It's beneficial for more people to drive investment into these tokens or coins because they're all looking for mass adoption. The more money that comes in, the more the prices will rise, until a tipping point hits where it's considered legitimate (that's the hope, anyway). It not only makes their own investment look stronger, but it also strengthens the company that's running the technology that the crypto uses on the backend. If more people adopt EOS, for example, then maybe more gaming companies will allow gamers to transact using the coin. Or more restaurants will allow you to purchase a sandwich with the token. It's what these currencies need to reduce this constant volatility.

...Broke the Next

But this market is far too new to have that level of consistency. In Rose's case, by late December, he borrowed nearly $14 million to pay for new cryptocurrencies, double the total worth of his account. It all came to a head when bitcoin crashed on December 22, 2017, forcing his account to liquidate.

The experience, he says, taught him about exuberant investing. Overall, Rose says despite the loss in his biggest account, he has still turned a profit during his time investing in cryptocurrencies because he had other accounts open. He's just not able to "take early retirement anytime soon," he added. Rose entered the market early and risked everything. Luckily for him, he can still sport a profit. But for you, there's no guarantee that the money will be there tomorrow.

ESSENTIAL

It's also important to understand how the bitcoin millionaires earned enough coins to reach millionaire status. If they were part of the early days of bitcoin—potentially even mining coins—then they could have gained a large supply of the coins when the price was cheap. Bitcoin didn't surpass $100 for the first time until 2013. Outside of a small surge that same year, it didn't sustain value above $500 until 2016. This meant early adopters could (and still do) hoard coins.

No, Seriously, Don't

One of the worst ways people go wrong while investing in general—and it holds true with cryptocurrencies as well—is by going into debt in order to fund the investment. It requires a return-on-investment (ROI) that's typically far more aggressive than the asset can provide. That's why you should wait, if you can't afford to invest now.

Take, for example, a situation in which you try to fund your crypto purchase with a credit card. A simple cash-back credit card comes with an average 13.12 percent interest rate. Since that's compiled monthly, you need your investment to return more than 13.12 percent monthly just to break even. If you buy $10,000 worth of ethereum using a credit card, then you're accumulating significant interest payments while you wait for your investment to appreciate. Sure, it could potentially work, if ethereum jumps like it did in a three-month period in 2017. More likely it's going to leave you in serious debt. Since that credit card payment would take twenty-five years to pay using the minimum repayment plan, you would spend $21,000 in total for that $10,000 loan.

More likely, you'll have to pull your funds out of the investment just to repay the bill, forcing you to sell early or suffer a loss.

Where People Go Wrong

It's quite simple: invest only what you can afford. It's exciting to see an investment jump 20 percent in three days. But removing all of your safety net in order to access one asset class that's performing well is the most common mistake investors make, no matter what they believe they've discovered. It's the assumption that past performance predicts future returns. It ignores all of the volatility and downside risk that will accompany that investment.

Don't Buy on Credit

Unfortunately, when bitcoin's price shows forward momentum, investors quickly jump on the credit card to try and secure an investment. Consumer group LendEDU found in a survey of 672 bitcoin investors that 18 percent used credit cards to fund the purchase of the coins. Nearly one-fourth of the group hadn't repaid the loan at the time of the survey.

Using a credit card doubles the risk of an already risky investment. By placing the funds into cryptos in the first place, you're betting that the investment will rise. But by using credit cards, you're also betting your financial security that the investment will increase more than the rate at which you're borrowing. It will make for a much more stressful experience, since you will ride every news piece and market fluctuation hoping that the price will appreciate enough to leave you in the black. You'll also find it difficult to make smart decisions about when to buy and when to sell if your hopes for a home or financial freedom are riding on the schizophrenic moves of a currency.

ALERT

Many of the coin exchanges allow the use of credit cards to fund the purchase. It's not a smart option, as we've seen. Plus, more and more credit card companies are beginning to limit the ability to use their plastic for crypto purchases. Card issuers such as J.P. Morgan Chase, Bank of America, Discover, Capital One, and Citigroup have banned the purchase of cryptos using their cards.

Don't Mortgage a Home

Since cryptos burst into the mainstream in late 2017, there've been a number of reports and message board posts claiming that people have taken out mortgages on their homes in order to fund a crypto investment. Sometimes it's $250,000, sometimes $75,000, sometimes $325,000. The cost doesn't matter: it's not a good idea.

It's a move done out of desperation more than intelligent investing, even for the riskiest. You don't want to lose your home just because the price of bitcoin falls. Plus, you could hurt the value of one investment—your home—by the dreams and prayers of a second one. You really shouldn't view your home as an investment vehicle that can be tapped as quickly as your savings or your more-risky investments, like very niche exchange-traded funds (ETFs). That's what you're doing if you take out a mortgage to fund the payment. Most of all, you shouldn't let one mistake cost you twenty years of your life, which is a common payment timeline for a very large second mortgage.

Why Aren't You Listening?

Cryptocurrency investing shouldn't be viewed like a Hail Mary pass in football, when late in a game a team that's losing will throw the ball in desperation, praying for a touchdown. On the field, it usually only results in a loss, which any team or fan can recover from. In real life, these Hail Mary investment passes can cripple your life savings.

Instead, consider your cryptocurrency investments as part of your overall portfolio. Will you own a yacht investing in this way? Probably not, but that's the case even if you invest all of your funds in cryptocurrencies. If you want the yacht, the best strategy is to develop the cryptocurrency that unites all cryptocurrencies or take a nice vacation and rent one. Yachts are expensive to maintain anyway.

If you treat your cryptos as a part of your portfolio, then you're able to protect against the downside and still have plenty to live off while preparing for the future.

FACT

Bitcoin investors are buying and holding. According to a survey of investors, 39.5 percent of respondents plan to hold the investment for one to three years. Only 16 percent said less than a year. What are they waiting for? When asked what price would encourage them to sell their bitcoin, the average mark came out to more than $196,000 a coin.

Continue to Invest in Other Markets

It's not nearly as sexy as a 1,000 percent return, but one of the few investment vehicles that has shown consistent, long-term results that beat inflation and is cheap to own is an S&P 500 index fund. With a 10 percent annual historical return, it won't light your pockets on fire. In fact, there are years that it won't perform even close to that mark. But over the long run, you will come out ahead of inflation. The most important goal for any investment strategy should be to save enough funds in vehicles that grow faster than inflation, so you have enough money to last the rest of your life when you quit working. You need a plan for that first.

Don't believe it? Take a thirty-seven-year-old making $50,000 with $0 invested in retirement today. If she invests 8 percent of her income over the next thirty years (with 2 percent annual income increases) in a traditional index fund that tracks the largest 500 US company stocks, then she will have $500,000 in the bank by the time she hits retirement age at sixty-seven, assuming a historical average return. It's due to the power of compound interest. You won't see that power today, as you invest. But the impact will show up fifteen to twenty years into your plan.

By pulling all the money out of the account and investing in cryptocurrencies, though, you're ignoring this compound component, especially if you're trading often. You shouldn't miss out on the strongest investing tool at your disposal.

ALERT

Remember that any index fund will have years in which it performs very poorly. That doesn't mean you should ignore these as investing tools, even if you want to increase your crypto exposure. Investors who stayed in an index fund tracking the Standard & Poor's 500 largest US companies throughout the 2008 recession earned back all of their losses within two years. Seven years after the bottom, the same index returned 160 percent, 23 percent on an annual basis, which are returns that shouldn't be ignored.

Continue Investing in Your 401(k)

It's rare to find free money in this world, yet the payments that you make into your 401(k) likely provide that. Since most companies provide some form of a match, which pays you 3–4 percent of your contribution to your 401(k) plan, assuming you pay in a certain threshold (for example, 7 percent of your pay), it's like receiving free money. You don't want to pass that up.

Even if your company doesn't provide a match, you still want access to the 401(k), since it's one of the cheapest ways to invest. You can find target date funds in a 401(k), which reduces your amount of risk as you move closer to retirement. Many of these funds will offer fees between 0.1 percent and 0.2 percent. These low fees can save you tens to hundreds of thousands of dollars during the life of your retirement savings.

Protection from the Unexpected

You also want to make sure you're covered in case anything unexpected comes up. Typically, for those who work at a company, you should have at least three to six months of expenses saved in a short-term savings account. This money will be easily accessible, in case something out of the blue happens to your home, you have to pay a large health bill, or you lose your job. You want to make sure your mortgage and expenses are covered from the unforeseen. If you work for yourself, then having six months' to a year's worth of savings is even better, due to the unpredictability that's prevalent in your employment.

Having this in place before you purchase cryptocurrencies will keep you from selling out of fear.

Okay, You're Ready to Gamble

If you're still reading, then let's assume you haven't been scared off by the warnings that have come throughout this chapter. It's necessary to understand the risk you're taking and the realities of the bets you're making.

It also means you're a risk-taker. That's an important first understanding of what it will take to gain from the future of cryptocurrencies. Since no one knows what will happen with cryptocurrencies tomorrow, two weeks from now, two months from now, two years from now, or two decades from now—and don't trust those that say they do know—it's a leap of faith to buy in. You're betting on the fact that there's hope in the technology, traction in the concept, and potential in the use of the digital coin as a currency.

You're Essentially Placing a Bet

You'll notice the words *bet* or *betting* used often throughout this book. It's the appropriate word for cryptocurrency investing because you're essentially placing a wager that a certain crypto will rise. Sure, you can improve your odds through research, but at the heart of your investment you're laying down money just as you would if you went to the racetrack and played the horses or flew to Las Vegas and placed it all on red.

It can be gone faster than it takes for a bitcoin to process a payment. The more you realize the risk involved, the better off you'll be.

Make Sure You're Only Losing What You Can Afford

It's also why you only want to invest in cryptos with money that you can afford to lose. Once you have made your selection, assume that money is gone. It can be hard to imagine, but it's the same strategy that people use when walking into a casino. If they can lose $100, then they will spend the money for the fun and enjoyment of the casino for the night. If their mark is $1,000, then all the better even if it can disappear just as quickly as the $100 can.

Keep the same mindset with your investment in cryptos. Typically, a portfolio will have about 90 percent of the funds in a series of retirement accounts, savings, IRAs, and maybe real estate. The remaining 10 percent of the portfolio is in areas that have a lot more risk, and potentially higher returns. Use this part of your portfolio to invest. Maybe this is where you place money in commodities or alternative funds. Reallocate this 10 percent portion, so you can use a percentage of it toward your crypto investments. It'll ensure you won't get too ambitious with your successes. If you end up wanting to use all 10 percent of this portion of the portfolio on cryptos, then that's up to you. You'll just have to expect higher volatility in that portion of the portfolio.

A Word of Caution from a Billionaire

In situations where there's money to potentially be made, like in cryptocurrencies, it's sometimes best to have those who have already made a large amount of dough weigh in. There are plenty of naysayers who argue that bitcoin or other altcoins are doomed. Although you probably disagree, there's wisdom in the voices that understand it's a nascent market, one that could become a legitimate asset class one day or could end up alongside other failed ventures, such as Google Glass, Microsoft's Zune, the tulip craze, and any other technological or investment bust that comes to mind.

FACT

Mark Cuban isn't a total fanboy when it comes to cryptocurrencies, but he's clearly watching the market closely and he's invested in some cryptocurrency startups. The Dallas Mavericks began accepting bitcoin and ethereum as a way to buy tickets starting in the 2018–2019 season. The franchise became the second NBA team to make the move; the Sacramento Kings did so back in 2014.

Billionaire Mark Cuban, owner of the NBA franchise Dallas Mavericks, puts it best. "You might take 10 percent [of your portfolio] and put it in bitcoin or ethereum. But if you do that, you have to pretend like you've already lost your money," Cuban told *Vanity Fair*. "I would limit it to 10 percent."

Can You Afford to Invest?

Determining whether or not you have the funds to invest—and figuring out just how much you can use—may be the most important part of the investing process. It gives you insight into how much wiggle room you have. Again, treat this money like a splurge; unlike that trip to Cabo though, this one has a chance to pay you back and then some.

This also allows you the opportunity to take ownership and understand your entire portfolio, by making an evaluation of your investing assets. To do this first gather any place you currently have money. This includes:

- 401(k)s
- Individual stock, bond, and mutual fund investments
- IRAs
- Roth IRAs
- Real estate
- Savings

When gathering your real estate portfolio, that should include investment properties only. Unless you view your home as an investment vehicle (i.e., you're planning on flipping the house), it's best to view your home as the place you're going to live for a number of years, and ignore it among these investments.

By gathering this information, you want to determine the total amount of money in your retirement and investment accounts. You also want to ensure that your 401(k)s and IRAs are distributed in safe vehicles, like an S&P 500 index fund, international fund, and bonds. Ensuring these tools have your long-term security in place, then it will provide you with freedom as you judge your crypto investments.

How can I outsource the picking of my 401(k) investments to ensure they're in safe vehicles?
Many 401(k) providers will offer resources to help you determine what funds match your risk profile. You can also look toward a target-date fund, which automatically shifts your investment allocation of stocks and bonds to less risky ratios, as you move toward retirement.

Now that you have those in order, you'll want to determine if you plan to use current cash flow to fund your investment or tap your savings or individual stock or bond investments. Avoid raiding your 401(k)s or IRAs because of penalties you'll pay on early withdrawals. Plus, it will add an additional burden, since you'll have to pay extra income taxes come April.

If your savings account has more than six months of expenses covered, then that's the cheapest way to provide a pool for your initial investment, outside of current cash flow, like your paycheck. If not, then tapping your individual stock, bond, or alternative investments will likely make the most sense. Make sure to calculate the fees and capital gains tax for cashing out your investment, since you'll need to include that in the calculation as you determine your ROI.

The easiest way to fund a new crypto investment is through current cash flow. Let's say you've earmarked 2 percent of your income for cryptocurrency investments; then you can automatically deduct that from your paycheck into a separate account linked to a cryptocurrency exchange. By doing so, you're not defunding any of your other investments and you won't have to pay capital gains tax.

Defining Realistic Goals

Part of what gets investors in trouble is they view cryptocurrency as a money grab. While there's no other investment vehicle that performed better in 2017, that's not the case in 2018. It's worth remembering that just because you decided today to invest, it doesn't mean your investment will come to fruition in a few hours. In fact, it can take years for substantial returns, if they come at all. Understanding what you want to gain from the crypto investments is important.

Should You Expect to Be a Millionaire?

The reason you've siphoned off a small part of your portfolio is so you have the potential for significant upside, if cryptos—particularly the coin you invested in—becomes a much more viable currency. This means there's a potential you could gain 5,000 percent. There's also a potential you could lose 65 percent or more. Both are possibilities on the crypto investing scale. Right now, since the asset class is so new, the probability of potential outcomes leans greater to the smaller ends of the scale.

This scale is how you need to view your potential outcomes, understanding that if the dream scenarios are on the left side of the scale and the negative or reasonable return scenarios are on the right side of the scale, then it's leaning heavily to the right, as of today. That's why you want to invest, in case that scale tips left. But don't put your entire hopes and dreams on the outcome of these tokens. It's never going to come out as well as you had hoped, if that's the case.

Are You in This for the Long Haul?

Since no one knows when exactly the scale could tip left, it's important to remember to keep a plan in place, and then continue to follow that plan, even if daily hiccups in the market make it seem treacherous. If you're investing in cryptocurrencies because you believe in the concept and technology, then it's years in the making, not days. Play it with years in mind. Don't look for a quick exit, unless the price suddenly flies upward beyond a point you believe it should.

If you want the quick exit, that's fine as well. But know it's like putting your money on a specific number on the roulette wheel. It might hit, but there's no rhyme or reason if it actually does.

Know What You Want and the Risk Involved

Instead, think about what you want from this investment. Keeping it as a best-case scenario tool, as Cuban suggests, then in a few years you could find yourself thrilled with your decision to place a portion of your portfolio in cryptocurrencies. If it's simply to chase hidden gold, then like the miners of the past, you could end up searching for a long time, unless you're one of the lucky few that hits pay dirt.

The "Should You Invest in Cryptocurrency?" Test

Answering these questions will solidify why you're investing and just how much you'll be willing to handle the volatility of the experience.

- Do you believe bitcoin or an altcoin will become a powerful currency one day?
- What do you want to gain from investing in cryptocurrencies?
- Do you have a retirement portfolio, and is it currently growing at a pace that will protect you in the future?
- Where will you get the funds to invest?
- Do you have to go into debt in order to invest?
- If you were to lose all the money you've set aside for cryptos tomorrow, would you be able to afford that loss?

Now that you've weighed the risks and answered these questions, are you ready to continue forward in the world of crypto investing? Then the next step is to start investing.

CHAPTER 3

Taking Those First Steps

Now that you understand why you want to invest, and the risk involved, the next important step is to purchase coins. But it isn't like other investments you've purchased in the past. Remember, this isn't like exchanging US dollars for euros at the airport, as you head for a European vacation. Since the cryptocurrency investment is done online, you can't actually hold your purchase (unless you splurge for a gold bitcoin, which some retailers offer). Instead, it's in the code-developed wind, and this creates complications in how you store and protect your investment. It will also require you to go through unusual hurdles to sell the investment. It's not like heading to your local bank. This chapter will discuss the basics of buying your first crypto.

The Xs and Os

Prior to the advent of the cryptocurrency exchange, the process for buying and selling cryptocurrencies took practically a doctorate degree in computer science, coding, or hacking. Now that exchanges and digital wallets exist in order to protect your purchase, it's a much more fluid and simple process. There are still some key points during your transaction journey, however, where choices will arise. Based on which path you choose, this will impact your experience, security, and returns.

It's Not Like Purchasing Stock

When you buy a stock or mutual fund on an exchange, there's little that you have to do post-purchase, other than maybe printing out the record for your accountant. The stock or fund share isn't going to disappear as soon as you walk away from the computer, satisfied with your decision.

That's not the case when you're purchasing a cryptocurrency. You have the responsibility to keep certain items in line, or else the coins could fall into a digital vacuum.

FACT

Think the possibility of losing your crypto investment isn't real? In 2017, Chainalysis evaluated bitcoins to determine how many coins owners had lost, never to be rediscovered. It found that 17 percent of the 16.3 million bitcoins mined at the time of the analysis were gone forever. Using a $9,000 per coin value, and that's about $24 billion worth of bitcoin.

First Sign Up for an Exchange

When you decide it's time to invest, you'll need to pick an exchange. While these are discussed later in the chapter, what you'll want to evaluate is which one works well for your region and which fee rate works best for you. When you make the purchase, say $50, then the exchange will take a portion of that amount as a fee for processing the transaction. Part of the money goes to support the exchange itself. In cases where the miners must process the transactions, then a portion of the fee also goes toward paying the toll to transact on the blockchain that your cryptocurrencies reside on. While you can easily find exchanges that have fees around 0.1 percent, it's important to remember that some tokens have high fees just for buying in. That can increase costs, especially if it's a more complicated coin to process and confirm.

How much you're spending will also dictate how much in fees you're paying, since they're typically a percent of the total amount you want to purchase. If you spend a significant amount, however, then most exchanges will reduce the fee percentage they need to process the payment. Buying just a small amount, you'll likely be subjected to the highest rate.

You'll Wait a Few Days

Depending on how much you plan to invest, expect to wait a few days before you're able to buy or sell your coins. Part of this time frame has to do with the coin itself; it's faster to purchase coins such as Ripple's XRP, since there's no miner who has to confirm the purchase. This produces speedier processing times. On the other hand, Bitcoin will often run slower, since the community must confirm it. While you're able to lock in the price of the coin at the time of the purchase, it means you're unable to sell for a few days. If the coin suddenly triples in value three hours after your purchase, you can't immediately sell. You'll have to wait a few days to a week before the coins actually reach your digital wallet. By then, who knows? Your bitcoin gains may be gone.

The wait period will also depend on how much you're purchasing. Buy a large chunk, and you could have that within a couple days (or minutes, depending on the exchange). Then it's just a matter of whether there's enough supply to support the purchase at the moment. For high spenders, there's no guarantee that your purchase will have enough supply in the market when you first process the payment, since it's dictated by how many coins are up for sale.

Paying the Piper

When you sign up for an exchange in the US, you'll need to decide how you plan to purchase the coins. Since many exchanges in the US, particularly the most popular, Coinbase, won't allow you to purchase the coins via credit card, you have three options:

- Link a bank account
- Use a debit card
- Set up a wire transfer

A bank account as the funder for the purchase is for intermediate to large purchases. Coinbase, for example, allows you to add up to $10,000 per week using a bank account approach. For most people, this is a very safe, cost-effective tool for funding the crypto investments, even if they never go near that top-level limit.

Debit cards are meant for smaller purchases. Some exchanges limit the amount you can add via debit cards to less than $1,000 per week. However, be careful about using the debit card, since there are fewer consumer protections if the debit card numbers are compromised through malware or a hacker.

The wire transfer is particularly useful for large, single purchases. Coinbase has a limit of $100,000 without extra verification. This amount can increase, but you'll have to convince the exchange that you can afford the amount that you want to transfer.

ALERT

It can be jarring when you sign up for the exchange, especially when you link your bank account to purchase a cryptocurrency. The exchanges will ask you to log in to your bank account. This isn't as scary as you might initially think. If you've ever signed into a budgeting tool, like Mint.com, then you're familiar with a similar process to these exchanges. If you're worried about it, however, be sure to request information about how the exchange holds your bank information before supplying your log-in.

Selecting a Wallet

When the popular exchange Coinbase first launched, it fashioned itself as a place to store and spend bitcoins and other cryptos. It was a wallet, not an exchange. As the idea of bitcoin investment grew and buyers and sellers held on to their coins, more like an appreciating asset than currency, Coinbase shifted to an exchange. But don't mistake it for a place to store your bitcoins and don't mistake any exchange for a wallet. An exchange is where you buy or sell the coins to other investors. A wallet is used to spend the coins, protect the investment, and hide the tokens from any particular threat.

ALERT

It's once you move your cryptos to a wallet that it's imperative for you to remember the private key that marks your coins. This series of numbers, letters, or even random words will tell you where your coins are hiding. Without the key, it's nearly impossible to retrieve your coins.

Selling Your Cryptos

As an investor, when you've reached the point where you want to sell, you will transfer the coins from your wallet and back to the exchange you plan to use as you flip the profit. It doesn't have to be the same exchange you used to purchase the coins. In fact, there are often arbitrage opportunities by selling the coins via different exchanges, since there's slight price differences between the various exchanges. However, by doing this, you might find yourself using an exchange that isn't as safe or reliable as the previous one you used. So before you make your move, be sure to double check whether it's a reliable platform on which to conduct your investing.

Finding the Right Exchange

Part of picking the exchange is personal preference. There are features and user interfaces that you might find more appealing in one exchange that are lacking in others. Another part of picking an exchange has to do with security. Since regulations have only begun to tighten around exchanges, you'll want to make sure any platform you use has passed the most up-to-date regulatory reviews. The last consideration in your exchange selection should be whether or not you can get the best price for your cryptos. Since prices can differ based on the exchange you use, it's worth monitoring multiple exchanges when you begin to think about selling your coins.

They Don't Owe You a Thing

What you need from an exchange, more than anything else, is the knowledge that if you use it as a regular way to buy and trade cryptos, you won't lose all your investment if it's hacked. However, because of the lack of regulation surrounding crypto-exchanges, there's still no such promise that an exchange will pay you back if it suffers a breach.

When Mt. Gox was hacked in 2014, it filed for bankruptcy. It's still winding its way through bankruptcy court, with many investors receiving nothing for their loss. Coincheck, a Japanese exchange, paid back some of the $530 million in losses it suffered from a similar hack in 2018. Whether or not an exchange will pay back what's lost will depend on the exchange and how much the hackers stole. It's a risk, no matter what exchange you choose, which is also why it's good to use various ways to store your coins, from multiple wallets to different exchanges; that way not all your crypto eggs are in one proverbial basket.

Stay Local

For those reading this in the United States, it's relatively easy advice to say stay within an exchange that's located in your country. Since there are plenty to choose from, you can easily find an American-based exchange that matches your aesthetic needs, as well as quell some of your security concerns. The same goes for someone living in Japan, South Korea, or Hong Kong. Since these locales have a high stake in the crypto game, they have local exchanges that have done the due diligence that's expected at this point in the crypto lifecycle, and will adjust to any changing regulations.

But it makes sense to stay local, since if something goes wrong, then you'll have an easier path to collect. It's not going to be as easy if you live in the US and trade in Japan. If a hack occurs, you're potentially dealing with language barriers. Plus, you'll have to become much more familiar with the Japanese government and judicial system in order to try and collect.

Monitoring Other Exchanges

Since there are more than 200 exchanges across the world, it creates an investing arbitrageur's dream in that there's plenty of ways that one exchange could price one coin significantly lower or higher than others. It's an issue that exchanges have tried to dampen, in an effort to create a unified price for each crypto. Yet, it hasn't completely been achieved. The price differences can become more dramatic, since there are certain altcoins embraced by one country, while other countries aren't as enthused by the same names. In these coins, opportunities arise, like through parts of 2017 when Ripple XRP was priced 25 percent higher on a South Korean exchange than on a US one.

While exchanges have taken steps to reduce the opportunities available through arbitrage, it's good to keep an eye on at least one South Korean, Japanese, and Hong Kong exchange, as you'll be able to start to notice what altcoins the local areas view more attractively than in the US.

If you decide to go the arbitrage route, be sure the price differences make up for any fees you might pay, either to process the payment on the blockchain or to pay the exchange for the service. If you do try to arbitrage, you'll probably want to have a number of different coins on different exchanges. It can take some time—up to a few days—to transfer coins between exchanges, which means price fluctuations could flush out the opportunity. Finally, don't forget to calculate the tax implications of all the buying and selling, as it will also play a role in your returns.

Check That It's Registered

If you're in the US and using predominantly a US exchange, be sure to check that it's registered with the Securities and Exchange Commission (SEC), a federal agency that's empowered to monitor investing markets in order to protect investors. Since the SEC has cracked down on exchanges, the reputable ones will have registered with the agency.

If You Don't Know, Ask

There are so many forums available to crypto investors, both for new investors and veterans in the space. If you're unsure about a certain exchange, ask a forum to get a sense of the reputation that the exchange has amongst the crypto community. While it's not fail-proof, there's a sense of relief if you're going with an exchange that the community overwhelmingly backs.

Some Exchanges to Consider

While many exchanges have come and gone, here are some names that remain prominent in the US and elsewhere:

- Coinbase (United States)
- Coincheck (Japan)
- Bitstamp (Luxembourg)
- CEX.IO (London)
- Coinplug (South Korea)
- Korbit (South Korea)
- Kraken (United States)

Selecting the Right Crypto Wallet

Once you purchase coins on an exchange, you have two choices for what to do with them. You can either keep them on the exchange or move the coins to a digital wallet, giving you the ultimate control over the investment. Since, as you will see throughout this book, exchanges have become common targets for hacks, it's not always the safest tactic to keep them on the exchange. By doing so, you leave your bitcoins at the whim of an exchange, which only has a minimal level of regulatory oversight. If you're investing any sort of significant sum of money, then it's highly recommended to move the coins into a wallet. It becomes more imperative as the size of your investment grows, since you could become a target and the loss would have a more dramatic impact on your bottom line.

Through these wallets, you can hold or spend your coins, since many of them were designed so you could use the coins for their intended purpose: buying things.

The one reason you might not want to use the wallets is if you trade often. It's not the smartest strategy—due to fees—but something to consider, since you likely won't want to continually transfer large sums to and from wallets when you're trading with a time frame of hours.

Wallets Abound

There's a plethora of options to choose from when you're ready to transfer your purchases from an exchange to a wallet. For those who will spend the crypto often, you have the option of digital wallets or mobile wallets, allowing you a way to transfer funds for goods or services as you go through your day. For others, who see this purely as a long-term investment, then you can find wallets that will remain completely offline, known as "cold storage," until you're ready to spend.

To give you a sense of some of the variations of wallets out there, here's a quick rundown of some of the options:

- Desktop wallets
- Hardware wallets
- Mobile wallets
- Paper wallets
- Web wallets

While this only touches on the most common, and safe, versions, it's important to remember that however you decide to spend or hold your currency, there's probably a tactic out there for you.

ESSENTIAL

There's an additional type of wallet that goes by the name brain wallet. In this version, you develop a key that's only known to you as the private key, signaling the location of the bitcoin. Then, when you spend, you access the coins using the phrase that you've developed. It's not hack proof because people are terrible at developing complex enough phrases that escape a hacker's tactics. If you forget the phrase, then you can also forget your coins.

How Wallets Store Your Coins

When you buy a crypto, there's a public key, which is used on the blockchain to signal that it's a recognized coin. There's also a private key, which you use to access the specific coin when you want to sell or spend it. The wallet stores the private key for you. If you lose this key, then you lose your ability to access the coin. They essentially disappear, since the wallet won't be able to find the coin you're referencing without the code and you won't be able to prove you're the owner of said coin.

Types of Storage

Besides the brain wallet, there are two ways you can store the coins. You can either link the coins via an online method, known as "hot" storage or you can store it offline, which is referred to as "cold" storage. How often you spend or sell your coins will dictate which type of storage you select.

Hot Storage

An easy way to remember whether or not your cryptos are at risk from hackers is this: if they're online, then there's a potential that hackers could grab them. It doesn't mean it's going to happen, but storing your investment on a digital wallet increases the chances because not only do the coins rest online, but also you'll have to give a third party—the digital wallet—your information. If the wallet company itself is hacked, you could very well lose your coins.

So why use them? Because you spend a lot. It's cumbersome to move coins from cold storage, back online, then back to cold storage. It will take a few minutes, in some cases, especially if you're using the hardware method, which is storing them in a tool that's similar to an external hard drive. People who spend the coins often will probably consider a digital or mobile wallet, at least for a portion of their portfolio, in order to have easier access to the coins.

If you have a sizeable stake in cryptos, only store the coins you plan to buy and spend in hot storage. Having a larger portion of your stake in cold storage will protect your portfolio.

Cold Storage

Holding your coins in cold storage means you're holding them in an offline account that has no access for hackers. It's the safest way to store your portfolio, and one that you should use for most of your coins.

To achieve this, you have a few different methods at your disposal. First, you can store them in hardware that looks similar to a USB drive, where you upload the key onto the tool, then unhook it from your computer. This stores the contents in the device, leaving it secure from any third party (unless someone were to rob you and take the drive). Another option is on a desktop wallet. Some large investors have a computer that sits offline at all times, storing their bitcoins and cryptos on the desktop tool within the computer. If they need to sell any of their coins, the computer comes online only briefly while the transaction processes.

Another method is by using the digital barcodes, known as QR codes, as your key, which you can print out onto a piece of paper. Known as a paper wallet, this piece of papyrus will hold both your public and private keys. It's one of the safest methods to shield your computer from malware, but if you lose the paper or the QR code becomes wrinkled beyond the point of recognition, then your bitcoins are gone forever.

ALERT

Just because you're in cold storage doesn't mean you're forever safe from the grasp of malware and hackers. In order to spend or sell your coins, you will have to reconnect them to the web. During these moments, your coins are susceptible once again. But it does limit the time frame in which your investment is exposed.

The Difference Between Investing and Spending

Cryptos are unlike any other investment you likely have in your portfolio. If you invest in other currencies or hide your savings in cash underneath a couch cushion, then you can spend the investment, but you can't expect much return from the strategy. The whole point of retirement savings is to gain more via the stock market than the rate in which inflation grows, since it will destroy the value of any dollar that's sitting within the couch. So you're definitely not profiting from the method.

Cryptos aren't like any stock you own either, because you also have the chance to spend the coins on regular, everyday purchases. What your intentions are—spending or investing—will dictate what coins you choose to purchase.

Spending

If you hope to not only have some currency for investing but also think about spending coins from time to time, then your options will be greatly reduced since only a few coins are accepted as a real form of currency, outside of video game operators and some niche online outlets. Therefore, if you really plan to spend the coins, stick primarily to bitcoin, since it has the largest breadth of retailers who accept the coin. There's also ethereum, litecoin, and bitcoin cash, which a number of outlets also accept.

Investing

If you're looking to invest, planning for long-term gains and price appreciation in the value of the coins, then the options open up greatly for you. Nearly every day, a new coin comes onto the market, providing another opportunity for you to purchase it. If it also has the right management team, technology, goals, niche, and market, then it could rise fast in value. Whether or not it does will have little to do with your crypto-picking skills and more to do with luck. That doesn't mean it's not worth understanding the ways in which you can invest, the ways in which new coins come to market, and the reasons they rise.

Initial Coin Offerings

Many of the cryptocurrencies that come to market are backed by a startup company. This company has developed the blockchain that tracks the coins for a specific purpose, whether it's to help send money across borders more easily, to improve tracking of supply chains, or some other attribute that might appeal to businesses and consumers. To raise money for the projects and to improve the appeal of the cryptocurrency, the company will run an initial coin offering (ICO). These are in some ways like an initial public offering (IPO) through which a company will raise money by selling stock. But there are major differences between an IPO and an ICO.

You Don't Own the Company

When buying into an ICO, you're purchasing the cryptocurrency that the blockchain firm has offered. This in no way entitles you to an ownership piece of the business. By owning XRP, you don't suddenly have a vote in how Ripple operates. By purchasing ether, you do not have a say in Ethereum's next upgrade. Instead, you're simply buying the currency and can decide when to sell it.

This differs significantly from an IPO. By owning stock in a public company, you *do* get a vote. If you have thirty shares, you have thirty votes. While this doesn't necessarily allow you decision-making powers within a large, *Fortune* 1,000 firm, it does give you some say in how your investment operates. It also provides you with some investor protections, offering recourse if the company acts fraudulently.

You Don't Get Insight Into the Company

ICOs have become a notorious microcosm of the crypto investing experience, since they've become a prominent way to scam investors. This has brought much criticism toward the regulations regarding ICOs, since companies releasing the coins don't have to provide much information about how they operate, what strategy they have for growth, and what plans they have moving forward. They don't have to share their balance sheets, provide documentation that they've even made a sale, or show profit figures. In essence, these companies are ghosts beyond what information they independently choose to share with potential buyers of the coin.

That's not the case when you invest in an IPO. Prior to the launch of the IPO, the companies are required to provide detailed financial information to the SEC. This becomes public prior to the date of the IPO, so investors interested in the company can weigh the health of the firm.

It's a Startup That's Launching the ICO

The companies that launch ICOs are fairly young firms. They don't have a long history of success, years of profits, or even a plethora of investors (although some do have angel or series-A investors).

Typically, a company launching an IPO has shown the ability to grow revenues or profits for some time. Since the financial information of the company will become available during the IPO process, institutional and retail investors will judge the company's performance, providing a harsh look at where it has been and where it's going. This weeds out companies that have no real reason to go public other than as a quick money grab. These bad players are more difficult to discover during the ICO process.

Does an ICO Make Investing Sense?

The appeal of investing in ICOs comes from the ability to get into a new coin for incredibly cheap, which gives you the opportunity to own a larger share of the name. The other reason? Bragging rights for getting into a coin early that then takes off. Both of these are fine reasons for owning an ICO name. Just know if you choose to go this route, there's a far better chance that the money you're spending will never be seen again.

You Can't Know Which Coins Will Rise

It took Ethereum's ether nearly two years to rise consistently above $20 a coin. Early investors in ether wouldn't have found it to be a particularly exciting investment until 2017. There's a likelihood that many early investors left, tired of waiting. The point is that investing in ICOs is extremely risky, since you can't know which coins will take off, because there's very little information about the blockchain that supports the coin, and it could take years before your initial investment thesis plays out.

FACT

It can take many years for an ICO to prove useful. Of the 902 different ICOs that went forward in 2017, the storage company Filecoin was the largest, raising a little over $200 million. Six months after its price posted on public exchanges, Filecoin's value had fallen 50 percent below its December 2017 mark. Yet, since Filecoin remains in existence, that's a success compared to most ICOs.

It Doesn't Hurt Too Much to Wait

The flip side of the ether story, taking two years to reach $20, is that it would have given any investor far more time to buy into the coin, as more information about the technology became known. Over the two years in which ether did very little, the world grew to know the founder, Vitalik

Buterin, and Ethereum had started to court large companies that showed interest in the blockchain technology. It gives you time to know which ones seem like legit businesses. Sure, you'll own fewer shares, most likely, but there's an improved chance you're not throwing your money at a bad business.

You Do Get More for Your Money

The reason you buy into an ICO is because of the number of shares you can get in a coin, if you purchased it from the beginning. If you had bought $100 in ether in September 2015, you would have about seventy-four coins. If you had done the same in September 2016, that would be about nine coins. The same in 2017? About one-quarter of one coin. By the end of 2017, the early investor would have over $53,000 in profits, while the person with nine shares would still walk away with a stout $6,500, and the late investor would have doubled that initial $100 investment.

It obviously pays to be early, if you're right.

Other Ways New Coins Come Onto the Market

As the popularity of the cryptocurrency market has grown, ICOs have become the most popular way for new coins to enter the market, but they're not the only way. As technologies grow more sophisticated and companies become more self-aware of the potential of cryptos, expect more offerings to be unveiled that will provide a whole new way to monitor the potential future players in the game. For now, consider these three other ways in which coins become available.

They're Mined

This is the process that bitcoin made popular. Deep within the blockchain's code, there are a certain amount of coins, and miners look for those coins to uncover new ones. Once they're uncovered, miners can then sell the coins to the market, just as you would sell them. The difference is the miners didn't have to pay market rates to obtain the treasure. If there's a market, as there is for bitcoin, then the coins will be snatched up quickly.

They're Controlled

The company Ripple used a controversial strategy when it launched its crypto, the XRP. Instead of an ICO, it mined all the coins, gifting a large portion of them to their executives. They then trickled out coins periodically, based on a number that the company determined would drive demand and ensure supply. The community turned against XRP due to this setup, so the company decided to take about half of the total XRPs and place them in an escrow account. The account funnels out 1 billion XRPs each month. If any of the coins go unclaimed that month, then the XRPs return to the escrow account until all of the XRPs are in circulation. It's a unique setup, one that might have an appeal to other companies, since it does offer some control in the coin.

They Fork

Blockchains are (typically) open-source software, and a community can sometimes tweak, test, change, and improve the system, seeking upgrades to the way it operates. Since there are weaknesses in the original blockchain—particularly when speaking of bitcoin—the community sometimes wants to tweak the blockchain that the crypto runs upon. If the community, in mass, approves the tweak, then a new coin isn't produced. But sometimes the community disagrees with a solution. In this case, the minority group produces what's referred to as a hard fork, where an entirely new coin develops. This will be discussed in further detail in the next section.

A Hard and Soft Fork

While the mechanics of creating a hard and soft fork can be complicated, generally speaking if the community of users and developers of a blockchain decides to make an improvement that the majority of the community or developers agree with, then it creates a soft fork, or a switch in the code that the original cryptocurrency will adhere to. This means the currency continues on under the new rules, without changing the makeup of the coin.

Sometimes, though, this change isn't approved by a vocal minority within the community, which leads to a disagreement on the future of the crypto. These disagreements can arise when the minority group believes the blockchain should change to improve the coin in some way, or it can arise because the majority believes a change must occur and the minority group disagrees. Instead of holding hostage the wants of the vast majority of the community, which agrees with the change, a minority forces a hard fork, in which a large percentage of developers will move with the original coin. The ones who disagree with the larger community will create a new cryptocurrency, which takes into account the less-popular decision.

What Happens in a Hard Fork?

When a hard fork occurs, creating a new cryptocurrency, it's similar to a stock split. Current holders of the currency will receive a certain amount of the new coin. For instance, when bitcoin cash was created during a hard fork of bitcoin's blockchain, a bitcoin holder received one bitcoin cash if she owned bitcoin at the time of the fork and the exchange she used recognized bitcoin cash. It's not always this one-to-one dynamic; there are instances where a split will lead to receiving multiple coins of the new token. It's dependent on the reason for the fork and those driving the change.

FACT

Cryptocurrency investing gets no more complex than when a fork of a fork occurs. This can happen though. In mid-2018, bitcoin cash experienced such a moment, when a hard fork was proposed, where a user would serve as a full node (or computer running the code) to create an alternative to bitcoin cash, increasing the block size for the coins from thirty-two megabytes to 128, among other changes. It eventually split in November 2018, and is dubbed Bitcoin ABC.

Other Terms to Know

There are a number of other terms that will come up throughout this book and during your time as a crypto investor. While there's a longer list of terms and definitions, which can be found in Appendix C, here's a brief rundown of a few terms to keep in mind:

- **Altcoin:** This refers to any coin in the digital currency space that isn't bitcoin. The term altcoin grew as the number of coins that tried to improve upon bitcoin's code multiplied.
- **Coin:** Nearly anytime you're referring to a cryptocurrency, you're referring to the coin. It operates as a currency on a specific blockchain, and only that blockchain, like bitcoin or ether. It's often used interchangeably with the term token.
- **Crypto wallet:** Crypto wallets serve two purposes: they're used to store cryptocurrencies in a safer environment, ideally separating the coins from hackers, and they also are used to spend the coins.
- **Digital contract:** This is a form of agreement developed on the blockchain, where two parties use the digital ledger to confirm the parameters of the relationship. The blockchain serves as the third party, providing verification of the agreement before passing along payments.
- **Private key:** This is essentially your user password for a coin. When you purchase a cryptocurrency, you're given two keys, one public and one private. The private key is similar to your personal signature, and only you will know the key. If you lose this private key, then you lose your coins.
- **Public key:** This is the identifier that the blockchain uses to confirm your crypto exists on its network. Your private key derives this key, and it informs the blockchain community that you own the coin and have the right to sell or spend it.
- **Tokens:** This term is often used interchangeably with the term coin, but in reality, there's a difference. Tokens represent a value of something or an asset. These representations can vary widely, from representing a unit of gold, a number of bitcoins, or customer loyalty points. The token doesn't operate on its own blockchain. Instead they are created by firms using a third-party blockchain, like Ethereum, to function.

CHAPTER 4

The Blueprint for Success

There are a lot of different theories and strategies that all claim to turn your crypto dollars into riches. Each one of those strategies can work; in specific cases they may have left someone with a profit. For instance, if you simply invested in bitcoin in January 2017 and then pulled out of the coin that November, you would have ended up returning a good amount of your investment. That doesn't mean it will work for everyone, especially since bitcoin hasn't had a jump like those eleven months since. It's also why you may hear someone say how many millions they earned by betting on the margin—or by borrowing money—to invest in the coins. It worked, but will it for you? That's a lot of risk to take on. Instead, this chapter will look at how to invest in coins because you believe in the technology, and you view it as a way to make speculative bets on a growing sector. In this chapter, we will discuss what this more prudent investing strategy looks like.

How Do You Pick a Winner?

There's a lot you must consider when thinking about individual coins to invest in, since there's an opportunity cost involved. Not only might you be wrong about where you're placing your money, but it's also preventing you from investing in another spot where you could be seeing significant gains. It's the problem with coin picking, or being forced to choose specific coins.

That's why you must come up with a strategy that you believe in. To do so, you'll want to consider a few areas that are ubiquitous across all cryptos. That way, you're at least evaluating the coins based on a set of criteria. You can then exercise that criteria across all layers of cryptos.

For instance, if you're someone who plays fantasy football, you wouldn't judge one running back by the number of carries the player gets per game and another running back on the number of plays. You would judge them both by the same criteria, whether it's a mix of carries, plays, touchdowns, yards, etc. The same logic applies with evaluating cryptocurrencies. As much as you can, evaluate them on the same criteria across all the crypto names, in order to ensure that there's consistency in your process.

Do You Believe in the Technology?

What's the purpose of the blockchain and, therefore, the cryptocurrency that's viable on the blockchain? How will companies interact or incorporate the blockchain? Will retail customers embrace the idea of using the coin as an everyday currency?

These are some of the questions you will need to ask about every coin that you evaluate. Despite the early days of mainstream crypto investing looking more like a run by speculators, as this sector grows, it's the technology leaders who will drive usage and investment. Right now, that isn't always the case, since customers are only beginning to understand the technology, its use within their business systems, and the startup companies providing the blockchains. At some point that will switch: the crypto market will be much more technology driven, and the money will flow toward those companies that have proven themselves useful. How beneficial that is for regular consumers and investors will be dictated by the purpose of the specific blockchain and the corresponding coin.

If it's simply a decentralized currency where no company operates the blockchain, like bitcoin, then decide whether or not the technology will allow enough users to spend coins on a regular basis to justify the market cap. If it's a smart contract tool, like Ethereum, then evaluate ether on whether or not there's enough demand among corporate entities to justify future gains. Starting with the technology will give you a base to begin evaluating more short-term indicators surrounding the currency.

ESSENTIAL

A good way to think about the potential of the technology you're evaluating is to determine how much trust the blockchain wants to automate. Remember, that's the purpose of the blockchain: to serve as an independent third party. If the technology replaces a process that typically requires a high level of trust—which banks, courts, and accounting firms provide—then the technology may have potential.

Do You Trust the Management Team?

Along with the prowess of the technology, learn about the management team in place. Do the crypto's leaders and founders fill you with confidence? How much weight you place in this could be based on what the blockchain company hopes to achieve.

For instance, if the crypto comes out of the development of a blockchain startup, in which its ultimate goal will be to eventually earn a profit from investors using its platform, then you need to research not just the technological prowess of the developer, but also the business acumen of its leader running the financial arm of the company. If you find that a crypto has a developer that's well respected in the engineering community or has become a star within the blockchain space, that's a good sign. If the company also has a cofounder who has a background in growing successful startups, it's another great indicator. If, on top of that, it has generated interest from top-name venture capital firms, that's a third indication that there's sufficient weight and intelligence going into evaluating this company as a value add. That will help the crypto that's the public face of this venture.

Evaluate the Transactions

One consistency across all cryptos, no matter whether they court big business or regular consumers, is that they need more transactions in order for the valuation of the coin to grow in a fashion that's not simple speculation. It's one of the few ways in which there's hard data that can be evaluated across the currencies, in order to highlight which ones have improved and which ones struggle.

For coins that have significant transaction rates, look at the growth of those transactions over the past year, past few months, and past few weeks. Do you see growth? Or do the transactions perfectly track the movement of the coin itself, which indicates all the buying and selling is done for investment purposes? If transactions perfectly track the coin, then that's a problem. It indicates that speculators have driven much of the transactions in the space, creating movements in the coin based on whether investors have decided to dump it or buy again. It's a unique wrinkle in crypto investing, since an investor buying and selling the coin is the same as a regular user purchasing and spending the token. When it comes to transactions, they all fall into the same bucket. Therefore, if you're seeing transactions track perfectly with the price of the coin, you're seeing how much speculation is at play in driving the price.

Most importantly though, you want to see a basement below which transactions aren't dropping. This indicates consistency in the number of transactions, and the higher this basement, the better off for the coin. If, instead, you're seeing transactions jump into the hundred thousands one day, then fall to practically none the next, you have to ask yourself why this is happening. If you then look at the price and discover a sudden jump then fall in value, one coming quickly after the other, it's an indication that the spending came from speculation, which won't sustain the coin.

The Coin Market Cap

It's not just transactions you want to look at though, since there's another layer to the spending puzzle, and that's how many coins are available within the blockchain design. Knowing the fundamental coin cap, or the limit on the number of coins in circulation, of the currency you're researching provides some clues into how the coin is spent (if at all).

Say you have a coin that has a total coin cap of 10 billion. That tells you something about the goal of the coin. Its creators have a design in place that requires significant spending in order for it to function as it's intended. You don't have a coin cap in the billions unless you expect significant transactions using the coin. This implies that businesses and large institutions are also part of the plan, since the large coin cap protects the coin price from large single purchases. The high cap ensures the price doesn't move too much from the single purchase and that there's enough liquidity in the system to process the sell. Bitcoin, for example, has a coin cap of 21 million, while Ripple's XRP has a cap of 100 billion. The difference in size is partly due to the fact Ripple wants to attract financial institutions, which operate using large-scale transactions.

The coin cap also shows you how much more run room the coin has before it hits its ceiling. Since most cryptos control for issues like inflation through limiting the number of coins that the market will ever see, there's value as a coin nears the top end of the cap. It's then that, theoretically, supply ends while demand continues to grow, driving the price of the coin higher. Bitcoin, for instance, has over 82 percent of the coins that will ever exist in the market currently flowing through its network. As that number reaches closer to 100 percent, which it will in the next decade, then it should improve the price of the coin (if bitcoin remains a strong draw for crypto enthusiasts). To reach the number in circulation versus the total coin cap, you just subtract the circulation supply from the total supply, to get the remaining amount left. Then divide it into total supply, and multiply that by 100, which will give you the remaining supply percentage.

FACT

To put that calculation explanation in number form, take the total supply available of bitcoins—21 million—and subtract from that the total number of coins currently in circulation, or about 17.2 million. With that 3.8 million bitcoins, divide it into 21 million and you see that there's less than 20 percent left in circulation once you multiply the decimal by 100. You can find the total number of coins in circulation by searching CoinMarketCap.com.

Calculating Owner Use

You can take the evaluation of this coin cap further, though, by then calculating how much of the coin is actually transacted on a daily basis. By looking at the circulation supply, or the amount available to currently spend, and the transaction rate, you can calculate the holding rate of coins, that is, how much users are holding on to the coins. These numbers will be high, since more users are holding on to coins, than spending. But if you do this analysis for a number of coins, it will at least tell you which ones are being spent more than others, as a percentage of the coins available.

FACT

What does this valuation look like? Take bitcoin. Let's say there's 18 million in circulation and there are 200,000 transactions a day. That means less than 1 percent of the coins are being transacted on a daily basis. Compare that with Ripple XRP, which has about 50 billion in circulation and it has 500,000 in transactions that day; in that case, a greater percentage of bitcoins are getting spent that day. How much you use this information depends on how much weight you place in this daily metric.

Other Valuation Models

There are a number of different valuation models that can show differences between coins. It's important to remember, however, that any of these comparisons are simply that: comparisons. The world doesn't know what it means if one coin is transacted at a slightly higher rate than another, since the information could be meaningless if the weaker-transacted coin catches interest from a large organization, giving it a sudden boost of legitimacy and stable levels of spending. Then that one coin that looked weaker will suddenly supplant the stronger coin. Again, none of these comparisons will predict the future.

Instead, what you're doing through this analysis is creating a way to compare coins on a holistic level, so you have some sort of basis for the coins you like versus the coins you don't. Inherently, it will eventually come down to your gut instinct, since there's no mathematical equation to provide an answer.

There are, however, a number of other valuation models you can use to compare two coins. Here's a quick list, which will provide a simple rundown of some of the tools that investors use:

- **Mining Profitability:** This explains how expensive it is to mine or approve transactions. Is there incentive for a community to embrace the coin? Has that incentive become too expensive?
- **Network Value to Transactions Ratio:** This compares the market value of the coin to the number of transactions a day.
- **Owner Concentration:** Do a small percentage of people own the vast majority of coins? This highlights the amount of interest from people not intrinsically linked to the coin.
- **Transactions per Second:** A higher rate per second indicates a stronger ability to scale, if the demand of the coin grows.

What Businesses Have Signed On?

As you're evaluating cryptos that are linked to a startup of some sort, it's going to be imperative that the startup grows its business in order to encourage further coin usage. As an evaluator of these coins, the onus is now on you to track and determine just how interested these businesses are in the technology. Having a running list of companies (or the number of companies) that have shown commitment to the coin will help provide a layer of understanding on just how much business interest remains in the coin.

If companies don't want to use the coin, then why should I?
You probably shouldn't. What you're learning about when looking at the specific customers is how much demand in the market there is for this type of service. You don't want to drive the only demand for the coin.

For decentralized currencies that target mainstream spending, you should keep a running list of places that will accept the coins. If the coin's transactions creep up, and there's no increase in the outlets where they're spent, that increase might have more to do with speculation. If, instead, a major online retailer or payment system accepts the coin, then a transaction move forward might indicate that there's a growth in the basement number of transactions you can expect moving forward. That's the growth you want to see.

Just because a blockchain firm lists a company as a customer, it doesn't mean that it will use the blockchain's coin. You should also look to determine if the relationship includes using the cryptocurrency, since a number of blockchains allow for the use of the technology without actually spending the crypto tied to the business.

The Information Hub

It's not always easy to find solid information about your coins. That's in part because cryptocurrencies are such a new asset that those covering the subject and providing credible data around it are only starting to take shape. This has brought in a group of startup news organizations centered on the coins. Mainstream outlets, on the other hand, often increase or decrease their coverage as prices rise and fall, since their readership climbs if there's a sudden outsized burst of interest shown via crypto price appreciation. That interest drops off though, as soon as the prices start to decline.

That means it's very difficult to always find the most credible resources for new information, especially as you dig into smaller altcoins. Here's a list of a few resources you can use, though, in order to stay up to date on the latest comings and goings within the space:

- BitcoinMagazine.com
- CCN.com
- CNBC.com
- CoinDesk.com
- Cointelegraph.com
- Fortune.com/section/ledger
- Reddit.com/r/BlockChain
- Reddit.com/r/CryptoCurrency

Evaluating Individual Currencies

There's a tendency when looking at the cryptocurrency landscape to fall in love with certain names. Maybe it's the management team of one currency that you find as an attractive quality in the coin. Maybe it's the transaction rate. Maybe it's the business narrative. Maybe it's just a gut feeling that has caught your interest. Whatever the specific reason, there's a danger in falling in love with one coin. It blinds you to the downside, which can be particularly damaging if the coin then jumps after you've committed your funds, convincing you to throw more money at the name. Remember that there's no clear winner in the crypto space, so even that gut feeling is just speculation. You don't want to get overly caught up in one name, mostly because you don't want to find yourself blinded by it. It's more than okay if you lose out on some of the gains. These crypto investments remain so speculative that it's better to come in a few days late than overcommit to a name that then plummets.

There are a few ways to account for this concern.

Reacquaint Yourself with the Downside

One of the reasons people fall in love with one coin is that they've had short-term success investing in it. If you plan to start out investing 10 percent of your crypto portfolio in the name, then find yourself increasing that percentage to 20 percent and beyond, well, you've forgotten about your original plan. You've fallen prey to the thought that what has happened will continue to happen, leaving yourself exposed.

Instead, pretend as if you never made a dime on the specific coin. Start over, evaluating the coin from the beginning, looking at how the coin is traded, why it's traded, and how often it's transacted. How do these numbers compare to other coins? What, inherent risk does the coin bring to the table? What hasn't shown its face yet? And what's driving the momentum forward? By resetting, and going back to the beginning, you might find that you have overlooked critical situations that could leave your overinvestment in the coin at risk.

If, instead, you're reaffirmed, then pick an appropriate percentage level within your portfolio to target based on your new analysis, being careful to not creep above the number. Technically, by doing this, you're still trying to time a market. But if it's the only way to prevent you from increasing your risk in an unsafe way, then at least you're managing your temptations. This is more understandable in the crypto market because it's so tiny, new, and lacking traditional investing structures, such as mutual funds and exchange-traded funds (ETFs).

ESSENTIAL

By becoming enthralled with one coin, you're buying as the coin gets more expensive. By purchasing coins on the rise, you're not spending your money on another coin that's staying steady at the moment. This leaves you buying fewer coins of the token that's growing since your money won't stretch as far in an expensive coin. Meanwhile, you're also losing out on the opportunity to buy more shares of the token that has held steady. That coin could actually benefit you more if it appreciates, since you'll have a larger share of the name.

Don't Change the Amount You Invest

If you've set aside 3 percent of your pay to invest in cryptocurrencies, don't change that amount in the belief that one name will rise. If you start to creep that up 1 percent or 2 percent, there's a very real chance you'll start investing more, and more, trying to cover a loss or risking your savings on short-term gains.

This is when you should display portfolio discipline. You have set a portfolio that you believe will provide you with a certain amount of return, if the crypto space moves forward. It's not a guarantee that you will gain untold riches, but based on what you can afford to invest and how much risk you can take on, this portfolio is designed to protect you and help you still profit. If at the first sign of excitement, you're trying to increase the size of your stake and changing the makeup of your portfolio, then you're displaying very poor portfolio discipline.

If you're going to make a mistake in this realm, though, then move part of your crypto portfolio into the coin you're most interested in. Again, increase the size of the percentage dedicated to the coin, and stick to that size, rebalancing every quarter. Do not increase the amount in which you're investing in the cryptocurrency space, since you chose the original percentage for a reason.

Don't Overweight Speculative Bets

As you do your research and become intrigued by smaller altcoins with less name recognition, invest in the coins. You should still, however, leave these names to the smaller corners of your portfolio.

There's a lot that goes into a winning cryptocurrency. Take a look at bitcoin. It doesn't have the best technological advantage in the blockchain space. It doesn't have significantly more transactions than some other coins. It doesn't even have a known founder. And a lot of the places that accept bitcoin also accept other cryptos. In trying to answer the question, "Should bitcoin remain the most important name in the space?" from a pure analysis perspective, probably not. Yet, because it was first and because of its name recognition, its brand, and its use cases, bitcoin remains atop this digital hill.

That makes it very difficult to escape the name. When you make a claim that XYZ crypto should become the market leader because of its superior technology, strong leadership, and everything else that's right for the coin, there's an important word within the mix. That's *should*. It doesn't mean it will. Plenty of smart, well thought out startups have failed. Just because the coin should appreciate doesn't mean it will. In fact, there's a significant hurdle before it can reach a status where it's disrupting the space or even becoming a more mainstream name, and that's actual use.

That's why you should invest in the name. But avoid overweighting these names too much, since you can't calculate many of the reasons that cryptos increase in value. At least not yet.

If You Find Yourself Trading a Lot, Stop!

A sign you've gotten addicted to trying to pick out specific names and riding their coattails is if you're starting to increase the amount you're trading on a daily or weekly basis. Since you have a portfolio construction, and there are fees involved with every transaction you make in cryptos, you have little reason to trade every day.

FACT

Humans are notoriously bad at picking investment winners. Just take a look at those paid for picking stock winners. Over a fifteen-year period, only 7 percent of large cap fund managers beat their benchmark index, according to S&P Dow Jones Indices. That number drops even further if you calculate the fees that one must pay to have access to such stock pickers.

What happens, when you start finding yourself trying to pick out winners, is that your mind changes regularly. One day, you have a gut feeling about NEM. The next, it's actually Cardano. The next, lumens. You can't keep up with this changing landscape because you can't actually know which one will gain.

If your trading picks up though, evaluate why it has started to grow. If you're trying to increase your gains using momentum, forcing you to move from one name to another, then it's likely because you're trying to time the market. If that happens, return to your long-term thesis around cryptos, and let that play out instead of trying to pick daily winners.

A Three-Point Mark to Judge Crypto Credibility

As you've probably gathered throughout this chapter, there isn't one tried-and-true way to bet on cryptos. They're far too new to create this level of reliability. That said, there are certain things you should make sure you understand and have accounted for, before buying into any new name.

This checklist will help you as you get started:

❑ What's special about the coin's blockchain? There must be something unique about the blockchain that the currency resides on. If it lacks differentiation from its competitors, any sort of short-term rise will soon fall back. Since you're not in the day-trading space, why would you commit funds toward the name only to see your gains rise then fall?

❑ What's unique about management? You want credible people at the helm of a cryptocurrency, and, more importantly, you want credible people who are willing to put their name on the project. While Satoshi Nakamoto gets a pass because he or she invented the blockchain, all other cryptos need to have credible management or founders. If those founders are impossible to find, then you have to ask yourself why.

❑ Do you have space in your portfolio? While you may have found a new name you have some interest in, which has a unique capability and strong founding partners, if there's not space in your portfolio, then you probably want to avoid it. This will keep you safe from yourself. Treat your portfolio like a zero-sum entity. If you're adding something, then you need to subtract from another name. If there's no place to subtract, then weigh whether investing in the coin is worth risking your financial security.

When to Hold

When to hold and when to sell your investment will become one of the biggest questions that new investors will face, once they've picked out the names that they decide they want to commit to. This question has many different factors and can go far beyond just basic investing strategy. While the vocal crypto investing community often talks about how they moved in and out of different coins, seemingly at a head-spinning clip, in fact your decisions to hold could prove to be the best one you make for the long-term stability of your investment. Don't get caught up in the day-to-day conversations that can make you feel inadequate or as if you're missing out on an opportunity by not selling. In fact, you don't know what the end result of the decision to sell cost the owners who are bragging about their remarkable gains, especially when you account for fees and the opportunity cost of fleeing.

Therefore, when thinking about holding, you should let your investment thesis be your guide.

FACT

We're a social society, and because of the weight we put on our peers' decisions, it can have an effect on our own financial well-being. Yale researchers looked at this, finding that when investors heard a friend knew about an asset but passed, the subjects bought the asset at a 71 percent rate. When they heard the friend purchased the asset, they bought it at a 93 percent mark.

Do You Still Believe in the Technology?

One thing you've read over and over again is how nascent the cryptocurrency technology and markets are. This means that you're on the ground floor of an asset for which there's no ceiling, yet. There's the potential for huge gains, when looking over the timespan of years. If your investment shot up 25 percent, while that's nice, there's no reason that over a significant time frame—say ten years—that you wouldn't see a 25 percent annual gain. Why would you want to exit when you're working with that potential?

That's why you have to ask yourself, do you believe in the long-term opportunity in cryptos? If so, and there's no reason that the crypto you have an investment in would become obsolete in that potential future, why leave? While, yes, it's true the 25 percent gains might be gone the next day, you're not playing this market in order to capture a small gain. Ideally, you're looking for a long-term shift in how we use and spend digital dollars, which provides plenty more long-term gains to capture.

FACT

Do You Need the Money?

Since you're only investing money that you can afford to lose, what's the hurry in cashing out? The whole point of this portion of your investment portfolio dedicated to cryptos is to find something that will prove exponentially profitable. If you're pulling out of the market at the first sign of gains, then you either invested money you couldn't afford to invest (which means you should get out of the market) or you haven't fully committed to the investment.

If you truly don't need the money, as should be the case, then there's no harm in keeping your funds in the crypto name, since you want to be there in two or three years, in case your investment has multiplied by three or four times. There's no harm in waiting, since you're gambling with the portion of your portfolio designed for this specific reason.

When Your Initial Investment Falls

There's a natural tendency, whether you're investing in stocks, bonds, funds, and, yes, cryptos, to run as soon as you see the value suddenly plummet. It feeds on the worst fears of investing, and that's loss aversion. It's the notion that we're more scared of actually losing money than the prospect of gaining.

This notion can get you in a significant amount of trouble in your investing life, if you do not check it carefully. That's because if you're selling on the downside, you're locking in losses. Take an investment of $100 into XYZ coin. Let's say the $100 falls by 30 percent shortly after the investment processes, and you immediately cash out. You've now locked in a $30 loss, guaranteeing you will end up in the red on the investment. Now let's say that three days later, the price of XYZ jumps by 60 percent. You could be up by $12, at this point, instead of down $30. You don't want to sell on the slide because it guarantees that you're going to lose money.

If anything, consider this time of depreciation an opportunity to buy, if you have the funds to do so. Why? Because you have a chance to purchase the coins at a deflated price, assuming you believe in the long-term potential of the currency. Say you're adding $100 into your portfolio every month, and the first month you bought the coin at $100, which is now priced at $70. If you continue purchasing the coin at the same pace that you originally planned, then the $100 isn't just purchasing you one coin, but one coin and nearly half of another coin. Your total portfolio now has almost two and a half coins. Now let's say the price doubles to $140 during the next month. You then have nearly $350 in coins, on an investment of $200. That beats the $140 you would have if you stopped buying when the coin's price fell. It also crushes the loss of $30 that someone would have locked in if they chose to walk away as the price fell.

When to Sell

One strategy you'll see as you talk to more people about their cryptocurrency investments is that they're almost looking to cash out their investment as soon as they place the funds into the market. It's as if such an investor believes that the market will move simply because of his small infusion, and eat away his gains just because he decided to enter. Or if he enters and immediately experiences gains, it's like an action movie stunt trying to get the money out, as if he somehow tricked his way into a profit. Don't be like this investor.

There's an inherent timing of the market when you're selling because it's at that moment when you're locking in whatever gains or losses you've earned over the time frame in which you've invested money in the crypto space. That's why you should be very careful about when you're deciding to make this move, since you're also locking in fees by making the transaction. And doing it too often can rack up those transaction fees, cutting into any profits you may have gained over the past days or weeks.

When It's Time to Rebalance Your Portfolio

Assuming you're not trying to day trade your way into profitable gains within the crypto market, then rebalancing your portfolio will likely be the most common reason you'll need to sell. What this does is move your targeted portfolio percentages back in line with their intended mark.

Say when you began to invest you targeted a 50 percent stake in bitcoin, 30 percent in ether, and the rest in a various number of other coins. Over time, as the prices of the coins fluctuate, these percentages will become completely out of whack. Say after three months your portfolio now has about 75 percent of its value in bitcoin, 10 percent in ether, and 15 percent in the other coins, after bitcoin propelled forward while other coins either remained stagnant or stalled. In order to get the balance back in order, you can sell the gains in bitcoin, and reinvest them into the other coins. This assumes you want to keep the original portfolio structure (which hopefully you do and you're not being swayed by some short-term movements in the coins).

In this case, you would sell the amount that makes up the bitcoin that has created a 25 percent increase in the portfolio, and spread the gains across the other coins in order to get them back in line. You would do this, while also accounting for your ongoing influx of cash that you commit to the market. You'll have to pay fees on these transactions, so you won't want to rebalance too often. A common habit is once every quarter or twice a year.

When Something Changed in the Structure of Your Investment

While you don't want to be in the business of trying to time the market, there's a reason to sell a crypto investment if the purpose of the coin completely shifts. Since many of the coins are backed by startups, these companies could dramatically change the focus or structure of the company, moving on a whim. If these changes alter your investment thesis in the coin, then it's probably time to escape.

The changes would probably occur for two reasons. First, say a blockchain, like Ripple, originally sought to court financial institutions with their technology. You liked this narrative and bought in. Now let's say the company suddenly announces that it can't find footing in the financial institution space, and will now look at retail suppliers as their main target. While this is a farfetched scenario, if something like this occurred then it opens up the coin to a much different set of obstacles and competitors. It could change the way you view the company and the coin, which means you should probably sell if you don't believe in the new focus.

The other scenario, which is more likely in the crypto space, is if a technological change occurs that you don't believe in. Say bitcoin decided to change its structure to allow for faster transactions. Well, this could hurt a coin like litecoin, which tries to sell itself on the basis of the ability to transact faster. Maybe you think this is a big enough change to escape litecoin. Or what if litecoin decided it wanted to change its structure to hide users even more, and you disagree with this technological alteration? Then you would maybe want to escape the investment.

ALERT

It's not a guarantee that you'll want to totally escape if a coin decides on a technological upgrade that you disagree with. If it's a contentious change, then there's a chance that more within the community will disagree to the point where someone will create a hard fork, developing a new coin. In that case, it's worth staying in, since as an investor in the mother coin you would receive the coins for the hard fork. Then you can exit the mother coin if you don't believe in the technology.

When You No Longer Believe in Cryptos

Right now, it's easy to see the potential in cryptocurrencies because it's based on new technologies, it's still finding its form in the larger economy, and most governments haven't taken significant steps in order to build their own cryptos. That could all change tomorrow, if something comes along that redefines how the world views the potential of this space. If there ever comes a time when you no longer feel optimistic that the cryptocurrency narrative will turn into a world-changing tool, then it's probably time to leave. That's not because your investment has failed, but instead due to your inability to support the trend. It'll make it nearly impossible to manage your investment with clear eyes if you inherently don't believe it can perform well. In that case, it makes sense to leave.

The Dangers of Evaluating Cryptos Like Stocks

Taking common investing strategies and using them for investing in cryptocurrencies makes sense, since there's a need to minimize risk and protect against overexuberance. Modern investing strategies help achieve just that. With that said, you can't take the strategy too far and treat cryptos as if they're stocks. There are significant differences in the return expectations, which prevent this one-to-one comparison.

There's No History of Returns

Crypto enthusiasts will try to predict future gains based on where a crypto has gone in the past. But when it comes to historical returns, a few years do not provide enough information or data to project based on those returns. It's dangerous to do this in any investing situation, but particularly damaging when you're basing it on only a maximum of ten years of data (in bitcoin's case). Just because bitcoin reached $20,000 in 2017 does not provide any evidence that it will ever reach that number again.

In the stock market, if you have a fully diversified US index fund, as long as the American economy continues to function, you can estimate that over time you will earn about 7 percent returns based on nearly one hundred years of results. Even that looks far different on a year-by-year basis.

There's No Dividends to Prop Up the Stock

Companies use methods to keep a stock moving forward through the use of stock buybacks and dividends. These dividends, in particular, can be reinvested in the market, providing an extra incentive to own the company.

This does not exist in the crypto market.

It's Not a Diverse Marketplace

At this point in crypto history, coins have not moved in isolation of one another. Bitcoin raises all boats, leaving it difficult to truly diversify within the crypto space, other than as a hope that one coin will break out of this lockstep movement.

When you're investing in stocks, there are eleven sectors within the S&P 500. While stocks within the sectors will often move similarly to each other, outside those sectors, you can find companies that move with each other, in opposite of another, or some level in between. It makes the ability to diversify so much more of a possibility. It's not 100 percent diversification, but it's much more than you will find in cryptos.

FACT

In a 2000 study by investment managers, the two authors found that with sixty stocks in your portfolio, you would still only capture 86 percent of the entire market. What's interesting about cryptos is that you can't diversify to capture the entire market. Instead, you diversify in case one coin becomes more prominent than all the others. You're not able to capture the entire market with diversification yet, because the big names all move with bitcoin.

There's Much More Volatility

The only true known reality within crypto investing at this point is that volatility will follow, no matter what coin you decide to place your bet in. It's not something you can control or avoid, if you want to take part in this space. It's another reason why you should stick with your portfolio strategy, since hopefully while one coin goes crazy, your other coins will provide some semblance of consistency. (It's not likely to happen in cryptos at this time, but it's worth wishing for.)

A successful investor either ignores the volatility or takes advantage of it.

It's Best to Ignore

If you only have a very defined amount of money you can spend each month on these coins, then your best bet is to ignore the daily fluctuations. This is much like stock investing, since you should also steer clear of checking your stock performance on a daily or even weekly basis. Instead, set reminders in your calendar to only check once a week, once a month, or once a quarter. If you're more prone to reacting to the volatility, use the longer time frames to check in; that way you won't be susceptible to changing your plans just because a coin is either up or down significantly.

When you do this check-in, be sure to look at the entire time frame's change, as opposed to that specific day you're checking in. Say you decide to check in every quarter, then gauge how your coins have performed over the three months. That way you can see a broader picture of the performance before deciding if you believe you should change things up. It allows you to also ignore what happened yesterday or the day before.

You Have an Opportunity to Buy the Dips

One option in your portfolio design is to keep a small portion of your monthly crypto investing allotment in cash. The reason for this is it will allow you to buy dips in coins. It's particularly apt strategy if you know your impulse will be to try and buy coins on a whim each month. This way, you're accounting for your investing inclinations or shortcomings. Again, you're in the business of timing the market, so you'll likely be wrong more than you are not. But say the volatility catches ether dropping 50 percent one day, but you believe in ether's long-term potential. Then you can take that allotment and buy more coins when they're depreciated in price. Will it always work? No. Don't worry about guessing a bottom. Instead, the goal is to buy when ether is slightly cheaper so you have more coins within your portfolio, in case it appreciates again.

How I Do It

It's fairly simple to find those who gained from the cryptocurrency ride in 2017; practically anyone that held their investment for a couple months that year would have seen significant returns. But it was easier said than done to get into the market and stay in. Those who did believed in the technology and researched the coins they sought to trust.

A Story of Gain

Calloway Cook first started getting into cryptocurrencies in college. He built a computer from scratch solely to mine litecoins. As you can imagine, he's not your typical cryptocurrency investor. While he managed to get a few litecoins this way, he didn't consider this investing.

That changed shortly after college, when he received his first tax return. With $1,700 in his pocket, he decided to put the check toward cryptocurrencies. He had other smaller investments in different coins at the time, but this was when he stepped into the space in a much bigger way. Specifically, he moved it into ether, which he had been reading about, studying the white paper that launched the coin, and evaluating the technology. "It's going to do what Napster did to music," says Cook. Luckily for Cook, that tax return came just in time for him to ride the 2017 wave that would turn ether from a niche coin into one of the primary investments within the space. He bought in while the coin was under $3. By the end of 2017, Ether had risen to just under $700.

What Went Right

Cook didn't realize all those gains, pulling out some of the investment to pay for his car and his student loans, all good reasons for selling out your stake in this speculative investment. But Cook is also very young, with forty years of working age left, unless his plans to retire by his mid-thirties come to fruition. He can take on more risk than the investor a few years from retirement, since he has plenty of time to cover any falls. He's seen plenty, like moving some of his money out of ether and into a couple other altcoins that have yet to show their value.

Still, the reason Cook remains in cryptos is because of his belief in the long-term technological benefit. Yet, with the gains, he's moved a large portion of his portfolio—80 percent—into traditional index funds and cash. As for the crypto investments, which struggled in 2018? "It's a matter of waiting" for them to turn back again, says Cook.

Now, we will look at the tactics that leave investors in trouble as they invest.

CHAPTER 5

The Mark of a Losing Bet

In the cryptocurrency space, there's plenty of opportunity to go down the wrong path, investing in a name that has no real basis for existing, or provides little benefit beyond giving the creators of the coin a quick influx of funds before they also flee. That's why it's often best to take a skeptical view of any new investment, leaving the onus on the coin to convince you that it's an eventual winner. Without that conviction in a name, you don't miss out by simply abstaining. Instead, it's those investors who move in and out of names without any reason, those who look for any sort of movement to change their strategy, and those looking to take a bet on any coin that comes to market that leaves their fees skyrocketing, and their returns minimal. This chapter will explain the mistakes that people make when investing in poor crypto names.

How to Avoid Losers

When investing in cryptos, your goal isn't to avoid all risk. In fact, by placing your money into the space, you'll be making one of the riskier investments you can possibly take. With that risk, you will end up experiencing losses in certain names. It's unavoidable. Instead, what you want is to take stakes in names where you have a strong belief and thesis backing your bet.

So you will invest in losers, in the sense that they will fall in price, leaving you in the red. But that's just investing. If you're taking stakes in quality technology or management groups, then that's not a loser bet. Instead, it's when you're doing your research and looking to place your hard-earned funds into anything that shows the slightest possibility for a short-term bump, where you will find yourself investing in some bleak coins.

FACT

While everyone looks at 2017 as a reason to invest in cryptocurrencies, remember it's the outlier to this trend. In 2016, bitcoin's price grew a much more reasonable (for a new asset) 123 percent, while by December 2018 it fell 70 percent for the year.

Part of this avoidance has to do with how you approach your investment, and view your portfolio. Here's what happens when investors make these common mistakes.

They Focus on the Short Term

It's tempting to take lessons from the technology sector when first beginning to evaluate your crypto strategy, since it's the closest comparison in terms of a new technology overtaking the way the world functions. With the advent of the Internet, the dot-com boom built thousands of new companies all looking to find a place within the market, developing tools to take what we already did, then transitioning it online. Entrepreneurs made millions (and even billions) in the early days, even if the companies lacked long-term viability, as traditional companies overpaid to purchase these startups. Of course, what would happen during the dot-com bust was that investors realized many of these companies were way overvalued on their profit potential and their protection in the market. You also saw some companies that were considered industry leaders made obsolete as stronger technology moved into the space. Netscape, Yahoo!, and GeoCities were once leaders; these names were replaced by the likes of Google, Amazon, and Facebook.

If you watched this space, trying to place bets on names as soon as they became hot, and then leaving shortly after for the next sizzling tech firm, you would have found yourself in a chaotic and hair-pulling investment cycle. Yet, if you had your money in the largest technology companies in the space through the years, you would have come out doing better than simply investing in the largest companies in the US, on an annual basis.

FACT

Just how much damage can the frequency of trading cause? University of California, Berkeley researcher Terrence Odean looked at trades that occurred between 1991 to 1997 at a large brokerage firm. He found those that traded frequently saw returns seven percentage points less than those that traded infrequently.

Looking at crypto investing in a similar fashion, keep your sanity in check by understanding that many things will change over the next decade and you can't possibly know what names will overtake the field or which ones will become laggards. Leave your focus on the long-term potential of the technology and invest in the companies best positioned for that future.

But a losing bet will get you in a spot where you're hoping for a short-term gain, moving from coin to coin, as these companies try to become the new-age Internet boom. It's not a comfortable place to watch this unfold.

You Convince Yourself You Know Something Others Don't

There's a common mistake that investors looking at individual firms often make, thinking that they've uncovered a morsel of information that no one else could possibly know in the market. These morsels then drive an entire thesis centered on the tiny piece of information. It's common in the stock market. For example, the fertilizer seller Scott's Miracle-Gro has a large business focused on hydroponics, which is a common method for growing marijuana. Some casual investors learn this and think they have found a path for Scott's stock to skyrocket, riding the legalization of marijuana trends. Yet, while it may not be common knowledge among the general public, within the sector's investors, it's very well known and has been for a long time. So if you were to invest in Scott's, you would need to price in a reason for its growth beyond the simple tidbit that you uncovered this marijuana exposure on your own.

This is common, like Overstock.com's exposure to the crypto space or Tesla's solar panel line.

In cryptos, there are more opportunities to form opinions that are based on the potential of the technology. It's entirely different to think that you've uncovered a use case that the market hasn't heard before. For example, if you realize that NEM is a popular source for video game payments, the market probably knows this and it has been priced into the coin already. It's better, as you do this research, to assume the world knows everything you've discovered, especially since your research will primarily involve reading other people's work (and you're presumably not the only person to read it). If you make this assumption that others know what you know, then you'll invest in the ideas that have long-term value, rather than trying to buy in just to take advantage of some lesser-known detail.

You Buy Based on Price

There's an important term when investing in stocks called the valuation. This term, used by investors and analysts of the company, determines whether the stock is at a price point that makes it attractive to buy. That's because in stocks, there's a difference between liking a company's narrative and whether it's priced at a decent level to buy into the name. For instance, if Amazon were to double its price and shoot up to $3,000 a share, there's nothing that changed about the investing thesis of the company—it's still working to overtake brick-and-mortar shopping, and doing a great job of it. That said, for an investor looking to buy into the company at that steep price tag, it means that they must evaluate whether or not the stock is worth it at that price point. Because, in stocks, whether you're looking long term or short term, there's a limit to how large a company will grow, how long profits will flow, and how strong the business will be, looking forward. Due to these limitations, analysts and investors use all sorts of mathematical formulas to try and determine if there's more room for the company to grow at its current price point. In other words, would Amazon be worth buying at $3,000 because you believe it can grow to $4,000?

When investing in cryptos, however, these mathematical tools aren't nearly likely to result in a rule that you can use to run your crypto portfolio. The tools investors and analysts use to analyze stocks have been built through years of research, and even then they're more like a best practice, rather than a hard-and-fast rule. Cryptos don't have these valuations because no one knows yet how large this market can grow or whether we've reached peak-crypto hysteria. No one knows when we will reach a point where cryptos show some formality and sanity in the way they trade, which will allow some form of projection. You can overvalue the current price of a coin that looks incredibly cheap, say $1 a coin, thinking the valuation is fantastic and worth a buy, when in fact that's the peak of the speculation that the coin reaches.

FACT

Part of the reason these valuations work is because there's a link between companies growing in the United States and the gross domestic product (GDP) of the country. If the GDP is growing, then the companies that make up the economy will grow as well. Crypto's growth, however, isn't linked with GDP.

Don't worry about valuation at this point in your cryptocurrency-investing journey. Focus more on the narrative and the technology. If you believe in the technology, the company, and its place in the blockchain universe, then that's a better guide than whether or not there's room for growth. Because if you're right about the technology, company, and its place in the blockchain sphere, then there's plenty of room for growth. If you're afraid to get in because you think it's too expensive and you're waiting for a drop in the price, then you're getting into the coin for all the wrong reasons.

You Don't Keep Track of the Crypto Company

These investments you've made aren't a bet into a stable, profitable, or even strong company. There are positive attributes, which leave them worth investing in, but they don't yet have the customer base, revenues, or track record to prove that the business will move forward for years to come. It's not like investing in Walmart, where you can as reasonably as possible assume it won't crumble into bankruptcy in the next month.

That's why you should remain vigilant about what's going on with the company, and check in from time to time to gauge whether it's still growing or not. These companies are only going to tell you when things are going well. They don't have a fiduciary duty to protect their crypto investors and aren't forced to share when profits fall or when expectations have changed. But you still want to see significant wins at this juncture in the growth journey.

Sign up for their press release circulation, if they have one, so you can be notified when a new announcement comes out. These are important for the crypto investor, since it's one of the few times when you will hear from the company. Also be sure to follow the company's leaders on social media, if they're active on a platform. While they won't share much about the specific tactics of the business, it's one of the few times you can hear their sentiment on the overall crypto universe—if they're sharing that information to their followers.

You don't want to be the person who puts his head into the sand, ignoring what's happening at the company that the crypto investment is reliant on. That said, you also shouldn't overreact to every piece of news. News items are a way to continue to challenge your belief in the firm.

You Constantly Check the Price

You've almost certainly known that person who checks his phone every minute, interrupting conversations to browse his email or social media networks, believing he needs to respond more than speak to you during your conversation. It's annoying. Heck, it might even be something you do. But if you act like that person with your investments, then you're not going to feel strongly about where you've placed your money. If you're following every up and down moment in the price of a coin, every day will be filled with anxiety, trepidation, and concern that it's time to sell. Mixed in there will be fleeting flights of optimism, although it will shortly be replaced as soon as the market turns once again.

If you feel as if you need to check your investments more than just quarterly, set a reminder in your calendar for once a week. At that point, check your investments, seeing how they've performed over the previous seven days. You don't want to become the irritable dinner guest, receiving real-time alerts that your purchase of lumens just dropped 10 percent. If you're in this for the long haul, 10 percent isn't a big deal.

ALERT

Many of the mobile applications you use for buying and tracking coins will automatically begin notifying you via phone updates. Make sure to turn these notifications off within your phone or app settings.

You Borrow to Fund Your Investment

It's something that needs reiterating: if the only way you can buy the investment you want to make is by putting it on a credit card, taking out a loan, or buying on the margin, then avoid the investment. Again, this isn't a get-rich-quick scheme. It sounds like it because there was so much forward momentum in the price of coins during 2017; people made thousands to hundreds of thousands of dollars investing in the coins. It makes it seem as if this is a short-term investment in which you can escape a few weeks after placing your funds into the center. It's not the case, and you don't want to risk your financial security on the hopes and dreams of these coins. Those who do are usually severely disappointed.

You Don't Ignore the Hype

When you first start to invest, a great place to gain some understanding about the weird world you've just placed your funds into is by going to the crypto communities online, for instance the ones on Reddit. These online communities provide a place to learn about how others view certain coins and which ones have fallen out of favor. It's also an extremely unsafe place to go as an investor, since you will get indoctrinated by the hype these cryptos can have within a very small subsection of the investing world.

Ignoring the hype in this market isn't about hiding from all of the communities. Instead, it's making sure you're using the information as only a guidepost for your strategy. While it's important to know what someone thinks the downside to certain coins are, it's just as important to clarify why you believe or disbelieve in a coin. Instead, you want to use the information while continuing to do the hands-on work of evaluating and forming conclusions of the technology on your own.

Where investors go wrong is that they read these communities, listen to the armchair crypto-psychologists, and then react to every changing opinion. You'll end up chasing around coins like a dog chases its tail: always moving but never getting closer to success. You don't want to be that person.

You Don't Read the Technology White Papers

To ignore the hype, you need to understand what the founders of the crypto originally intended the blockchain for and what that could mean from a business perspective. This will give you a way to research this market, and help you come to a conclusion about how much potential there is in the space, whether you believe it's ripe for blockchain disruption, and if you think this particular company has a chance to produce that disruption. To get that information, first look at the company white paper that started the entire project.

ESSENTIAL

Sometimes it's not always easy to find certain white papers, especially if you're looking for small crypto names. The cryptocurrency database at WhitepaperDatabase.com, however, does offer a wide selection of current and past white papers, which you can review at no cost.

Nearly every credible blockchain has its origination beginning with the development of a white paper that lays out the blockchain's plans, why it's unique, what problem it solves (from a technical standpoint), and why it's needed in the space. It's from these concepts that the company builds a cryptocurrency. It's the most important insight you can gain into the way the company thinks, their view on the technology they're producing, and the potential their creation has. It's here where you can learn what in the heck this specific blockchain will do.

Someone who invests without reading these white papers is going on hype. They hear ether is special, so they invest. They've read there's something unique about Cardano, so they invest. This will lead them to the whispers of the online communities, and put their investment in danger, especially when they're looking to exit at the smallest sign of retrenchment.

You Don't Consume Trusted Resources

As the world has seen from the proliferation of fake news stories and sinister companies with the goal of turning false ideas into a reality, it takes skill to consume information correctly. It's not just about the news outlet, but also what stories you're choosing to read.

That lesson is important in the world of cryptocurrency. Since there's an inherent goal within some crypto-specific media organizations to propel the coins forward (and ensure their content is read), you have to watch out for overenthusiasm from the cryptosphere. That said you also have to be careful of mainstream outlets, as they don't yet understand or accept crypto ideals that have turned these coins into a potential legitimate tool, currency, and investment. Therefore, you need to consume the articles you're reading with the right grain of salt, sifting out facts from opinion.

When a news outlet reports that an exchange was hacked, and someone walked away with $500 million NEM, then that's a fact. You can use that information, since it will likely devalue NEM. When someone writes that the founder of Cardano believes it can reach $10 a coin, that's useless to your investing thesis. Why? Because the news is just the opinion of the founder of Cardano, who benefits from any jump in Cardano prices, claiming it can reach $10. It's a very biased opinion. Avoid this kind of "news." It shouldn't have any impact on your investing strategy. (It's important to note that this is just an example, and the founder of Cardano never made such a claim.)

ESSENTIAL

Think you're adept at spotting stories that are meaningless or fake? You can try testing your ability by using the site Factitious.AUGameStudio.com, which has created a fake news quiz to help people understand how fake articles are developed and read.

An investor who loses money in this space will use all of these types of articles to sway his thinking on a daily basis. When Cardano's founder talks about appreciation, the naïve investor will buy in, thinking it's due for a rise. Don't be fooled by this propaganda.

You Don't Go to Blockchain Meet-Ups

To understand what the technology is capable of, you also need to understand where it's going. You can find a significant amount of proselytizing and preaching in the online communities, but one of the best places to find out the future of the technology is through blockchain events or meet-ups, which are in-person gatherings where people discuss and debate the technology. These get-togethers bring enthusiasts in your area, including many who work within blockchain firms. They will discuss the practical future and potential of the technology. It's a lot more hands-on than, say, if you were investing in an index fund. But that's the case because you're deciding to become a venture capitalist by entering this space. You need to understand what's happening in this world to bet on it. These events are some of the best ways to hear real case studies, and meet people who actually create in the blockchain field.

Don't invest based on your intuition and beliefs. You'll guess wrong far more than you will right.

The Day-Trading Mistake

In the late 1980s and into the early 2000s, day trading became a common activity for people. They sought to use timing to jump on a deflated stock, scoring small wins that would add up into a big gain. The Internet age made this tactic possible for the regular at-home investor. Companies like E*TRADE Financial became huge businesses, profiting off their ability to make this activity available to people at home. In exchange, the companies charged fees for each trade. It also quickly became clear this wasn't the financial activity to use if you wanted to safely save for retirement. Why? Mostly because people are really bad at market timing and predicting when companies' stock will rise and when it will fall. While there are plenty of investors out there that still tout this strategy, it has largely been devalued.

Yet, in cryptocurrency investing, the idea of trading on a daily basis remains an embraced move. Nothing is special about cryptocurrencies when it comes to day trading, though. It's still a solid way to lose money.

There are inherent reasons in the structure of investing that makes it very difficult to come out ahead when trying day trading. Even if those structures weren't in place, it would require more than getting two or three bets correct in order to profit. Instead, it would require you to get multiple picks a day right, if you're to wind up in the black. All that timing puts the possibility of ending up on top very slim.

Those Fees Remain

The biggest structural challenge to investing and trading out coins throughout the day is fees. You're going to be racking up a .01 percent exchange fee or more on every trade of every coin you make. That doesn't seem like much, but let's say you make a trade that is equal to $1,000. Then you need that trade to make more than $10. But actually, that's not true, because you also have to sell it, so now you have to make sure it makes $10, plus whatever you sell the coins for when the sale goes through. While these fees will always be part of the equation, they become more onerous the shorter you hold your coins in one spot. Say you make ten different trades that day with the $1,000. Then you would need to make $100 more than you invested, and you'd need to make it in hours, as opposed to months or years.

Since you're day trading, not all of your bets will end up with profits. With 10 percent of your original investment coming out in fees, based on this scenario, you have to perform better than 10 percent that day just to wind up ahead.

ESSENTIAL

In this scenario, the fee includes an exchange fee. With cryptocurrencies, however, you also have to worry about the transaction fee that miners collect to approve the transaction. For some coins, this fee is incremental, remaining a very tiny portion of your cost. But for others, like bitcoin, it can become prohibitive, especially if the currency's price climbs; it's often a certain percentage of the price of the coin.

You're Presuming You Know More Than the Market

There's a big assumption underlying the idea of day trading, and that's that you somehow know more than the market does about the short-term future of cryptocurrencies, as well as specific coins. It's a tough thing to pull off day-in and day-out, as you're trying to determine which coins will spike that day and which ones won't. You will get lucky and find that you're picking a few correctly. It's luck, however. A person who goes to the poker table to play against pros will likely win a few hands. But she will still walk away with little to show for her efforts (if she doesn't choose to walk away in time).

The odds are stacked against you in any day-trading venture. That holds true with cryptos. Now that more investment firms have started to enter the market, they have state-of-the-art equipment and backchannel ways to invest faster than anyone else—in cryptos, stocks, or any other financial instrument.

FACT

A reason that people trading stocks at home have little chance to profit over the long term is due to technological advances, like high-frequency trading, which are available to institutions but not at-home investors. This allows institutions to conduct trades faster than you. Coinbase has made this high-frequency trading option available to institutions, indicating this disadvantage could transition to the crypto space.

It's an Exhausting Way to Invest

An underrated reason for avoiding this day-trading tactic is because you have to monitor the movements of the coins—meaning the entire world of crypto—all day, every day. In crypto investing, there's not a time when cryptos shut off for the night. It's a 24-7 operation, meaning your short-term investing strategy would leave you at risk every time you go to bed, try to get other work done, or even when you sit down to have dinner with your family. It's another reason why you can't expect to get it right all the time, since you can't work with the precision of a robot. That's required in the day-trading world.

You're Not Investing in the Blockchain's Future

There's another subtler issue with day trading, and that's it's not really invested in the future of cryptocurrencies. You're not actually trying to gain because you believe one coin's technology stands above others. You're, instead, investing in the idea that you've uncovered an undervalued coin and think it will jump in price in a few moments. It's not exactly conviction in the technology; rather it's a guesstimation in the valuation of the coin.

What's the problem with this strategy? No one has found a valuation method for these coins that stands the test of time, so it also takes significant assumption on your part. Over the long term, unless you happened to stumble upon that valuation method that surpasses all other valuation methods, you will lose more than you gain.

You could take the same tactic for any investment: whether it be coins, or stocks, or other currencies. But at least there are some methods in those other vehicles to come out ahead, even if the chance that you will turn a profit this way remains a small one. If you're going to day trade, why not try your hand at established markets, which have some sort of clarity. If you're going a super-risky route while investing, at least give yourself a chance in a world where there are more research and tactics available.

There's Nothing to See Here

While there's no hard-and-fast rule about what investment will work within the cryptocurrency world, there's one piece of advice that may serve as your strongest protection against bad investments: assume that the coin you want to invest in will not ever do anything. By putting the onus on the cryptocurrency to prove its worth, you can separate out the coins that may look decent on paper from the coins that actually catch on in the market. It will mean you get in a little later, but it will also make it more comfortable to invest with long-term thinking in mind.

Those who struggle with their cryptocurrency investments assume that every new instinct or gut feeling they have when it comes to their crypto investments will turn out prescient. It's simply not going to be the case. When you think this way, money goes into the investment before the coin actually produces any real-world results. You have the desire to be right and have something to brag about to your friends. That's the wrong motivation driver. There's no reason to be that early into a coin, especially since if you do so, you'll have a large number of other investments that will perform terribly, which you will avoid bragging about with others.

Selling the News

Part of the jitteriness and volatility in the crypto market has to do with the fact that it's a very new environment in which to place your dollars. This newness creates constant change, so investors are trying to read the tea leaves to determine where the market will go from here. This environment encourages many to enter, even though they have little conviction about the space, leaving them fluttering in and out of the market with the latest news.

There's a problem with this strategy. If you're constantly selling based on the news, you're not a faster seller than the investment firms and institutional investors that monitor the space. They have the technology and resources to react faster than anyone else in the market, which leaves you multiple steps behind them. Because of this, you're usually selling shortly after the news hits and after the price of the coin has already begun to fall. Why would this become an issue? It's quite simple. Investors who are always buying based on the news are selling as the price falls and buying as the price rises. That leaves them with less than if they had just stayed within the coin.

You're Selling on the Downturn

Let's say Japan decides to add restrictions to their cryptocurrency space, which leads to a short-term fall in the price of the coin in which you invested. You're working and receive the alert from Google about this latest movement. You check your bitcoin exposure, and it has dropped 5 percent to $9,500. Because of this sudden movement, you sell your stake, fearing this will lead to a long-term fall in the coin. You've now locked in a loss of 5 percent. If you bought the bitcoin at $10,000, then you've locked in only losses. If you bought in at $9,000, then you've locked in a smaller gain than you may have earned if you just waited.

The question becomes, do you want to constantly lock in these losses? If you're doing this for every coin you own, the losses increase exponentially. Say you have five coins, all which dropped 5 percent. Then the real value of what you've lost will be significant.

You're Missing the Upswing

What may sting worse in this news-selling strategy is what will happen after the news has made its way through the market. Let's say you sold your bitcoin at $9,500, locking in that 5 percent loss, and it continued to fall to $9,250. You may look at the price and feel satisfied with your decision. However, what happens if the next day, the SEC announces it will approve the first index fund made up of cryptocurrencies. This would be huge news in the crypto space and likely lead to immediate gains. In the minutes after the news hits, the price of the coin jumps to $10,250 before you get a chance to repurchase coins.

What does your opportunity cost look like? If you had stayed in from the beginning, you would be up $250 or 2.5 percent over the two-day span. By selling, then buying back in, you've actually lost $750, since you locked in the $500 loss, and now you're purchasing the coins again at a slightly higher rate, costing you $250 more than you originally had in the coins.

Don't Fall for the Market-Timing Assumption

Some will look at this scenario and believe where the investor went wrong is not buying back in at $9,000. That's the easy assumption to make with hindsight, since Monday morning quarterbacks have a perfect record of success. It's not a realistic criticism though, since you can't possibly predict every movement of the market. You won't know when a coin will fall or rise. You just have to be a part of the game to enjoy the experience and reap the rewards.

If you believe in the market, the news remains only a backdrop to the long-term investing thesis.

Yes, These Were Once Real Cryptocurrencies

Among the vast array of crypto names, there's a whole lot of fluff. Some of this fluff isn't necessarily a scam, although it's a way for the owners to make a quick buck, or for the creators to market new features or offerings on their non-crypto products. Some may simply be bad business ideas. Yet, in these coins, you find just how ridiculous some of the offerings can be. They look silly now, but at the time of launch, people bought in. If you're ICO shopping, for instance, you can find yourself buying into some absolute head-scratchers if you're not careful. It's also why constantly ICO shopping won't prove useful in the long run, since so few names have actually produced significant gains and traction.

Dogecoin

This cryptocurrency may accentuate the enthusiasm that unfolded in late 2017 more than any other coin. It was developed as a joke cryptocurrency, based off the popular Internet meme "Doge" which usually displays a Shiba Inu dog looking toward the screen with skepticism. Its tagline, says the coin is an "open source peer-to-peer digital currency, favored by Shiba Inus worldwide." Yet, at its height in January 2017, when investor enthusiasm reached peak levels, the Dogecoin somehow reached a market cap of $1.5 billion even though there's very little use for the cryptocurrency. It looks like the real joke was on the investors buying in. Then again, it's still trading.

WhopperCoin

At the height of the cryptocurrency surge, companies got into the mix, using cryptos as a marketing tool for new offerings. In August 2017, Restaurant Brands International, the parent company of Burger King, released WhopperCoin in Russia, providing a way that customers could use cryptos as a way to purchase their hamburgers or fries. It was only offered in Russia and served more as a loyalty program for the fast food giant. You would get a WhopperCoin if you purchased a Whopper, presumably giving the coin the value of one Whopper. It never caught on in the secondary market, and it certainly hasn't helped that Russia's government has gone back and forth on what it views as legal cryptocurrency behavior.

Dentacoin

When you think cryptocurrencies, surely the dental industry wasn't the first place you thought needed the innovation. Yet, that's what Dentacoin markets itself as, "transforming dentistry" through blockchain software and the cryptocurrency. Why, you ask, would dentists need their very own cryptocurrency? While there are surely areas within the business that could be improved through the right blockchain technology, why that would require its own cryptocurrency, instead of one already on the market, remains a mystery. The coin hasn't caught on, remaining below a penny in value.

TrumpCoin

The TrumpCoin was developed as a way to support then-candidate Donald Trump during the 2016 election. Within the fervor that led to his election, supporters developed the TrumpCoin to donate to the campaign or to trade with other Trump enthusiasts. It reached its height shortly after Trump's inauguration, and sort of like his presidency, it has been a rocky ride since.

How I Lost It

It's easy to go down the wrong path, if you don't have the right goals or strategy in mind, when it comes to crypto investing. You can be investing for all the wrong reasons, looking to jump in with every phone notification, or not researching the technology.

Hopefully, if you make such a mistake, you're in a position where it's not leaving you financially insecure or unsafe.

A Story of Loss

Alan Santillan had just gotten his first paycheck as a newly minted member of the working world, shortly after his graduation from college. Living in Seattle, he suddenly had some money to throw toward an investment. Many of his friends were making profits in cryptocurrencies, so Santillan thought he should too.

He put $400 toward bitcoin in 2017, enough to gain about one-tenth of one coin. The investment started to show some rewards, and he thought he could afford to extend his investment into litecoin, after a friend mentioned its performance. In a few weeks, he turned $300 into a $700, cashing out with a $400 gain in the altcoin. Then followed an investment in ethereum and bitcoin cash. This was at the time when the entire market rolled forward leaving Santillan nervous that everything would go away at any point. So after a couple months, he pulled out of all the coins. He had turned his $2,100 total investment into about $5,500. Not a bad take for a couple months of nervousness.

But after he left, bitcoin continued to climb. And climb. His friends had mentioned that ethereum was the most stable of cryptos, so Santillan felt as if he should get back in. He took all the money he had taken out, and placed it back into ethereum. Unfortunately, he bought it near ethereum's peak. The value of the coin fell 63 percent in the six months that followed. Santillan is afraid to check the price of the coins because "it's depressing to look at."

What Went Wrong

Santillan, like many of the investors in the crypto space during 2017, didn't actually understand what cryptocurrencies or the blockchain were. He invested more because he took the advice from his friends, and a quick look on message boards confirmed what they had to say. But he didn't look deeply at the white papers or the technology to understand why he was investing and for what cause. It was simply to make a quick buck.

That's also why he jumped in and out of the coins so quickly. Santillan said he received price notifications on his phone, which dinged him often about the movements of the coins. This encouraged him to react out of fear that he would lose his funds.

But Santillan is also young, in his early twenties, with a job as an SEO specialist. While it hurts to lose a couple thousand dollars now, it's not going to ruin his chance at long-term stability. He's going to "forget about" the investment, he said, meaning he's going to keep it in until it either disappears altogether or it reverses course. That's what long-term investing is about. Who knows? This short-term loss could turn into a long-term gain over time.

CHAPTER 6

Knowing the Players

It's still early days for the cryptocurrency space, but there are already a number of prominent names that have popped up, providing intellectual weight and experience behind some of the most well-recognized coins. Having experience is relative when it comes to the crypto landscape. The technology is so new that the early adopters with interest and the technical acumen jumped out ahead. This creates situations where some of the crypto management includes young geniuses, barely able to drink alcohol in the US. Others, on the other hand, have developed businesses in the past, before being awed by the potential of cryptos. In this chapter, you will learn about a few of these industry leaders. Since this space is so new, however, it's also important to remember not to get too infatuated with the current group of crypto superstars.

The Importance of Management

Since many cryptocurrencies, particularly altcoins, that you may throw your dollars into also have a business side based on a blockchain startup, it's important to know who makes the decisions that shape the future of the business and, therefore, the coin itself. Even if the coin, like bitcoin or litecoin, doesn't have a company working behind the scenes, it's still vital to recognize the person who created the network. As you perform your analysis, evaluating whether or not there's a technological need for the blockchain component or coin, it's going to help if you know something about the management. Does it come from a background of creating such cryptos? Has it shown a technical superiority over peers? The answers to these sorts of questions provide a base level of trust. If you trust the person, there's a better chance you will trust the technology. That doesn't mean that some important technology won't come from some unknowns—after all, almost everyone was an unknown at some point. It's just that if you research a coin developed by someone who doesn't have a long track record in the space, then you should require a higher bar for the technology before you decide to place your funds in the investment.

ALERT

Don't mistake a major investor, though, from a technological savant in the space. The Winklevoss twins have placed a significant amount of their worth—$11 million initially—in bitcoin. But they were far from the earliest adopters, taking a stake back in 2013. While this has netted them millions, and potentially billions, it's not as if they saw the trend before it happened. They saw the trend as it was happening and had the funds to invest.

When looking at an altcoin that has the blockchain company behind it, though, there's a difference in what to expect from the management, depending on who the person is and the background they bring to the project. For some, it's the technology that they have their hands on, leaving the business building to others. For other leaders, those focused on growing the company, it's about looking at the startups that they've developed, proving a track record of success. You'll want to see both types of leaders within these companies, since both areas of the business have some major technological and business marks to reach before they find long-term success.

Then, there's a third group, which might not run a crypto or own a blockchain company. Instead, these are the prominent investors and thinkers in the space, which will help shape the future of the coin through their ability to conceptualize what will come or the power (or lack thereof) they have to shape policies. Knowing where they invest—or understanding where they're looking next—can provide clues on how the cryptocurrency market is moving in the future.

What's Their Reputation?

In order to evaluate whether or not the company leader you're investigating has the stuff to pull off the success you need, first look at the reputation they have within the crypto-space. Do they have a name that resonates on message boards and blockchain circles? Do people talk about them with respect or revulsion?

This is where going to the message boards and crypto groups can help you gain some insight on how the community views the technical acumen of the founder.

This tactic, though, really only works for the leaders that develop the product, as opposed to the business leaders, since the community has only so many facts at their disposal to evaluate the company. Also, you're going to find stronger opinions on these boards about the philosophy behind the code, rather than whether or not the CEO knows how to negotiate, for example. Since the code is open-source, there are a number of other engineers weighing in and outlining strengths of the platform. There's hard proof in that discussion, which is why it's worth listening to.

ESSENTIAL

When on these message boards, you'll need to practice understanding what is good information to use and what you can ignore. Since these Internet commentators can't sit in a boardroom and watch a CEO negotiate, if they're calling someone weak at the boardroom table, take that with a grain of salt. How do they know? They probably don't.

What Else Have They Done?

It's rare that a superstar coder or gem of a business leader comes out of nowhere to fully surprise the world, developing a technology that no one could solve. Of course, in the history of innovation, it has happened. But for your sake, don't bet your dollars on the whim of a shooting star, until others have touted the technology.

Instead, you want to view the technical leaders based on what they've created in the past. While this might be the first time they've developed a blockchain tool that has gained steam, there's usually a sign that there's interest, intrigue, and legitimate talent prior to the launch of the specific crypto you're studying. You can search a name online to get a feel for someone's past work. Also, check out GitHub.com, a platform for developers, and see if the person has created projects in the past. You want to see that this isn't some get-rich-quick scheme, but a general interest in the space. It will better protect you from scams or uninteresting technology.

FACT

You can search for Ethereum founder Vitalik Buterin on GitHub. If you do search him, you can find results that go back to 2012, when he participated in a discussion or provided code. In 2012, he was eighteen years old. That's a good sign of his dedication.

From the business side of things, it's easier to research. The talent that has started to lead the development of a company has certainly fallen more on the shoulders of CEOs and presidents who have a history of creating within the business world. It's not always going to be someone that has already made billions—after all, if he was that successful in another sector, he would probably stick with where he's most knowledgeable.

You want to see proof that the business leader has some success in leading startups, building them into larger companies, and sticking around. Has he been a CEO before? Where? How did that company do while he was there? These are specific searches you can make when evaluating a leader, which help provide some clarity around the talent you're investing in.

Are They a Part of the Conversation?

When it comes to technical leaders, since the blockchain space is so new, there are a number of outspoken developers, all having a conversation about how specific blockchains are developing, and the philosophy of the science behind improving chains in the future. This creates a back-and-forth between these crypto billionaires and the community of developers that follows the space. Since there's an effort to prove the validity of the technology, and help shape its future, these crypto creators remain a part of the everyday conversation, either through Twitter, Reddit, or by creating white papers and videos outlining their most recent additions. These leaders will provide regular analysis, which allows you to form opinions on the ones you find most insightful and intriguing. Follow the names through their social media outlets and, over time, you will form stronger opinions, separating out the leaders you don't agree with or find intellectually shallow.

Do They Explain Themselves?

The thing about talent is that they don't shy away from promoting and cheerleading their creation. They're not necessarily shilling their crypto or blockchain, but they're unafraid to defend it. Buterin is a perfect example of this. While he has gone on record to say the crypto enthusiasm has become too exuberant at times, he's also at the forefront defending his technology and the blockchain in general. It's important to see a leader so willing to defend the technology, since right now it's all cryptos and blockchains have. It will lead to more adoption and understanding of the space and provide you with a comfort level that this person actually knows what he's talking about.

Have They Proven Their Technical Acumen?

For most of us who didn't study cryptography or the outer reaches of computer science, understanding whether or not a founder's technical acumen reaches a high enough bar is tough. After all, there are only so many times you can read a white paper to determine if the actual concept makes sense from a technological standpoint. You shouldn't have to make such a leap.

That's why the community remains a resource, to help you with the technology side of things. What have others said about it? This world is full of opinionated developers, all willing to call B.S. on the technology if it begins to make headway. Rely on these discussions to decide whether or not you believe it has technological value. If 100 percent of the community is against the technology, then it's probably a situation you want to avoid. If it's split, take the discussion holistically and determine which side of the aisle you come down on.

But don't outsource your opinion on the need for the tool. Does the blockchain solve a legitimate purpose? Does the crypto serve an audience that's currently overlooked by other offerings? Is there a market for the coin? These are factors you can weigh on your own. Don't be afraid to form opinions on that, even if you have to trust others to outline why the code is legit or not.

ESSENTIAL

The world of cryptocurrencies is filled with evangelicals who have placed their hard-earned money into the coins—often more than they can afford to lose—and have the belief it's the key to riches. This is why you must form these opinions yourself, since these types of investors fill the message boards, scraping any reason to try and boost the coin.

Who Is Vitalik Buterin?

With every technological breakthrough and trend since the development of the personal computer, investors and media are all on the lookout for the next young savant that ushers in a new way of viewing the potential in the code. It's where we learned of Steve Jobs, and Bill Gates, and how the founders of Google stepped into the mainstream. Then social media ushered in the rise of Mark Zuckerberg. In the crypto space, the leading candidate for this illustrious honor (at the time of this writing, anyway) is Vitalik Buterin, the creator of Ethereum.

Where Did He Come From?

Born in Moscow, Russia, Buterin grew up predominantly in Canada, after his parents immigrated to the country when he was six. According to an interview Buterin gave *Wired* magazine in 2016, he first learned about the concept of cryptocurrencies in 2011, when he was just seventeen years old. His father, who worked in programming as well, introduced him to the concept, and bitcoin specifically. At the time, Buterin didn't see much worth in something that had no intrinsic value, and he ignored the coin. But then, reportedly due to a change in the computer game *World of Warcraft*, which Buterin played extensively, he realized that centralized control created problems. Those problems become extreme when expanded to the size of our financial system. This turned him back toward the fight to decentralize the monetary system.

Some have claimed Buterin was a savant in mathematical concepts and programming as a child. Funny enough, it wasn't his programming that got him the earliest attention though. Instead, it was the written word.

Buterin, according to *Wired*, wanted to obtain bitcoins in order to take advantage of the growing currency, but he didn't have any money to invest. He was a teenager after all. Instead, he found someone who would pay him in bitcoins for blog posts that he wrote. Romanian bitcoin investor Mihai Alisie read these blog posts and reached out to Buterin about a bigger writing gig. From these discussions, the two created *Bitcoin Magazine*, the first cryptocurrency magazine, in 2011, with Buterin serving as the lead writer. To recap, within a year, Buterin heard about cryptocurrencies, dismissed them, changed his mind, built a small stake in bitcoin, and then founded the magazine that has become a trusted resource for crypto enthusiasts. It's one of those stories that make you reminisce about what you did when you were seventeen. And it probably wasn't anything like Buterin.

FACT

In 2013, due to the success of *Bitcoin Magazine*, Buterin decided to drop out of the University of Waterloo, where he attended college. He spent so much time every week writing about bitcoin, that he felt school no longer made sense. This gave him the chance to travel around the world, to research how other crypto startups took off.

The Ethereum White Paper

After a few years of writing, travel, and further analyzing of the crypto space, in 2013 Buterin published a paper that outlined a different version of the blockchain than the one bitcoin had developed. Instead of building upon bitcoin's blockchain, Buterin argued for using an entirely different programming language. This language, known as the Turing-complete programming language, not only made the code more expandable, but it also conceptualized what others had only surmised, expanding the potential of the blockchain. Buterin showed how two entities could create contracts on the blockchain, with the code providing the support, oversight, and approval of the agreement. No longer did someone require a third party—like a lawyer—to approve such a contract, since once both sides agreed, the chain handled the confirmation of the terms. No payment would be received without the approval of all the terms within the contract.

From this simple white paper, sent to a handful of friends, Ethereum was created, and the cryptocurrency, ether, was developed. The ether coin ICOed in 2014, in an effort to raise money as Buterin and Ethereum's cofounders looked for initial funding in the business. Buterin continues to serve as the technical lead on the project and voices his vision and opinion about the future of the crypto space and ethers through his Twitter account and other outlets.

FACT

In June 2017, an Internet rumor spread that Buterin had died in a car crash. In the hours following the fake news, the price of ether fell by 30 percent. Buterin, of course, hadn't even been in a crash. He proved that he was still alive in the most Buterin way possible, by posting on his social media channels an ethereum block number and its corresponding hash, proving he still lived.

Who Is Charlie Lee?

If Buterin represents the potential and future of the crypto world, foreseeing what's to come, Charlie Lee, the creator of litecoin, encompasses where cryptos currently sit. That's because the way in which Lee developed litecoin has become a common tactic among crypto enthusiasts who try to branch out and build their own highly valued coin. It's not something Lee shies away from; he has said on multiple occasions that he doesn't view litecoin as a bitcoin disruptor. Instead, he sees it more as the silver to bitcoin's gold.

Where Did He Come From?

Lee was born in the Ivory Coast, which is where his father landed when he emigrated from China. At the age of thirteen, Lee moved with his family to the United States, and he would eventually attend the Massachusetts Institute of Technology, before going on to take roles at prestigious companies such as Microsoft and Google.

But where Lee would gain attention is in the crypto space. He first heard about bitcoin while reading an article on the Silk Road and a few months later he launched his first attempt at building a coin, which was dubbed Fairbrix. To create the coin, he used much of the code, with a few adjustments, from another alt-offering dubbed Tenebrix. But the coin wouldn't last long because some of the security controls weren't strong enough to protect it from an attack.

FACT

In developing litecoin, Lee said he decided to make it four times as lite as regular bitcoin, hence the 84 million coin limit (21 million × four). It also processes transactions four times faster, which is how Lee came up with the name, litecoin.

The project didn't set Lee back for long because by October 2011 he had developed and launched litecoin. He took a similar approach as he had with Fairbrix, but this time he borrowed from bitcoin's code. He copied the code and then made changes to fix what he felt was problematic in bitcoin's makeup. This included increasing the number of coins available to be mined to 84 million and reducing the transaction time. When the coin launched, Lee's life didn't change much, other than watching his crypto bank account rise as litecoin did. At the time of the creation, he worked for Google, and he continued there for another two years.

In that time, he became an outspoken voice within the crypto space; his Twitter following still stands above most other crypto-ites. Then, in 2013, he left Google to join Coinbase, becoming only the third employee at the now prominent crypto exchange. He remained there until mid 2017, as coin prices exploded, before turning to promote litecoin and other cryptos full time.

The Backlash

Lee has garnered negativity toward his efforts and coin, particularly among a small sub-group of crypto enthusiasts. Some feel as if he simply cribbed the bitcoin code and has used it to prop up a coin that doesn't offer much in return. But Lee has long argued that he views litecoin more like an everyday spending coin, whereas he sees bitcoin as one you buy and hold, using it for very large purchases. It's complementary to bitcoin, not a competitor.

The other area where critics attack Lee concerns his Twitter proclamations. Some argue that his comments on social media are simply made to drive up or down the price of litecoin, in an effort to benefit Lee. To avoid further speculation of this, in December 2017 Lee announced he would sell all of his litecoin, outside of a few physical coins he created for collectible purposes. "When Litecoin succeeds, I will still be rewarded in lots of different ways, just not directly via ownership of coins," wrote Lee, via Reddit, in announcing his decision. "I now believe this is the best way for me to continue to oversee Litecoin's growth."

ALERT

As you know, litecoin is very similar to bitcoin, including in that there's no need for one person to run the coin or for Lee to develop an organization with the specific purpose of keeping the coin alive. Instead, computers all over the world that have connected with the code, sustaining the life of the coin, allow Lee to handle his apostolic duties.

Who Is Chris Larsen?

Chris Larsen doesn't have the technical skills that many of the big names in the crypto space possess. Instead, he brought business ability to the development of Ripple Labs, which has made him among one of the richest crypto investors in the entire market. But it has been accompanied by one of the more controversial and stressful battles for cryptocurrency control to date.

Where Did He Come From?

You could call Larsen the grizzled veteran among the group of crypto billionaires, because heading up Ripple Labs wasn't his first rodeo. When Jed McCaleb created the concept of Ripple, his partners felt they needed a financial savvy lead to help run the ship. That's how they came to meet Larsen, who had headed up two Silicon Valley startups. In 1996, he launched E-LOAN, which allowed customers to search for loans directly online. It was one of the first such loan tools to connect home buyers with lower rates, and it came around during the height of the tech bubble. It survived, and the company continues to function to this day as a part of Banco Popular de Puerto Rico. But Larsen had long left the company, launching a peer-to-peer marketplace for loans, Prosper.com. Again, it performed well, gaining praise for the concept. But a few years after the launch, the idea didn't have the same cachet in the market, and Larsen stepped down as CEO in 2012. That's when he would have the chance to take on the reins of Ripple Labs.

Ripple's founders mined all the coins upon the creation of the coin XRP. Within that, Larsen received a reported more than 9 billion coins, which, at a $1 value takes very rudimentary math to figure out. His stake has reportedly fallen to about 5 billion, but along with a 17 percent ownership of Ripple Labs, *Forbes* valued his worth at about $8 billion in mid-2018, making him number one on the publication's list of richest cryptocurrency leaders.

FACT

At the height of the crypto craze, it was estimated that Larsen had more wealth than Elon Musk. That can quickly fall in the cryptosphere though, as the price of Larsen's XRP stake was cut by 65 percent within a month and 85 percent two months later.

What Happened?

By the time Larsen joined the crypto rich list, he had left the company as CEO, continuing on as chairman. But his partner, McCaleb, had divested entirely from XRP and launched a competing company, Stellar. *The New York Observer* reported that in 2013, Larsen won a power struggle between McCaleb and his girlfriend, entrepreneur Joyce Kim. Kim had joined the company in 2013 but wouldn't last long there, as she clashed with Larsen and others. The argument over Kim's role would eventually lead to McCaleb calling for himself and Larsen to return all XRPs back to the community. McCaleb also reportedly demanded that Larsen be fired, which the board voted down, five to one (McCaleb was the lone dissenter). Months later, McCaleb would exit. Larsen would retain the CEO position until 2016.

Who Is Brian Armstrong?

Brian Armstrong is a name you should know due to the power he has within the crypto space. While he's not a well-known investor or crypto creator, he's become a growing icon for creating the platform in which the majority of US investors use to access bitcoin, ether, litecoin, and bitcoin cash. He's the founder of Coinbase, the popular US exchange, launching him among the most famous entrepreneurs, worldwide, under age forty, propelling his weight forward in the cryptosphere.

Where Did He Come From?

Armstrong is the quintessential technology founder. Growing up in San Jose, California, he learned how to code and design websites in high school, giving him some of his first paying gigs. He went to college at Rice University to study computer science and economics. While there he founded UniversityTutor.com, which provided college tutors an online platform to find and teach students. Armstrong led UniversityTutor.com as CEO until 2012, when he left to form Coinbase.

Armstrong Delves Into Cryptos

In 2012, after leaving UniversityTutor, he and Coinbase cofounder Fred Ehrsam sought to build a bitcoin wallet, or a safe place where you can store the coins. The duo soon realized though that what people needed was a safer way to buy and sell bitcoin, which is why Coinbase moved toward the exchange design, leading to investor capital and interest.

FACT

Coinbase is one of the more successful cryptocurrency startups. It became the first crypto startup to receive backing from financial institutions when the New York Stock Exchange and the Spanish bank BBVA invested during a $75 million funding round in 2015.

He Holds Power

Since the coins that show up on Coinbase will receive more interest from casual investors, Armstrong has become a powerful arm within the crypto space. The decisions to add coins come with careful insight and thought, but it can lead to ire if Coinbase decides not to provide access to a growing crypto.

In mid-2018 Ripple Labs began a public push to get its coin on the exchange. Coinbase has long held the view that it will only post coins that regulators will undoubtedly view as cryptos, instead of securities. Since Ripple owns many of the coins, some argue it's more of a company offering stock via crypto, as opposed to a separate digital currency. Ripple leaders disagreed with the notion and even reportedly tried to pay Coinbase $1 million to add XRP to the exchange (Ripple Foundation has denied this as rumor).

However, the concerns were diminished in August 2018, when Coinbase announced it would consider adding thirty-seven cryptos to the exchange, including XRP. It's not a guarantee that Coinbase will add XRP, which further highlights Armstrong's decision-making power.

Who Is Nick Szabo?

Consider Nick Szabo the cryptocurrency philosopher. He has long been a part of the rise of digital coin, even before Satoshi Nakamoto launched the idea of the blockchain. In the 1990s, Szabo coined the phrase "smart contracts," or the idea that a code could enforce a series of protocols on the users, serving as the trusted third-party when confirming the contract. It's the concept that Buterin turned into a reality with his design for ethereum. In fact, one of ethereum's units is named szabo, in a nod to his contribution.

But not much is known about Szabo, outside of his opinions of money. He's a computer scientist, cryptographer, and money philosopher, but beyond that he provides little information about who he is and where he comes from.

The Idea of BitGold

More than a decade before bitcoin came into existence, Szabo theorized in a paper that you could potentially mine currency through code. He surmised that if a puzzle that someone solved took time, then the currency developed from solving the riddle would have value. It's the basic concept by which bitcoin functions: miners seek to solve algorithmic problems in order to obtain new coins, which are then verified by the code and the network of computers. The puzzle that bitcoin miners must solve exerts large amounts of energy, which is the "buy-in" Szabo surmised was needed to add value to a coin. In fact, a week before bitcoin's white paper published online, Szabo asked an online forum if anyone wanted to help him code up BitGold.

FACT

It's easy to see why, from Szabo's writings, he might be Satoshi Nakamoto. Many people have accused him of this, but he has always denied his involvement in bitcoin.

Who Are the Winklevoss Twins?

If you have followed the rise of Facebook, then you've probably heard of the Winklevoss twins. Tyler and Cameron Winklevoss are notorious for suing founder Mark Zuckerberg, claiming that they had come up with the idea for Facebook while at Harvard University. The twins claim they hired Zuckerberg, for some coding work and he stole their idea. Facebook settled with the twins, reportedly in exchange for over a million shares of the social media company, plus cash.

While the brawny duo's launch into individual wealth and riches might have been controversial, through their early investments in bitcoin they're paving a new potential path toward notoriety. Now, with reportedly billions in cryptocurrency gains, they are seeking to develop a cryptocurrency financial ecosystem.

Where Did They Come From?

The Winklvii, as the Internet has come to refer to them as, hail from Connecticut. Their father built a technology firm, turning it into a highly profitable source of revenue, according to *Vanity Fair*, leaving Cameron and Tyler often interacting with the upper crust of society. For college, they attended Harvard, which is when they claim they met Zuckerberg and first mentioned the idea of Facebook to him. Since that time, and through Facebook's IPO in 2012, much of their time was spent trying to discredit and seek reward for their perceived injustice.

They also were Olympian rowers, finishing sixth in the 2008 Beijing Olympics.

Their Bitcoin Interest

With part of the payout from the Facebook settlement, the Winklevoss twins began accruing a large interest in bitcoin starting in late 2012, when coins were under $10 each. *The New York Times* reported that their ownership grew to 1 percent of all bitcoins on the market. Part of the reason their initial investment was scoffed at was because they also invested in the exchange BitInstant, which crumbled when its founder Charlie Shrem was arrested for helping to transfer $1 million of bitcoin to the online black market, Silk Road. Shrem went to prison for two years for his involvement in the marketplace.

This didn't deter the twins, who have continued to hold their stake, which was valued at over a billion dollars when the coin reached its height in 2017, making them potentially the first bitcoin billionaires.

What They've Done Since

Where the Winklevoss twins may make their greatest mark—beyond investing in crypto startups via their venture capital fund, Winklevoss Capital—is in the creation of a crypto ETF. They've been at the forefront of trying to convince the SEC in allowing the coins to be used as support for an ETF, which would open up potential for greater institutional investing, along with the development of more retail-focused options, like similar index funds. The two have tried multiple times to get approval from regulators. The SEC denied the claims, in part, because it fears the bitcoin market is too easily manipulated.

FACT

The twins have also started a very popular crypto exchange, Gemini. They got the idea from how they stored their keys to their early bitcoin investment, which included printing out the codes onto paper wallets and mailing them to safety deposit boxes across the country. The idea was that someone seeking to steal their bitcoin couldn't find the entire vault in one spot. Gemini takes a similar tact, just in digital form, to secure investments.

Don't Overweight Management

It's important to look at and evaluate management when researching a coin. It should be included as part of your decision process to invest. However, you don't want to rely on this aspect of the crypto evaluation process too much. Why? Well simply, you don't truly know the people who are leading these companies or creating the technology. Sure, you know the information they've provided you with. Their resumes look great. But if the growth of the #MeToo movement has taught investors anything, it's that the public knows very little about the people who lead these firms, as many showed a solid history of success and a very quiet track record of sexual harassment.

You can't possibly know how well a CEO of your favorite crypto coin commands a boardroom when he walks into a potential customer's office. There's no one explaining why certain customers passed on a blockchain company's offerings, whether it's price, the tech, or because the management of the blockchain company didn't strike confidence in the people who make decisions. These unknowns create a wide range of possibilities that you can't possibly have access to. It can also fool you into thinking a leader is far better than she actually is.

Just take a look at Wells Fargo as an example. For years, its CEO John Stumpf headed lists of the best leaders in the world. It turned out though that Wells used tactics to fake customers and add services to customers' accounts that they didn't want, all in an effort to reach unrealistic quotas. So, while the world thought Stumpf was a genius manager, in fact he has caused multiyear struggles and billions of dollars in fines for the bank, due to his leadership. How would investors have known that? They didn't. The only ones who knew were the jilted customers, the Wells Fargo employees, and the leaders of the company.

That's why it's important to take note of the leaders running these crypto-firms, but it can't replace analyzing the coins themselves. To do that, let's take a deeper look at the coin that started it all: bitcoin.

CHAPTER 7

The Basics of Bitcoin

When getting started with crypto investing, you will almost certainly have some of your investment in bitcoin. It's the dominant name in the space, and avoiding bitcoin is like not investing in Apple within your stock portfolio. It's foolhardy to eschew it altogether, unless you want to bet against how the entire market currently moves. That said, you should still understand why it became the prominent coin and, even more so, if it can continue to remain the domineering presence in cryptos. This chapter will discuss why bitcoin has continued to stand above all the rest, and explain its weaknesses. The latter have led to new types of coins that investing dollars have embraced.

Bitcoin's Origin

Where bitcoin comes from has become the most told and infamous story in the crypto universe, while also the least understood. If you have ever looked into bitcoin, then you have probably come across the pseudonymous founder Satoshi Nakamoto. It's he who began the craze by publishing a white paper on how to develop the blockchain. This paper provided the blueprint to launch the technology craze, the blockchain, which you've heard so much about. Then, only a few weeks later, Nakamoto released the opportunity to mine and buy the digital coin, bitcoin.

This set off a digital gold rush as people joined the craze to seek out and uncover the coins. While you may have heard this story, what's missing is what happened in the years after Nakamoto launched his project. Circumstances allowed bitcoin's value to appreciate as people adopted the coin in greater force. It's a story that's also relevant to you, since you must understand why people adopted this random digital dollar.

The Problem Bitcoin Solved

Prior to bitcoin, a number of different digital coins were developed, touting the idea that you could spend the currencies through digital means, and they didn't require, in theory, a third party. But the problem was that they *did* require that unaligned party, because in the early days of digital coin development, no one had solved the issue of double spending. This term meant users could theoretically spend $5 of digital coins on a movie and $5 on a couple slices of pizza, and there wasn't a repository that verified the fact that the same $5 digital coin wasn't being used for both.

ALERT

You shouldn't believe in bitcoin simply because it was first. There's a whole line of failed businesses that came first, launching a new trend, only to putter out once better solutions came around. Netscape once dominated the web browsing space before Internet Explorer and others showed up. AOL did the same with email, until Gmail came along. And Myspace had cornered social media until Facebook.

The open sourcing of bitcoin's blockchain allows the community to verify that there isn't double spending, since each coin has its own mark, and each mark has its own transaction history (within the code). Every transaction is checked by looking back through this digital ledger. It ensures a safe marketplace; when you spend $5 worth of bitcoin, you can only spend it once.

The Early Days

The community of digital coin enthusiasts, libertarians, and online anarchists jumped at the idea of a decentralized currency. It's something that they had long sought, since it provided protection against the federal government and it served as a practical way to conduct transactions. As miners leaped into bitcoin, seeking new blocks of the chain that would unlock more coins, another group found that the digital asset served another purpose. Criminals believed they could use the currency anonymously to buy products on a site called the Silk Road. This site served as a hidden black market online, becoming a prominent spot to buy and sell drugs, guns, and other illegal services. It's this use that drove the early appreciation in price.

Since criminals commandeered the early transactions, it unfairly stigmatized bitcoin as merely a tool to conduct illegal activities. Cryptos have struggled to remove this stigma, even to this day.

ESSENTIAL

It was foolhardy for criminals to use bitcoin. As investigators learned how to track and follow bitcoin, these early criminals found themselves in trouble because they trusted the anonymity they thought existed on bitcoin's chain. Startups have even been built to help authorities catch this group of users.

A Way to Exchange

Another major problem that faced bitcoin for the first year of its existence: there wasn't a way to turn the bitcoin into cash. Even to this day, bitcoins can't survive on their own without another currency to describe their value. So there must be ways for users to turn the bitcoin into US dollars (or other currencies) in order to cash out, if that's what you wanted to do.

It wasn't until the Bitcoin Market was developed as the first bitcoin exchange, which provided miners and users the ability to exchange bitcoins for cash or cash for bitcoins. This also provided the opportunity to use the coin as a way to exchange services, leading to the first real-world transaction, which took place in May 2010. Florida programmer Laszlo Hanyecz sold 10,000 bitcoins to purchase $25 worth of pizza.

A couple months later, Mt. Gox, another currency exchange, was launched and would become the industry leader until its demise in 2014.

Bitcoin Goes for a Ride

Since these initial hurdles of allowing people to use bitcoin to buy and sell goods were solved, bitcoin has hit new and remarkable heights. WikiLeaks began to accept them as a form of donation in 2011. Existing bitcoins surpassed $1 billion in market cap for the first time in 2013. That same year, bitcoin crashed after surpassing $100 for the first time because a hack exposed the precariousness of the coin. Venture capitalists jumped into the scene, providing startups in the cryptos and bitcoin space the funds to grow. Bloomberg even added bitcoin's ticker to its terminal. Yet, it wasn't until mid-2017 when another turning point occurred. Bitcoin finally hit a tipping point in the eyes of the mainstream media, investors, and spenders. This set off a frenzy of buying that created the 1,700 percent appreciation in price, and officially secured the coin as a potential investment option.

What Makes Bitcoin Unique?

Bitcoin's status comes from the fact it was the first. Many of the cryptos that have followed use bitcoin's blockchain as a starting point to produce variations of the crypto that got the whole market started. When bitcoin is compared to other cryptos, the other cryptos often solve a problem that bitcoin didn't plan for, expect, or find worth fixing. Yet, even though that's the case, bitcoin remains the most high-profile, important crypto in the space. That brand recognition provides some safety for bitcoin investors.

It's the Bellwether

When media organizations report on the rise and fall of the crypto market, what they base it on is bitcoin. It's the S&P 500 of the crypto space, and its performance will determine how crypto sentiment is perceived. Because of this status, it has the most eyes focused on it, so if it suffers a 10 percent fall, comments will follow, usually asking if this signals the end of the crypto bubble.

This attention leads to more trades in bitcoin than any other crypto, which creates side effects, both good and bad. Since it's the most traded, the impact of momentum has a significant effect on how your investment performs. As prices rise, the rush into the bitcoin market will suddenly increase. If prices fall, then they will fall lower than they should, most likely because of the momentum that the fear brings to investors. These momentum shifts create roller-coaster rides that have very little to do with whether or not bitcoin has grown as a potential currency.

It Moves All Tides

When bitcoin moves upward, so does the rest of the crypto universe. It's the bellwether of the crypto space, driving status for a number of the other cryptos in the investment sphere. When bitcoin performs well, suddenly there is more interest in altcoins, like litecoin or ethereum. When it does poorly, then so will the rest of the crypto space. As an investor, you want to have your money in investments that will do well on the products' own merits, undeterred as much as possible by larger macroeconomic issues. Within the crypto space, bitcoin's the investment that's closest to achieving that goal.

ESSENTIAL

As of now, it's very difficult to find coins that don't simply move with bitcoin's fate. It's the biggest weakness within the space, since bitcoin has an undue influence on the rest of your cryptocurrency investments. The cryptos that don't move with bitcoin are typically the smaller, less-known coins that may not have much of a long-term future.

It's Decentralized

Bitcoin doesn't have a startup sitting behind the code, trying to develop blockchain technology that has a specific use or targeting a specific niche or seeking a specific customer. It's decentralized, so unlike other cryptos, the performance of bitcoin isn't determined by whether or not the startup also does well.

Instead, what you want to see from bitcoin is that it's growing as a tool for transactions. Therefore, as an investor in bitcoin, you want it to become a more prominent way for people to conduct business more than become a tool for business. That's a higher bar for adoption, in many cases, since it takes a more mainstream need to grow and prosper.

Bitcoin isn't alone as a form of decentralized currency. It has a number of forks, which are currencies that were developed to solve problems within bitcoin's original code. These have now become prominent currencies on their own. These forks are decentralized. Other decentralized currencies have also launched to solve bitcoin's issues, which could potentially cut into its mainstream appeal. That hasn't happened yet, though.

It's Adaptable

Since bitcoin grew to such heights as the first crypto and the most prominent name in the space, there's a bevy of entrepreneurs who have sought to fix problems within the bitcoin code, which leaves it at a disadvantage to other upstart cryptos. For example, since bitcoin's transactions are public, a number of cryptocurrencies have used the idea of anonymous transactions as a tool to increase investment interest in a new crypto. This problem isn't just one to attract criminals. Businesses would prefer to ensure that there's greater privacy to the transactions they make, and for what those transactions are made. A number of developers have discovered ways in which bitcoin can be conducted anonymously. While these strategies haven't reached the status of implementation, it could become a feature one day.

The Investing Community Has Bought In

Unlike most other cryptos, for the most part, the investing community has shown a willingness to at least test the waters in the bitcoin pond. A futures market has been developed where investors can trade future contracts, betting on the fact that bitcoin will rise or fall. Electronic trade funds (ETF) have invested in bitcoin in order to ride the momentum waves, providing a buffer for returns. Goldman Sachs has opened a bitcoin-trading arm. And a number of different entities have asked the SEC for the opportunity to develop the first crypto index funds targeted to retail investors, which would be heavily weighted toward bitcoin. It's the one crypto that has driven all of this momentum, which improves the adoption rates and provides security, creating a floor for your investment.

It's Synonymous with the Crypto Image

While all cryptos have a stake in the perception and marketing of cryptocurrencies, there isn't one that has more of an image and fan base than bitcoin. It's a fad all its own; T-shirts, paraphernalia, bumper stickers, and actual gold coins have been developed around it. It represents something far bigger than itself: decentralized currency, freedom, liberation from a central government, isolation, technical achievement, and riches all wrapped up in its simple name. It has become not just a cryptocurrency, but also a status symbol. This helps protect it as the main coin within the crypto space, since the imagery helps sell bitcoin's use.

The Bitcoin Fundamentals

Developing fundamentals for your crypto investments will depend on what you look for in the cryptocurrencies you prefer, and what you expect to see from solid performing names. So the basic fundamentals that you eye will differ based on your individual preferences. You should keep that consistent when evaluating bitcoin as well. There are certain fundamentals, however, that you will be required to at least take notice of, since it's a decentralized currency. No matter what, you'll need to know how the adoption of bitcoin as a currency has grown and why it has improved. If it has failed to grow, you need to understand why. Beyond that, there's some other fundamentals that most investors will at least take note of.

Transactions

It's worth mentioning once again that bitcoin's transaction rates have not grown significantly since the price reached impressive new heights in 2017. At this point, that's fine, since it's still about generating interest in cryptos. The more people interested in the idea, the more likely they are to provide some funds to the mix until there's a tipping point that leads to a vast improvement in the usage rate. That time hasn't come yet. Transactions remain the biggest black eye for bitcoin investors, providing some fuel to the notion that bitcoin could be a bubble that will pop as soon as people realize few want to actually spend the digital coin.

Correlation with the VIX

If you're looking to find an index to track volatility, seeking to find an opportunity to buy into bitcoin, there's no clear answer. Since bitcoin remains a very new investment vehicle, institutions and universities are only beginning to understand what drives the bitcoin price. But there's one index that has shown an early relationship with the price of bitcoin, and that's the Chicago Board Options Volatility Exchange Index (VIX), also known as the Fear Index.

FACT

Surprisingly, the Fear Index has shown more levels of volatility than bitcoin. The CBOE measured the volatility of the two vehicles in 2017, finding that since 2013 bitcoin had less volatility during three out of the five years measured. The most surprising find was that it actually had less volatility through ten months in 2017, when the VIX stood at all-time lows.

The VIX tracks market volatility. The more the volatility, the higher the VIX goes. It's known as the Fear Index, since this volatility indicates that there's a lot of concern in the market, if it rises. Over the past couple of years, the VIX volatility and bitcoin's volatility have been remarkably similar, according to the CBOE Global Markets, which developed the VIX.

As the VIX rises, so does bitcoin. When it falls, there's some evidence that bitcoin will fall as well. Again, it's still early days in this analysis, so it's premature to link it as a certain connection or causation, but early indications show some relationship.

Track Coins in Circulation

As bitcoins are mined, it reduces the amount of potential new coins that could enter the market. The ongoing theory is that this will eventually lead to a tightening of the coin—remember that supply is fixed—which should lead to increases in the price of bitcoin, assuming demand remains at its current levels (or hopefully increases). It's unclear if this theory will prove true, since there are a whole bunch of other cryptocurrencies available, which could impact the supply side, reducing this impact. But bitcoin investors won't actually know if this works in their favor until the market reaches the point where this dynamic can play out.

Still, as the supply tightens, expect a run-up in prices while investors prepare for this potential result. You can track the number of bitcoins in circulation at Bitcoin.info, which updates daily as additional coins are discovered.

FACT

Since bitcoin has had a number of hard forks, its circulation numbers are more complicated than simply stating a 21 million cap. With Bitcoin Gold and Bitcoin Cash added in, then there's actually 63 million, with about 52 million in circulation. It could force the need for a much higher rate of demand than originally anticipated, in order to create the supply crunch that many investors hope for.

Track New Uses

What bitcoin needs for significant price gains are more transactions. But you can't have those transactions without more opportunities for mainstream users to buy and spend coins. If there are significant gains in the number of companies accepting bitcoins and ways that users can spend them, it will further protect the coin from a loss in value, leading to improvements in price.

It's a good idea to set up Google Alerts, which will send you a notification when a change in bitcoin uses occurs. You can do this by going to

Google.com/Alerts, and add in search terms like "now accepting bitcoin" or "will accept bitcoin" to receive these alerts as they become published content. (You can also select to receive them once a day, so your inbox isn't overwhelmed by the updates.)

Track New Legislation

The biggest underlying threat within the bitcoin price is what happens if regulators crack down on the use of the coin. It's something that some countries have done, banning the ability to spend the coins at all for local purchases. Russia has come down hard against cryptos, for instance, limiting citizens' access. Similarly, China has made it nearly impossible for people to exchange the coins. Meanwhile, countries such as Japan, South Korea, and the US all are developing laws that could either hinder the use of bitcoins or make them a safer entity, driving up usage rates.

No investor knows for sure how the eventual legislations will look, if crypto adoption continues to rise. But you should still know the current laws that will dictate the fluctuations of your bitcoins. To understand what laws have been put in place, there's BlockchainLawGuide.com, which provides a useful rundown of the current legislations and rules for your crypto investment.

The Problems Lurking in Bitcoin

The idea of a bitcoin bubble has grown in prominence over a number of years now. When bitcoin first surpassed $100, investing experts came out in full force to argue that bitcoin was a bubble that no regular retail investor should purchase because it was doomed to fail. But when bitcoin grew through 2017, to about $20,000 a coin, the debate grew more heated, since the stakes in the game had become much larger. This has drawn out the debate on a much grander scale, as more voices enter the fray, while some are bolstered by the subsequent 2018 collapse of bitcoin's price.

The arguments are rather repetitive, and you've possibly heard them before (and even thought them yourself), but they remain important factors in what could potentially lead to a fall that will leave bitcoin investors aching for the days when exuberance had reached near ecstatic levels.

ALERT

There's No Store of Value

Gold has something referred to in currency circles as "store of value" meaning there's some sort of inherent value in it that people want. Over centuries, gold has been sought after and bartered due to this value component. If the world's currencies suddenly disappeared tomorrow, people could still trade gold for goods.

Bitcoin doesn't have this inherent store of value, even though its founders tried to create it through the mining process to uncover new coins. This remains true, even as the price of bitcoin jumped to nearly $20,000. There's no getting around this argument. At the core of bitcoin, there isn't a store of value, like gold may offer, since it's not tangible.

But does it matter? Since it's a supply and demand question, meaning there's a supply and still a very strong demand, the fact that bitcoin doesn't actually hold any real value becomes moot, as long as people continue to seek them out. It's the same with a $1 bill. Inherently it is just paper with an extravagant design. If everyone in the world said that this bill is worthless, then that paper would only be worth the material it's made from. There's no store in value of the paper bill.

Of course, it's much more likely that the whole world decides that bitcoin serves no purpose and, therefore, has no value, as opposed to people turning on the US dollar and its economic system. That's why this issue still lurks deep within the bitcoin debate.

A Spending Problem

There's not enough growth in the number of transactions that take place with bitcoin to justify the significant increases in price that the coin has seen over the past couple of years. With transaction rates near 2016 levels, it should concern you as a bitcoin investor. Why haven't transactions increased?

Part of the reason for this lack of transactional growth is because consumers need easier ways to spend bitcoin (and cryptos in general). There are so few opportunities to spend them in the real world, that it becomes difficult to actually use them, outside of online shopping.

The other issue is that the bitcoin mix of owners has predominantly viewed it as an investment tool instead of a currency meant to buy and sell goods. It's an oxymoronic relationship, in many ways, as early adopters hold on to their bitcoins in anticipation of continued increases in value. But with all the bitcoins wrapped up in the hands of these early adopters, there are fewer people to actually spend the coins. This makes it very difficult for mainstream users to find the purpose in bitcoin transactions, when there's not enough demand to transact using bitcoins from these early adopters.

The third reason transactions have stumbled, particularly in the US, is because bitcoins are not treated as currency for tax purposes, which puts an onus on tracking each transaction. This stymies the flexibility and usability of the coin, hindering adoption.

Transaction Speeds

It takes minutes to hours for bitcoin to actually sell, when you look to transact your coins. It's a fundamental problem with investing in bitcoin. The only way to speed this up during times when the rate of transactions is high is to pay more in fees, which no one wants to do since it cuts into returns.

This headache has to do with the process in which the blockchain verifies the transaction, limiting the size of each block that holds the transactions. Other cryptos have worked to solve this issue, and it's a lag time that will become of greater concern as more businesses use bitcoins to process transactions. For example, since athletic stores have fixed costs, managers can't always wait days for them to access their funds. This will make them hesitate on the idea of using bitcoin, since it adds a risk to their bottom line.

It would take a significant change to the bitcoin code to address this concern.

Transaction Fees

To speed up the transaction, you can pay fees, which the miners that interact and monitor the bitcoin transactions will receive if they approve the cost. The higher the fee paid, the faster miners will ensure the transaction processes. But this can become costly, particularly for businesses that are conducting a number of transactions via bitcoin. While it's often under a $1 average per transaction, these fees tend to cool a hot market. When 2017 price rises jumped into full gear, average fees on the transactions surpassed $50. The fee became so high that companies such as the video game developer Valve stopped accepting bitcoins altogether. Some companies turned to other cryptos. This reduced demand for bitcoins, which led to some of the cooling in the market that bitcoin saw in 2018.

Obviously, as an investor, you don't want to see your investment suffer because of the costs involved to participate, especially when your investment needs mass adoption.

The Bitcoin Forks

Bitcoin forks help improve upon the current bitcoin blockchain. They're ways in which the software can change, creating new rules and components, allowing for easier use. The forks create new tokens that investors can now access and will move somewhat independently of the parent coin. These forks, though, aren't always agreed upon by the entire bitcoin community.

There are two types of forks. Understanding what they are—without getting too far into the technical weeds—will help ensure they don't hinder your current investment. At the same time, you can keep an eye out for a new opportunity involving newly fashioned tokens.

How They Occur

For your purposes, forks improve upon the code that runs the blockchain. They're not conducted without significant buy-in from the community of miners and users interacting with the blockchain. It takes a near complete buy-in for a soft fork to occur. When there's a strong disagreement around the blockchain changes, then a hard fork takes place.

Soft Fork

A soft fork won't create a significant hurdle to your bitcoin investment, in all likelihood. Instead, since it requires a near unanimous agreement from bitcoin participants, it's usually done for the good of the coin. For instance, when the community felt a need to change the signature validation requirements in 2015, a soft fork occurred. It meant a new part of the chain was created, incorporating the suggested tweak. At first, only 95 percent of participants agreed with the change, creating two separate blockchains. Eventually, the remaining miners fell in line with the new blockchain. At this point, the entire blockchain that had existed before moved with this new coding, keeping bitcoin intact.

It's what's referred to as "backward compatible," which means soft forks comply with the legacy chain of code, so no other coins are created.

Hard Fork

Sometimes, when these forks occur and a new chain exists, a large group of miners and community members don't agree with it. This creates a hard fork, where the split from the original chain becomes a new entity, since it's not backward compatible. In these cases, an entirely new token is created. This is what happened in the formulation of bitcoin cash. Its supporters increased the size of each individual block of transactions, which improved the speed of transactions. Much of the bitcoin community disagreed with the split, and therefore a new coin was created.

FACT

The first significant hard fork to occur in bitcoin was in 2014, with the split of Bitcoin XT. It sought to improve transaction speeds, and at first looked as if it would catch on as 1,000 nodes moved toward the new rules. It didn't last though, and a cofounder of the split left the project in 2016, although it's still trading to this day.

When such a fork occurs, you typically receive one of the newly created coins for each bitcoin you currently own. Theoretically, in these cases bitcoin will fall in price by the amount in which the market values the new bitcoin fork. So with bitcoin cash valued at $300 at the time of the fork, in theory, the bitcoin price would fall by $300. Of course, cryptos don't always act based on the theory, since hype, exuberance, and speculation have driven a number of the price increases.

QUESTION

If I invest in a bitcoin fork, will it trade similarly to bitcoin?
Yes, but not because it's a fork. Theoretically, a fork could become its own entity, trading on its own fundamentals. But, as of now, forks trade similar to bitcoin much like the rest of crypto space.

The Problems with Hard Forks

One thing to think about as hard forks occur is whether they create a viable threat to bitcoin itself. Since they're a legacy of bitcoin, only created to improve upon the code, there's a possibility that such a fork could lead to the loss of confidence in the mother coin. This could lead to a replacement of bitcoin, in the eyes of investors and consumers. It obviously hasn't been an issue yet, but it could become one, if there's ever a fork that truly provides value that bitcoin can't already offer.

Too Many Forks

There's a dichotomy in bitcoin's transaction times. From one perspective, it paves the way for new entrants looking to improve transactions. Take litecoin. Since transaction fees had become too onerous, leading to delays in transaction times, litecoin was created to reduce the target time to conduct transactions at around two minutes, as opposed to bitcoin's ten minutes. But a fork can also occur when two miners simultaneously discover new blocks, or accept new blocks. Eventually the community determines which one earned the blocks. With faster transactions, like the ones you see with litecoin, more soft forks will likely take place.

Investing in Bitcoin Cash

The bitcoin cash fork took place in August 2017, in an effort to increase transaction speeds of the crypto. It did so by increasing the size of storage that each block within the chain could hold from one megabyte to eight. This boosted the number of transactions-per-second to sixty-one with bitcoin cash, up from seven for bitcoin.

Since transactions move much faster, the fees drop in size. It's another added bonus to bitcoin cash, which is why when the fork occurred, it already stood at $310 and has remained in the top four cryptos by market capitalization.

It Will Mimic Bitcoin

While all cryptos have an at least thin relation to how bitcoin moves, bitcoin cash will have a significant correlation, as long as bitcoin remains the stronger of the two currencies. As bitcoin rises, bitcoin cash will increase for much of the same reasons. If laws pass that help the spending of cryptos, they will both likely rise. If transactions suddenly fall, they will both likely drop. It's not a diversification method to move into bitcoin cash, if you already own bitcoin. It's a protection against the appeal of faster transactions, in case bitcoin cash's speed becomes a requirement for users.

ALERT

While hard forks come about from general disagreement, they can also be used for more nefarious reasons. Scammers will use a fork to try and trick bitcoin owners to buy into the upgrade, only to use the split in the blockchain to launch attacks on the coin owners. Others will use the bitcoin name to try and lure them into supporting a fork that isn't actually using the bitcoin blockchain. Once again, it's playing off the lack of knowledge around forks, and trying to steal coins in the process.

Investing in Other Bitcoin Forks

Bitcoin cash isn't the only hard fork that bitcoin has experienced. While many new coins use part of the bitcoin blockchain code to develop a new name, there are certain coins that were developed out of the disagreement between miners (as opposed to a group wanting to launch a new coin). These haven't had the success that bitcoin cash has had, but still exist among the options of altcoins.

- **Bitcoin Gold:** It forked shortly after bitcoin cash as an effort to change mining protocols. The support of bitcoin gold hasn't held up, unlike bitcoin cash, and it has fallen in price even as bitcoin and bitcoin cash rise.
- **Bitcoin XT:** Among one of the first hard forks, XT was an early attempt to improve transaction speeds in 2014. While it still technically exists, it has fallen well below a single penny per coin.
- **SegWit2x:** It became a point of contention in the bitcoin community, as an attempt to improve transactions by reducing the size of each new block. It had a number of prominent supporters, who then backed out. This led to a canceling of the fork before it could occur.

More than bitcoin forks, it's the larger universe of altcoins that provide the greatest opportunity to replace bitcoin one day. The largest altcoin name that has the most support to replace bitcoin has become ethereum, which we'll turn to next.

CHAPTER 8

The Basics of Ethereum

Ethereum has become the most prominent and popular name within the long list of altcoins and is behind only bitcoin in the size of its market cap. Unlike bitcoin, though, there are two sides to ethereum. There's the startup firm that's building a business around blockchain technology. There's also ether, the token that's used to conduct business within the ethereum network and the currency you purchase when buying into the name. This chapter will discuss what you need to know about Ethereum and how you can invest in ether.

Ethereum's Origin

Ethereum is the brainchild of Vitalik Buterin and was developed as a tool to provide developers a way to create decentralized applications on the blockchain, launching in 2015. To pay for services, such as creating an agreement with a developer to build such an application, ethers are used.

Buterin's primary breakthrough was the development of smart contracts. These allow two parties to agree to terms, without the requirement of a third party to confirm the results. Conditions are set by both parties on the blockchain, which allows the payer to track the efforts of the payee, without having to fund services that the developer doesn't provide. Once both parties agree to a set of services, the blockchain checks each box as the developer reaches each benchmark. It doesn't require a third party to watch over the transaction and the developer doesn't have to be concerned that the client might stiff them on pay, once the work is completed. It's beneficial to both parties because it removes the need for trust within the arrangement. Remember, when Satoshi Nakamoto developed his blockchain thesis, it hinged on removing the need for this trust from the financial agreement, which allowed bitcoin to become viable. Buterin advanced the theory, providing a way to remove trust from the contractual portion of an arrangement as well.

For reasons that may be obvious to you, this smart contract has immense potential in the business world. Ethereum is the platform that developers can use to build applications, while also using these smart contract concepts.

Business Interest Blossoms

Unlike most other crypto names on the market, companies have moved quickly in developing their understanding and building potential use cases for Ethereum's technology. The Enterprise Ethereum Alliance launched in 2017 so companies could come together to discuss the possibilities of the technology and develop best practices for conducting business on the platform. It's filled with heavy-hitters, including representatives on the board from Microsoft, Accenture, Intel, and J.P. Morgan.

Ethereum's appeal stretches to the largest corporate entities because this blockchain contract could have immense impact on compliance efforts. Imagine if a company could simply place within the blockchain all the rules and checkpoints a transaction must go through, from a compliance standpoint, trusting the technology to handle the checking and confirmation. It has the potential to reduce the complexity of the compliance needs, from manpower to the paper required to assuage government and accounting oversight.

FACT

If Ethereum's technology can help with compliance issues, how much potential does this area of business have? In the first year, startup costs for small businesses related to compliance average a total of $83,000, according to a survey by the National Small Business Association.

But it's not just the compliance efforts that have businesses excited. It can be used in supply chain contracts, remove middlemen (like agents) from the process of purchasing certain products (such as music), and can even cut into the law field, executing contracts without the need for legal representation to enforce the agreement.

How It's Used Now

Startups and legacy organizations are starting to adapt the Ethereum blockchain for a number of different reasons, both for business and consumer purposes. It has served as a platform for startups to launch new services. These adaptations by startups include developing a predictions market, which allows you to earn money by betting on the results of future events, including the fluctuations of individual stocks. JAAK wants to use the Ethereum platform to provide music rights holders a fluid and decentralized way that will allow consumers and businesses to play and have access to music without a need for a label to coordinate the sale. And there's Transactive Grid, which allows energy contract holders to sell energy rights to third parties.

Then What's Ether?

Ether is what Ethereum built to conduct transactions on the blockchain and to raise ICO funds. When referring to the cryptocurrency, you will hear experts and analysts use ether and ethereum interchangeably; Ethereum the company has become synonymous with ether the cryptocurrency. But by owning ether, you're not in some way owning the company that is operating smart contract technology. You're linked, since what improves adoption of Ethereum will also improve the transaction rates of ether.

FACT

The largest holder of ether is believed to be one of Ethereum's cofounders, Joseph Lubin. He reportedly joined the project shortly after Buterin released his white paper discussing smart contracts and purchased the most coins during the ether ICO. In 2018, *Forbes* estimated his holdings to be worth anywhere between $1 billion and $5 billion.

What Makes Ether Unique?

In order for the cryptocurrency market to become a standard, one of two scenarios must play out. Either one cryptocurrency becomes the ultimate cryptocurrency, ensuring all other iterations or designs are obsolete. In this scenario, many cryptocurrency investors could find themselves disappointed with their investments, unless it's clear early on in this hypothetical coin's rise that it will become the preeminent name in the space or, if it's like bitcoin, where there's already millions invested in the name.

The other scenario is that while one coin rises to become prominent—kind of like bitcoin today—there's a whole plethora of other names that are used for specific purposes and needs. It's in this scenario where ether really shines (unless it would somehow become that crypto to thwart all cryptos in the future). The reason it has proven to function well under these circumstances is that the company behind the crypto has shown itself to offer real value to businesses. This provides Ethereum with a layer of protection against the normal concerns that face startups, such as not enough demand for the product. Instead, you have a coin that has become the second largest name in the space because its use is growing through the improvement of the company. This means there's legitimate demand for the coin (even if it remains small) that can help justify the rise it has seen over the past two years, even with the struggles in 2018.

ALERT

It's important to note that much of ether's gains came during the 2017 crypto bull run. It's then that the coin jumped from $11 to over $1,300 a coin. Since that time though, the coin has struggled to reach those high marks, and moved similarly to bitcoin's fluctuations.

A Corporate Darling

Cryptos don't just benefit from blockchain adoption. There are plenty of companies, like Walmart for example, that have built internal blockchains to help them track movements of supplies. They don't require a cryptocurrency to use this sort of blockchain. Instead, for cryptos to flourish, adoption of the blockchain would also require use of the blockchain's crypto that the companies have developed. It means actual financial transactions are required on the blockchain to make it worthwhile, from an investor's perspective. And the larger the transactions, the stronger the crypto will become.

That's the sweet spot that Ethereum currently sits in. It has become the blockchain for business-to-business transactions, which creates a layer of security when evaluating the safety of the coin. As long as businesses see a need for the platform, they will continue to use it. And the stronger the businesses that enter the platform, the more reliable those transactions and rates will become. All of this will help the value of ether, since it would see incremental increases in its transaction rate, as the price rises. That's allowing for a legitimate upward movement in demand, which creates a reliable price increase.

Despite ether's early popularity, it hasn't reached that level of reliability. When companies like Microsoft and J.P. Morgan see use for the blockchain, though, it's a positive sign that they also see potential in the currency used to transact on that chain.

Value Within the Internet of Things

An industry that has seen significant value in Ethereum's blockchain in the early days of development is within the Internet of Things (IOT). Since more devices have become connected via the Internet, using the ethereum platform has proven a powerful way to ensure they remain functioning in unison.

As researchers at the Heider College of Business at Creighton University point out in a working paper on the values of bitcoin and ethereum, a house connected to the ethereum network could unlock doors for an apartment the moment it's rented by a new tenant. "Ethereum has a better technological foundation than Bitcoin does to take advantage of these [IOT] needs," write the authors Julianne Harm, Josh Obregon, and Josh Stubbendick.

Its Contracts Were First

There's nothing like being the first to market with an idea, like Ethereum was in the creation of smart contracts. The ability for it to join the blockchain movement, by reshaping the movement like it did, creates armor for the company. Since the founder of smart contracts, Buterin, remains at the company, it also gives businesses comfort that the mind behind the firm is engaged in the business.

Now other blockchain firms are offering smart-contracts similar to Ethereum's offerings. With that comes a layer of competition. But because Ethereum introduced the concept and provided the initial framework, it prevents it from getting lost in the shuffle, at least for now. Of course, another tool could come along, blowing away Ethereum's offerings and therefore rendering ether obsolete. But that isn't likely in the short term, and, therefore, allows for some runway in the ether investment.

It's Easier to Mine Blocks

Unlike bitcoin, new ether blocks don't have nearly the hurdle to mine new coins. It's this way in order to encourage miners to validate the contracts that take place on the blockchain more quickly. Each one of Ethereum's blocks holds five ethers, and a set of blocks are expected to be uncovered every nineteen seconds. For bitcoin, that rate is every ten minutes. This allows for speedier transactions and improves the buying or selling of ethers. It also reduces the fees for those buying and selling coins, since there isn't the need to pay up to have a quick result.

ESSENTIAL

The fact that ether has simplified the mining of coins vastly improves the fees you can expect to pay in the future, when transacting in ether versus bitcoin. At its peak, ether transactions reached a fee of just over $4. Bitcoin, on the other hand, surpassed $50 per transaction. It's another reason why businesses favor the idea of ethereum over bitcoin, since that number adds up when conducting thousands of transactions a day.

The Ethereum Fundamentals

What you'll find as you look further into ether is that as volatile as bitcoin is, ether can be even more so. This is because there's so much potential for the Ethereum blockchain, but as a corporate entity, it also has the potential to become obsolete. This results in a nauseating ride that will pump up sharply when there are new businesses that sign onto the Ethereum blockchain. It could also drop dramatically if those businesses don't conduct the number of transactions as hoped when they signed onto the platform or when other players offering competing services join the market and start to show signs of momentum. You don't want your entire portfolio in the Ethereum space, but you also don't want to ignore the opportunity either.

Ethereum's Rise

While the layman investor will be wowed by bitcoin's height in total value, in many people's eyes, it's actually ether that saw the most remarkable increase in 2017. Since it ICOed in 2015, it's six years younger than bitcoin. At the time, 60 million ethers were released into the market. This meant that it had far less momentum heading into the penultimate year for cryptos and there's a much larger supply. Theoretically, this would suppress large forward movements, since there would be plenty of supply to match the increase in demand. That's not what happened in 2017. Heading into the year, one ether cost $8.30. By the end of the year, that price had risen to $722, resulting in an 8,600 percent increase in price.

But ether's rise comes with significant falls. By middle of January 2018, ether had surpassed $1,347 only to see it lose 72 percent of its value by early April, as the entire crypto marketplace saw significant losses when investors tried to cash in on their unexpected gains and the exuberance in the market waned.

It's a symbol of cryptos' unique volatility, but also what you can expect from ether at this point in Ethereum's history. There can be significant highs, but they come with those potential lows.

There's No Coin Limit

Unlike bitcoin, Ethereum didn't set a limit on the number of potential coins that could come onto the market. Bitcoin has a 21 million coin ceiling (if you don't include its forks) while Ethereum hasn't set such a strict standard. This could potentially mess with the supply side of the coin, especially if too many coins come to market. Since ether launched with an initial coin offering, providing about 60 million ethers to the marketplace, it has added 18 million ethers a year. The code does limit the amount of ether that can be added on a yearly basis, leveling it at that 18 million mark. However, there's no upside limit, although even Ethereum's cofounder Buterin has argued one should be set.

Transaction Volume Rises

If you were to sync up the transaction volume of ethereum with the price of the coins, the two graphs would look almost identical. In early 2017, transaction volumes were near 40,000 per day, before exploding in usage, surpassing nearly a million transactions by the end of the year. Much of this, though, was due to the increase in speculation surrounding the coin as new crypto users entered the market, hearing that ethereum had become a crypto darling.

ALERT

The fact the transactions changed so dramatically indicates that a large percentage of buyers and sellers were speculators. The goal of these transactions is to become much more constant. When you see transactions fall and the price immediately follows, you know it's because of speculators losing interest in the name. If companies were leading the charge, you would expect fewer peaks and valleys in the transactional data.

This trend also highlights that ether's price moves more on perceived value than bitcoin. If a large company decides to enter the ethereum platform—and transactions jump—it could provide hard data to support ether's continued price improvement. But you want that transactional data to serve as an early indicator to price movements, not one that move hand-in-hand with the price of the coin.

The rise of transactions also speaks to the benefit of becoming a tool for business purposes. As more businesses adopt the platform, however, you'll expect to see greater increases in the size of transaction volume.

The Problems Lurking in Ethereum

What makes ether unique as a cryptocurrency investment has a flip side, which can create the potential for problems. While some of the problems aren't unique to Ethereum, like the continued reliance on bitcoin, others are simply a function of how Ethereum operates and how it's currently designed. It's the downside risk—and potential reality—that comes with the investment in this cryptocurrency, one that you must keep in mind if you're thinking of placing your hard-earned cash into the coin.

ESSENTIAL

It's important to note that even Ethereum's founder, Buterin, has warned against the rise of ether and other cryptocurrencies. In February 2018, he tweeted a reminder that "cryptocurrencies are still a new and hyper-volatile asset class, and could drop to near-zero at any time." He continued to add that traditional asset classes remain the safer bet for investors.

Linked to Bitcoin

Bitcoin's success and trickle-down impact on the rest of the cryptocurrency market also plays into ethereum's price. Despite that fact, ether's price can move based on the function of how the business performs. However, it's not a coincidence that ether's massive price increase in 2017 coincided with bitcoin's price acceleration. As investors saw bitcoin's price move, they began to seek other opportunities in the crypto space, leaving one of the strongest business cases in the blockchain universe as the most likely party to also see gains. But it doesn't mean ether's price has separated from bitcoin's movements either.

When these movements happen, keep in mind that ether will likely move a little more dramatically (whether it goes up or down). Ethereum's thirty-day volatility index stood above bitcoin's both during the rise in 2017 and the fall in 2018.

Coin Limits

When Ethereum launched, the founders put no limits on the total amount of coins that would be available. While they did limit the number of new ethers that could be created on a yearly basis to 18 million, this lack of a ceiling on the total amount of ethers reduces the degree to which supply can play a role in improving the price. It creates scenarios where demand must remain extremely strong to outpace the growing supply, before a crunch can occur. The same isn't the case for bitcoin; since there's only 21 million in existence, there's some natural supply crunch built in.

As ether has grown in popularity, its founder has called for the community to install a supply limit. He originally issued the suggestion as an April Fool's joke. But after reading developers' responses to his gag, Buterin's opinion changed and he's now indicated that he believes that the token should have a ceiling at just over 120 million ether, in part because it would ensure inflation doesn't become an issue within the ether-space.

It Can Be Replaced

Just like any company that forms with an innovation at the forefront, Ethereum is at risk of another startup improving upon what they do, making the technology obsolete. While it's not expected at the moment, due to the number of enterprises interested in the ethereum blockchain, you never know what technology awaits around the corner. That means Ethereum, like any startup, will need to continue to innovate and grow. Ether is dependent on that growth.

The Ethereum Forks

Since Ethereum hasn't existed as long as bitcoin, it has fewer hard forks within its family tree. Yet, it has had some contentious moments, which have led to prolonged discussions among the Ethereum core developers about the best way to move forward. This has threatened the potential for forks, but to this day, only one hard fork has taken place that has produced a potentially viable currency: ethereum classic.

Close Call

Ethereum has had a number of forks go forward or threaten to take place, yet they never seem to quite catch on with a large enough community to make them viable. A hard fork that took place on January 20 created the cryptocurrency EtherZero. The developers wanted to fork from the original ethereum blockchain, in order to produce a coin that could conduct thousands of transactions per second, as opposed to around fifteen per second like Ethereum targets. It also claimed it would completely wipe away fees from the transaction process.

The fork took place on January 20, 2018, but never saw any support. In the months after the fork, the price of the coin dropped from nearly $120 to under $4.

Ethereum Upgrades

Since Ethereum launched the blockchain, it has undergone a number of updates in order to improve the smart contract process and allow the contracts to become more dynamic than originally designed. In order to implement these changes, a fork must take place. But because Ethereum developers support the forks and the community is warned when these upgrades will take place, the main currency moves with the change. That allows for the upgrades to take place, without the development of a new coin, since the rest of the developing community and miners move with the fork.

It does create a potential hiccup if, for some reason, developers began to disagree on future upgrades. This could result in a hard fork that produces a new currency. If that happens, and enough of the developers support the new currency over the old one, then ether's price could suffer. That hasn't occurred yet, but it remains a possible outcome.

Ethereum Hacked

In 2016, Ethereum faced an existential crisis that would determine how it would function in the future. A hack occurred on the Ethereum blockchain, targeting the decentralized autonomous organization (DAO), which was a fund built by Ethereum investors as a decentralized concept to invest in companies. The hacker, who remains unidentified, took off with $50 million worth of ether.

This left Ethereum developers with two options: to continue, accepting the fact that the thief would now own a large percentage of ethers, or to create a hard fork that would disavow the hack, acting as if nothing happened. Ethereum developers ended up siding with the latter, moving the ether with the hard fork.

Not everyone agreed with that solution, including Charles Hoskinson, one of Ethereum's cofounders. Those that remained on the original ethereum blockchain, which concedes the hack, became ethereum classic.

Investing in Ethereum Classic

What's unique about classic is that it split from ethereum prior to the dramatic 2017 price increase in ethers. This means that over the past two years, it trades somewhat independent of ether. That didn't work out for classic during the 2017 rise, since it never reached beyond $46 per coin. At this point, it has become the coin for those ethereum traditionalists who still disagree with the move to forget the hack. It hasn't moved much beyond a statement investment for hard-core Ethereum philosophers.

CHAPTER 9

The Basics of Ripple XRP

Unlike bitcoin and ether, the Ripple blockchain was built with controls that allowed the company to determine when and how much currency to distribute to the community. From this control, it created a unique characteristic within the currency, until the crypto community forced a change. Critics have likened it to the Federal Reserve, which controls the money supply. Despite attempting to stem the criticism, this aspect of Ripple XRP turns off many cryptocurrency enthusiasts who believe the currencies should operate independent of the company. Meanwhile, others view the technology and strategy as innovative, supported by the growth of customers reaching out to Ripple to participate on the blockchain. In this chapter, we will discuss the inner workings of this controversial cryptocurrency.

Ripple XRP's Origin

Ripple launched in 2012, developed by Jed McCaleb and Chris Larsen. McCaleb brought instant credibility to the project, which was originally named OpenCoin, because he's the creator of Mt. Gox, which would become the world's largest cryptocurrency exchange before its collapse (long after McCaleb had sold the exchange). At the time of launch, OpenCoin was striving to create blockchain protocol that would improve payment systems, like the ones banks use to transfer money across borders.

The Partners Split

In 2013, Ripple held its initial coin offering for XRP. Despite McCaleb's name on the project, it didn't lead to overnight success. However, months before the ICO, third-party investors grew interested in Ripple, providing an angel round of investing. This helped further fund the project, while the coin took time to take off. It wouldn't be until 2017 when it would finally pull above a penny per coin.

McCaleb wouldn't be around to watch the rise though. He and Larsen had a falling-out, leading to McCaleb's departure. Instead, McCaleb sold his Ripple stake and created the Stellar framework, which has also done extraordinarily well in the short time it has functioned.

Larsen would remain as the CEO of Ripple until mid-2016, when he moved to chairman of the company and hired Brad Garlinghouse as CEO.

What Makes Ripple, the Company, Unique?

Ripple, in many ways, mirrors a traditional startup, when looking at how the company operates and the focus of its customer base, targeting specific industries with its technology. In this new world of decentralized currencies, this polished look stands out. Its founder, Chris Larsen, had started ventures in the past, including peer-to-peer lending companies Prosper and E-LOAN. Ripple's investors include names like investing firm Andreessen Horowitz, known for investments in Airbnb and Lyft, or LightSpeed Venture Partners, which invested in Snap, the parent company of Snapchat. Its board of directors matches this heavyweight backing, with members such as Stanford professors, a former White House National Economic Council advisor, and bank executives. In a universe where scams run rampant, it's reassuring to see this level of legitimacy. That's not all that helps Ripple stand out.

ESSENTIAL

How much you weight the fact Ripple has venture capital and traditional backers will depend on how much you weight this old investment experience. Cryptocurrencies, in many ways, draw on the notion that there's something different about the blockchain and the currency, which traditional investors don't understand. For some, they will turn away from Ripple, due to this traditional support. Others will find it comforting that smart people also like the technology.

What It Targets

Ripple the company targets a very specific purpose in unleashing its blockchain: to improve the way companies conduct payments. These payment systems, as Ripple quickly points out, were made years ago, before the advent of the Internet. This leaves them slow and expensive, which is why fees can grow so high when processing transactions across borders.

ALERT

Just how big is this cross-border payment market? By 2020, consulting firm McKinsey & Company estimates it will reach $2.2 trillion in revenue, growing 5 percent annually since 2015. Where cryptocurrencies will first make their mark is within emerging markets and Asia, a region that accounts for 45 percent of cross border payments.

Because of this very specific purpose, Ripple has a number of banks and financial institutions that have at least tested out the "RippleNet," including Santander, Royal Bank of Canada, American Express, and MoneyGram. It's this high-level interest from large organizations that brings a level of cachet to Ripple. Santander, for instance, has a pilot program open to employees that allows them to make international payments through an app developed by the bank, using Ripple's blockchain. The payments post almost instantly, as opposed to days later, without the significant fee that follows a cross-border exchange.

That Doesn't Mean They Use XRP

Despite the interest in Ripple, banks can use the blockchain without using Ripple's cryptocurrency, XRP. Companies have begun to test out XRP for certain types of transactions. Cuallix is a non-bank financial firm based in Mexico, which conducts transfers to the United States. In October 2017, it began to test XRP as a way to process these transactions, in an effort to cut down the transfer time.

If Ripple can convince more institutions to use XRP to conduct the transactions, the better off XRP as an investment will perform. Ripple's CEO claimed that by the end of 2019, multiple banks will incorporate the Ripple product that uses XRP to conduct the transfers. You should keep track, noting the size of the company, and the amount it expects to transfer daily using XRP, if these customers materialize. It provides a potential boost for XRP that's foreseeable (if it comes true).

Ripple Doesn't Use Miners

Bitcoin and Ethereum blockchains use miners, that is, members of their community, as the method by which transactions are approved and verified. Not Ripple. Instead of going the mining route, it uses an algorithm that connects trusted servers, which essentially vote on whether or not a transaction is validated. Once the servers agree, then the transaction is verified. This process reduces the fees it takes to conduct transactions, since you're no longer relying on a group of miners to provide the verification.

This also cuts the buy-in from a nascent community, since there's little way for a group economically linked to the coin to gain, other than investing and hope there's an appreciation in the coin's price. While that's why you might invest in XRP, others, whose livelihoods are based on the mining and authenticating of coins, aren't interested in this side gig. Instead, XRP is entirely wrapped up in the performance of the company and the number of banks it signs on as customers.

What Makes XRP Unique?

Since Ripple has developed this establishment reputation, and because of certain decisions the company made while creating the cryptocurrency, there are unique factors that impact the movement of price within the cryptocurrency, which doesn't happen to most other names. The most controversial difference? It's a cryptocurrency that launched close to the corporate vest, meaning it originally controlled supply to a degree that causes significant disagreements about whether or not the coin is decentralized.

All the Coins Have Been Mined

As soon as Ripple launched its blockchain, it mined the 100 billion coins that would exist within the digital framework. Twenty billion of the coins were given to the founders and early executives, while the rest were held by the company. This brought on fears that the business could flood the market with Ripple coins at any time, feeding concerns of inflation within the digital coin.

In response to the community's fervor over this wrinkle, Ripple placed 55 billion coins in an escrow account in December 2017, saying that the account will release 1 billion coins each month, based on the smart contract that controls the distribution. Every month, 1 billion XRPs will come to market. If they go unused, then they will return to an escrow account and rerelease once the original 55 billion XRPs have a chance to launch within the marketplace. This will repeat until all the XRPs have entered the market.

About 40 billion XRPs have been released so far, including the 20 billion the founders originally owned. Why billion coins instead of millions, like other cryptos? If banks latch on to the cryptocurrency, they transact in large denominations. It's surmised that Ripple's founders didn't want XRP's prices to fluctuate dramatically just because a client did one large sell. With banks, that means billions of coins were needed to protect against this specific market manipulation.

The Setup Angers Some

Since cryptos have upended some established ways governments view securities and currency, the original setup that Ripple employed caused an uproar among those who said it's a security (like stock ownership); by releasing them in this highly controlled fashion, it's breaking the law, this group argued.

In 2018, a crypto investor, Ryan Coffey, sued Ripple Labs, claiming that coins the CEO, Brad Garlinghouse, sold represented a sale of unregistered securities. Since Garlinghouse didn't sell through an ICO, Coffey argued it was an illegal distribution of the coin. While Ripple disagreed, it highlights the unique dangers cryptos can bring and even more specific downsides Ripple can engender. Coffey pulled the lawsuit in August, but Ripple faces similar lawsuits. As these cases—or future cases—move through the court system, it could also shape how the legal institutions view cryptocurrencies. It could alter how the market views cryptos, depending on whether courts get a chance to evaluate the case, and whether they judge XRP to be a currency or a security.

How serious does Ripple take this fight? Think about the heavyweight lawyers whom they've employed. Ripple hired the law firm of Debevoise & Plimpton to represent them, and one of the lead lawyers on the cases is the former SEC chairwoman under the Obama administration, Mary Jo White. You don't hire that level of representation unless the threat is of significant importance to the long-term health of your company (and the industry at large).

It Was a Victim of the "Kimchi Premium"

In December 2017, Ripple traded at a significant premium on the Korean exchanges. Due to South Koreans' interest in cryptocurrencies, when prices in the space were rising, investors could sell cryptos they bought in the US for more if they sold them back on a South Korean exchange. This became referred to, somewhat offensively, as the "kimchi premium."

One of the world's largest coin price indexes, Coinbase, removed prominent Korean exchanges from the price listing in January 2018 to avoid the South Korean price inflating the actual demand for the coin. From that simple decision XRP's price fell by one-third overnight. Ripple had a large following in Korea, so it was hit harder than most other coins. It also dropped it as the second largest coin by market cap to where it typically sits now, at third (although that can change quickly).

It Benefits from the Business

The positive aspect of having a coin that's linked to a startup, like XRP's connection with Ripple, is that when the company does well, so does the coin. Early in its life, Ripple has shown an ability to garner attention from significant businesses. While the number of transactions these companies make remain a mystery, particularly the number of transactions they make with XRP, it's encouraging when you see banks and financial firms publicly highlight their testing of the RippleNet, the term Ripple has given its product it offers on the blockchain. This leads to a short-term boost of XRP, but also can lead to significant improvements in the transaction volume, which is the ultimate goal. If more companies do buy into Ripple's products that use XRP, then transactions could increase quickly and a fast price appreciation would follow.

The XRP Fundamentals

As a tool for investing, XRP has some specific attributes that help it stand out from the rest. Since it's a controlled entity, it creates some unusual trading considerations; remember you're only seeing the demand that Ripple wants you to see. This creates a more difficult scenario in analyzing and understanding how the crypto itself performs. And since the company isn't public, it can limit the information it provides investors in XRP.

ALERT

While it's an unusual setup for a cryptocurrency, the idea that a startup would closely control how it grows and its strategy for such growth isn't shocking. It can actually be healthy for a company, since it knows better than others the amount of volume and scale it can handle. It wouldn't be surprising if more cryptocurrency and blockchain firms use this structure moving forward, since there's an attractiveness to controlling the currency.

Its Market Cap Is Misleading

At its height, prior to the reduction in price from the removal of South Korean exchanges, Ripple reached just over $3.30. Over 2018, it hovered below $1. Why, if the price remains so low, can it command such a large market cap? It's simple math.

You probably noticed that its circulation is in the billions, as opposed to millions like Bitcoin. (Ethereum just surpassed 100 million coins in supply last year.) For Ripple, that circulation is above 40 billion. It means there's a whole lot more coins in distribution, so the value gets spread out among the coins that are available. This also requires significant increases in usage if the coin price you've invested in will appreciate in a manner that will be worth the investment, from a real dollar perspective.

ALERT

Market capitalization is a measurement that highlights how much value the investment has within the market. In stocks, it's determined by the number of shares outstanding multiplied by the stock price. For cryptos, replace the shares outstanding with the coins outstanding, and multiply by the price of the coin. It's why XRP's market cap looks strong. Even if it were priced at just a penny, the market cap would be worth $400 million, placing it within the fifty largest cryptocurrencies.

Because of its deflated price tag, if you're going to invest in Ripple, then you'll likely gain a lot of coins. For example, if you invest $500 in XRP you'll own about 500 coins. The same amount of money invested in bitcoin would gain you just a tiny fraction of one coin. This could have a dramatic impact, if Ripple rises significantly. Let's say Ripple jumps to $100 over the next five years and you have 500 coins. That investment has turned into a gross value of $50,000. That's significant, while the bitcoin investment probably doesn't have a 100× jump in its short-term future, unless bitcoin suddenly becomes a $1,000,000 coin.

Of course, XRP's usage rates would need to climb dramatically if the price were to jump to $100 a coin, since it would require a substantial increase in demand to counter the large supply of coins.

Transactions Track Price

The positive point about XRP's transaction volume is that it has grown from 2016, when the price of one coin was less than a single penny. From May 2016 to May 2018, the number of transactions per day more than tripled. That's a good sign.

If you're looking day-by-day, then you see transactions that even now appear to track at about the same rates as they did two or three years ago. Considering this transaction volume looks very similar to the graph of price changes, it implies that many of the transactions remain linked to trading among investors. For the price to move the way you want, you'll need to see those bank customers of Ripple start to use the coin on a regular basis, so the transaction volumes increase at a much more significant rate than they're currently moving. Then the price will likely follow. As an investor, you will have to wait for that link.

Transaction Speeds Add a Boost

One benefit of the Ripple platform is that it can conduct a number of transactions within a second. If you're looking to trade the XRP coin at a certain price and you sell, you know the transaction will go through before there's a significant time-lapse, which might allow for the price to fall. This adds an extra bonus to Ripple. Since the fee per transaction is minimal—a fraction of a cent—outside of what your exchange may charge, it ensures you can maximize your investment gains. It's a benefit that bitcoin doesn't have, since it can take minutes for a transaction to process on bitcoin's blockchain. When that price rises, bitcoin's fees become significant. You don't have to worry about that with XRP.

It Tracks with Bitcoin

If this sounds like a broken record, it will tell you what you need to know about cryptos, until their transaction volumes increase independently of speculators. XRP, like most popular cryptos, move very closely with the price of bitcoin. This suggests this movement occurs because of trading and speculation within the market. As bitcoin rises, investors look for altcoins to take stakes in. XRP has become a popular coin of choice within that altcoin universe, leading to interest in times of bitcoin bull runs. It's why it's difficult to diversify within the crypto space, since so many of these coins move with the one crypto, bitcoin, which remains the outright leader.

Following XRP's Roller-Coaster Ride

The reason XRP has jumped into the discussion of top altcoins isn't just because of its structure and creative core, but also because of its almost miraculous rise in late 2017 and into 2018. This rise came when the coin itself cost less than a penny to purchase and hadn't yet reached many people's notice, other than as an interesting blockchain technology.

What changed, as bitcoin's price rose? Investors started to look for other cryptos that have narratives behind them that could lead to growth as well. And there's not a stronger narrative than a blockchain company that has funding support, a strong technological acumen among its founders, and large banks and financial institutions as clients. However, that hasn't resulted in ongoing gains.

It should be noted that those who invest in Ripple's XRP fall in love with the narrative. Maybe they were early investors, enjoying the 4,157 percent rise in 2017, and convinced themselves that the runaway train would return. Maybe crypto investing has become a lot like cheering for your local team, blinding you from what's happening within the space. It's impossible to say, but you shouldn't fall too much in love with the narrative. Instead, ask whether or not clients begin using XRP. That's the key to your investment success.

Will Ripple Fork?

Since Ripple runs a much more closed system than other blockchains, there's little concern that a fork will occur. Instead, it uses an amendment system, where the developers provide potential amendments to the blockchain to help it run more smoothly. If the amendment receives a significant majority of support—typically 80 percent or more—then the amendment will pass, and the past blockchain will change to support it. Without the consensus, no change will be made. This reduces any possibility that a hard fork could occur, unless the company itself decided to institute such a measure.

While XRP has become a popular choice among altcoins, there are other, smaller names that show potential as well.

CHAPTER 10

The Other Altcoins

The cryptos discussed to this point receive more publicity than the countless other altcoins due to the momentum they saw in the marketplace, due to their standing within the blockchain world, and due to their track record. Yet, that doesn't mean there aren't a number of other coins that have come to market with the potential to develop into a name that more people know, have their prices appreciate, and create a nice profit in your portfolio. This chapter will take a look at a few of these coins that have become better-known names in the space, even if the popularity in the larger market remains very small. What's exciting about these coins is they still have the potential for vast changes that the larger coins lack unless there's a significant shift in how consumers or businesses spend money.

Defining Altcoins

It's really easy to explain what an altcoin is. Technically speaking, it's any coin that isn't bitcoin. Since bitcoin was the first to hit the scene and build a mainstream following, it's as conventional as this space can get. The rest of the coins that make up the cryptosphere are referred to as altcoins. Yes, that includes ethereum and XRP. They got the name because they provide alternative services, functions, and usability features that bitcoin either lacks or chooses not to offer. From an investing perspective, they also provide choices for crypto enthusiasts outside of bitcoin.

FACT

The first altcoin produced went by the nomenclature namecoin, and it launched in 2011, two years after bitcoin's unveiling. It largely borrowed bitcoin's code, although it also tried to add a layer of reduced transparency by hiding user domains. It does continue to trade to this day, remaining a very small coin by market cap.

How Does the Technology Differentiate?

Based on the way the developers of bitcoin created its blockchain, certain rules are in place that guide its use and capabilities. It's not a perfect piece of code, which produces opportunity for blockchain developers to improve upon and market new blockchains that solve a piece of the riddle. These weaknesses, like the inability to process many transactions per hour or the heightened cost of transactions as the price of bitcoin rises, also highlight why bitcoin may not remain the end-all and be-all of cryptocurrencies. It's just the first and currently most recognized name in the space.

Some of these concerns that other coins address weren't ever expected to be an issue, since who could have predicted when Nakamoto first introduced his white paper that the price of bitcoin would rise to the heights it has seen. While bitcoin's blockchain is adaptable, it does take almost the entire community's buy-in, which prevents any swift changes to the structure.

These weaknesses produce an environment where a new cryptocurrency could rise, garnering a significant adoption rate, leading to a reduction in bitcoin's usage. Most notably now, though, it creates situations where companies or users that need cryptos to solve certain pain points, like cross border transactions, may turn to the altcoin universe since there are coins that transact faster and more cheaply than bitcoin.

Why Differentiate As an Investment?

Altcoins provide two benefits within a portfolio: protection against bitcoin and opportunity from increased interest in the token.

Since it's such a new market, no one knows what the future will hold for any coin within this space, and that includes bitcoin. While right now it's the preeminent coin, there's no guarantee that another coin won't come along and replace it as the bellwether for all cryptos. If such a coin were to grow, it would come from the altcoin universe (unless it was one of bitcoin's forks). While you're not necessarily taking stakes in the names you think can completely wipe out bitcoin, there's a benefit to having exposure to a few altcoin names, in case one of them begins to climb as a result of its growing market strength, independent of bitcoin.

Right now, corporations are only beginning to try and understand the full potential of the blockchain. This leaves them turning to these startup coins to test whether they can provide the solutions to their digital currency needs, with safety, security, and legitimacy in mind. When certain blockchains pop up, they will be tested, and the most legitimate ones will begin to show favor with a community outside the initial investors. When this happens, these altcoins can rise in price. Since they're much cheaper than bitcoin, you can often gain a larger share of the coins at a reduced price. They also provide hope that companies will latch on to certain coins that add value to their business through the token's blockchain.

That Doesn't Mean They Will Appreciate

You invest in altcoins on the hope that they will appreciate. But there's no guarantee they will, which is why it's prudent not to put your entire crypto portfolio in the altcoin space. Many coins have done little to show that the company will transition into a viable business, or that the transaction volume will grow at a significant enough pace to provide ammo in an investment thesis and justify a higher valuation. They remain unproven. Like most unproven investments, it's more likely that your altcoin investment will fail rather than succeed.

The Wild Ride of Altcoins

While, it's prudent to invest some of your crypto portfolio in altcoins, remember that it's not like any other investment you will be taking stake in. Cryptos as a group have a high level of volatility. Bitcoin, in its own right, sees significant ups and downs within a few days (or even hours). Altcoins, particularly smaller altcoins, have an even higher level of volatility, unless no one invests in them at all. It's something you will have to accept if you buy in. While some will use this volatility to sell as soon as there's a spike, if you keep that volatility in mind with regards to your entire crypto portfolio—and your crypto portfolio's place in your entire investment holdings—then you shouldn't have to worry too much about the daily ups and downs of these coins. If you track them on a daily basis, however, don't be surprised if you're grabbing the champagne one day and nausea medicine the next.

ESSENTIAL

At this stage in growth, you should be more concerned if a coin doesn't have volatility, as opposed to those that do. Since no one is sure what these coins will do over the long term, investors jump in and out hoping to catch lightning in a bottle. But the names without volatility are those where there's no interest, meaning they've lost investor attention, momentum, and possibly hope for success.

They Move with Bitcoin

Like the more mainstream altcoins discussed in previous chapters, less mainstream altcoins will also move very similar to bitcoin. Except, since many of these coins have much less value per coin, it creates higher highs and lower lows, as people rush into the names to take advantage of a bitcoin rally. It's speculation that's driving these movements, instead of anything tangible within the coins itself.

Let's take Stellar's lumen. It peaked shortly after bitcoin reached its apex, moving from $0.20 a coin in late-December 2017 to $0.75 a coin by early January, a jump of 275 percent in about two weeks. By March, that had fallen back to the $0.20 mark. With bitcoin, there's the potential that prices could stabilize if transaction volume were to increase. But these coins are much younger, and there's less adoption so fewer transactions. That's why when prices rise that fast, it's speculation driving the train. And the speculation occurs when bitcoin does well.

Nothing Will Happen for Some Time

Many altcoins will sit with very little action for months and even years. There's little interest and buzz around the coin. Maybe they're new coins. Maybe they've been abandoned. It's important to understand why some coins remain in the cellar. Just because the price is low doesn't mean that it's a good value. There's a chance the reason the price is low is because no one in her right mind will ever use the coin. Don't mistake cheap for value.

ESSENTIAL

In investing, there's a term, "value trap." It occurs when a company that's priced cheaply receives interest from those who believe it's certain to rise based on the low price point. The problem is, there's an inherent issue with the company that makes it impossible to rise. It's similar to the trap when you buy a home that is cheap, but needs so much work it becomes a money pit.

The History and Fundamentals of Stellar

It's not surprising that a token that developed from the Ripple protocol would have an unusual setup, and that's the case for Stellar and its token, lumens (XLM).

In 2014, Stellar.org was created with the goal of bringing banking capabilities to the areas of the world that lacked such opportunity. Since it's often not economically feasible for large companies to service areas with significant poverty, these communities get overlooked. But they need the ability to send and receive money, sometimes from other countries, in order to conduct business or other common needs. Stellar wants to bring the ability to transact easier to these areas of the world.

At the time of its launch, 100 billion lumens were created, with 5 percent going to the organization and its founders, while the remaining 95 percent were given away.

The People Involved

The development of the Stellar network was based on concepts that were developed by chief scientist David Mazières, who is also a professor of computer science at Stanford University. In the paper, he set his theory on how to develop more open financial systems, which would reduce costs for transacting cross-border transactions, among other uses. In the paper, he laid out the concept of the Federated Byzantine Agreement (FBA). It's the notion that allows for speedier approval of transactions. In a regular block-chain, nodes are used to approve transactions. Once a large percentage of nodes approve of the transaction, it moves forward. In the FBA, nodes are verified and trusted, so each trusted node can approve a transaction and the entire community recognizes it.

While Ripple created the first FBA system, Stellar offered the first "provably safe FBA," which allows it to stand out from a technological perspective.

It has another similarity to Ripple, as well: Jed McCaleb, the original founder of the exchange Mt. Gox, helped create both networks. He first developed Ripple and then moved over to Stellar after a falling out with his business partners. He continues as the lead developer of the Stellar Consensus Protocol, the blockchain that runs the network.

They've also reportedly received $3 million in seed funding from the venture capital firm Stripes, which has a seat on the nonprofit's board.

How Do Businesses Use Lumens?

Stellar's goal is to open up areas of the world that didn't have access to financial systems and markets. To do this, they need partners that will not only use the technology, but also use lumens as the third-party currency that can be cashed in for whichever country's currency it's being transacted in. Early in its lifecycle, Stellar has shown an ability to attract large players to at least test out its technology.

They have a number of partnerships with banks in parts of the world where economic hardship remains high: India, the Philippines, and parts of Africa. It has also signed with companies such as IBM, which uses lumens to conduct cross-border transactions in the South Pacific. When this news hit in October 2017, lumens became a hot new topic of potential crypto gold. But there are parts of the Stellar network that limit its upside as an investor.

FACT

Lumen Fundamentals

When investing in lumens, you're not just investing in the coin. You're also investing in the nonprofit that developed the coins, which has the stated goal to encourage financial activity in smaller economies. This also means you have to deal with the fact that Stellar.org plans to give away all the lumens that are available. For some this will be a deal breaker. How can you invest in something that's given away for free? It will deflate the demand, until there's only a third-party market controlling the coins. By the end of 2018, Stellar had released 20 billion lumens, with 10 billion provided for free. Stellar intends to give away every remaining lumen within ten years.

The Value of the Nonprofit

One way to evaluate the true value of a lumen, is to look at the money that the nonprofit brings in. This is the approach that Brian Koralewski, founder of Austere Capital, used in its early valuation of the firm. One way the Stellar nonprofit brings in funds is through fees that you pay in order to transact and trade in lumens.

Within its code, Stellar requires a very small percentage—equivalent to .00001 XLM—per transaction. This limits the amount Stellar can collect in fees. Koralewski estimated that if there were 1,000 transactions per second, the limit that Stellar can collect in fees would be just over $115,000 a year, assuming a $0.36 lumen price. As Koralewski points out in his analysis, it makes sense because Stellar wants to keep costs low to increase access. As an investor, though, it caps how large lumens can grow.

It's Trying to Commercialize the Business

Since more business will further appreciate the token, which will further drive adoption, Stellar has developed a group called Lightyear. It's a separate, for-profit business that seeks to find ways to commercialize the Stellar network through services, such as consulting and maintenance contracts, by working with organizations already using the network. It's early days for this outlet, and it hasn't yet made significant gains that have impacted the value of lumens.

Other Factors Play Into Lumen Adoption

While the Stellar foundation has a noble goal, it creates some barriers for adoption, since many factors play into improving financial access for those who don't receive significant banking services. It requires many more partners, such as IBM, to invest in these areas and in the Stellar infrastructure. Those partners also need to use lumens in order to improve the currency long term. Whether or not that influx of cash moves forward will depend greatly on the opportunity the companies see.

There's Still a Significant Amount of Supply Coming

With a little more than 100 billion in total lumens that will eventually hit the market, Stellar has a long way to go before it reaches its cap, and only about one-fifth of the supply has currently become public. This leaves a significant unknown in what will happen as the rest of this supply reaches the hands of those that plan to use them. It could severely crunch the demand of the coin, reducing the price. Again, it's an unknown, but one that would require significantly higher transaction rates to make the large supply worthwhile.

The History and Fundamentals of Litecoin

When bitcoin came onto the scene, developers and engineers entrenched in the digital currency community quickly jumped on the idea, exploring ways to improve and grow the concept. But bitcoin's code is open-source, which means others can crib much of the program, with only a few tweaks, to then grow their own cryptocurrency. These coins that come from bitcoin's code are numerous, but there's one in particular that has seen its value rise over the years.

Charlie Lee developed litecoin in October 2011. He took bitcoin's code, altered areas within the code that he viewed as holding bitcoin back, and then released it into the wild, drawing users and investors. The reason it has appeal is because of the tweaks that litecoin offers, plus the credibility that Lee brings to the table as a cheerleader for the coin.

The Creator of Litecoin

Lee has credentials that add a layer of legitimacy to the litecoin name. Prior to developing litecoin, he worked as a Google engineer. In 2011, as a side gig, Lee developed another cryptocurrency that went by the name Fairbrix. It was an offshoot of another coin, which had a mismanaged ICO. But Lee thought the design of the coin deserved its own opportunity, so he launched the code under a different name. But the results ended up similar to the initial ICO, as it collapsed soon after. Out of the gate, it was hacked, leading to a loss of more than 51 percent of the coins. Another bug within the code prevented new coins to be created, collapsing Lee's initial effort in the crypto space.

By October of the same year, Lee decided to combine parts of bitcoin's code and Fairbrix to create a more stable coin, which he named litecoin. Since he used a large part of bitcoin to create litecoin, some believe it's a fork of bitcoin. It isn't a hard fork, like bitcoin cash or other such changes to the code. Instead, like many other altcoins, it's heavily inspired by bitcoin's code. By 2013, Lee had quit his job at Google to become chief engineer of Coinbase. Then in 2017, as litecoin's valuation grew, he moved to proselytize the coin full time.

ESSENTIAL

Lee announced he had divested nearly his entire litecoin stake in late 2017, near the coin's height, and donated the returns. In the announcement, Lee declared he wanted to avoid a "conflict of interest" as he promoted the coin and cryptos. In the six months after he announced the sale, litecoin's price dropped 71 percent.

How Litecoin Differs from Bitcoin

While Lee used bitcoin as its design inspiration, there's significant differences between the two coins, one that makes litecoin appealing to a group of investors that view it as a potential everyday currency.

It Has a Larger Coin Base

Instead of total market size of 21 million coins, like bitcoin, litecoin has an upper coin limit of 84 million. Lee's decision to have a larger coin base fits with the goals of the coin in that it wants to be viewed as an everyday option to conduct transactions. Lee has compared bitcoin to gold, where it's used for large purchases, like a home or car. Otherwise, investors hold on to the coin as an investment. Lee has likened litecoin to a tool for everyday purchases, no matter how small. In order to provide that service, there's a greater need for coins, hence the larger supply.

FACT

At this point in litecoin's growth, it hasn't caught on as an everyday tool to purchase items. The number of transactions per day of litecoin remains a fraction—often 10 percent or so—of bitcoin's. You'll want that gap to close, if litecoin can truly become a purchasing tool of everyday items.

It Has Faster Processing Times

One of bitcoin's greatest weaknesses and a reason for complaints is the time it takes to confirm transactions. The ten-minute processing time is a significant drawback, and it's why developers first began creating altcoins, trying to court others by fixing this dilemma. Litecoin was one of the first altcoins to do so, reducing the processing times to a little over two minutes. This also reduces fees to process transactions.

What You Want to See from Litecoin

Since litecoin wants to become the decentralized cryptocurrency for the masses, what you really want to see is transaction rates that tick forward. The more these transaction rates increase, the better off this coin will do, since there's no company that's working behind the scenes trying to court customers of the coin. Unfortunately for the coin, transaction rates haven't increased in a way that doesn't just track the price of the coin. This indicates that speculators drove up most of the transactions as they moved in and out of the crypto.

That doesn't mean litecoin hasn't had significant gains in the industries and companies offering payments via the coin. It's still prominently offered from small, niche merchants. Tracking when new names offer the coin will provide opportunity for this token to jump.

It Hasn't Broken from Bitcoin's Grip

Like many altcoins, litecoin remains at the mercy of bitcoin and its price movements. You can actually see when litecoin has grown simply by looking at bitcoin's price. Outside of a short blip in 2013, litecoin's price remained consistently below $5 a coin until March 2017, when the price suddenly shot up to $366 only to lose 80 percent of the value within a few months, as bitcoin also fell.

As an investor, you'll want to see this connection between the two coins break, but that can't happen until litecoin's transaction volume increases. Without the commitment for using the coins for everyday purchases, it's going to be difficult to have sustained forward movement. Yet, it has decent name recognition and a clear goal of becoming a coin for everyday purchases. It makes it easier to evaluate and understand the purpose of the coin, which may help as more investors and spenders enter the cryptocurrency space.

The History and Fundamentals of Cardano

When research firm Weiss Ratings developed their list of secure crypto names, a lesser-known startup in the space, Cardano, received one of the best scores from a technology and adoption standpoint. This is a newer coin, which only launched in October 2017, but based on the Weiss ratings, it's clear there's already significant interest. Despite its status as a very young name in cryptos, it has already become a stalwart within the top ten coins, based on market capitalization.

What has propelled this coin into the upper-echelon of crypto options? Cardano, whose crypto goes by the name ADA, has produced an innovative new concept, propelling it forward in the eyes of blockchain enthusiasts.

The Development of Proof of Stake

When bitcoin came onto the scene, the algorithm it used to validate transactions went by the name proof-of-work. This required the community of miners to validate transactions and new coins by solving an algorithmic puzzle. But this leads to a significant energy cost, one that has gotten worse as bitcoin's tokens become more difficult to find. Ethereum also uses proof-of-work concepts. Cardano's breakthrough was using a "proof-of-stake" concept, and securing the network to protect it from bad players. This proof-of-stake gives coin holders voting rights to determine "slot leaders." These slot leaders confirm new nodes (remember, this means computers or electronic devices hooked to the code) and blocks of coins, which reduce the number of confirmations that a transaction must go through before it's confirmed. Cardano wasn't the first to use this concept, but they're among the early adopters that have received praise for their solutions. Theoretically, this will allow Cardano to increase the number of transactions per second, as the number of users grows. It creates scalability, something that other coins lack.

This proof-of-stake concept helps the coin scale faster, making it a potentially more attractive option for larger organizations.

The People Behind the Coin

Since the coin bills itself as one developed through scientific philosophy and research, it's probably not a surprise to learn that it has some blockchain heavyweights behind the name. Charles Hoskinson was a cofounder of the Ethereum Project, which created the popular crypto ether. He left in 2014, and founded the technology firm IOHK. He, along with cofounder Jeremy Wood, worked to create a solution for the proof-of-stake concept. Once that was viable, the group launched Cardano in late 2017.

FACT

Interestingly, Wood and Hoskinson first worked together while at Ethereum, and they're the drivers of the largest ether fork, ethereum classic. This coin, which remains just a fraction of the mother coin, ether, broke from the community following a 2016 hack. Ethereum decided to pretend that the hack never occurred, returning any stolen coins. Classic doesn't ignore the hack, staying true to the original ether timeline.

The Purpose of Cardano

While ADA has become a popular altcoin early in its public life, Cardano still remains a very early-stage platform geared toward attracting financial firms by offering their platform as a way to run financial applications. Eventually, Cardano will incorporate smart contract computing via its platform, of which ADA will serve as the cryptocurrency for the network. It seeks to balance needs of users, including privacy, with just enough access for regulators, to approve the transactions. It's a fine line, one that Cardano hasn't yet fully achieved. But it's early days for this startup.

Beyond that, Cardano is developed with scientific rigor in mind. It's the college professor to Ripple's entrepreneur. This could create a solution that proves viable for years to come. It also has the potential of becoming fixated on solving solutions, while ignoring the growth needed to sustain a company. It's worth watching, though, since from their beginning, they've created solutions that have earned blockchain enthusiasts' respect.

FACT

Cardano has a cap of 45 billion coins, of which about 26 billion coins were delivered via an initial coin offering. Another 5 billion coins were given to three entities: IOHK; Cardano business incubator, Emurgo; and the Cardano Foundation, the educational-minded arm of the Cardano system. The rest will be discovered in the proof-of-stake process as rewards for approving blocks of transactions.

It's Still Tweaking

Since Cardano is growing and upgrading in stages, it's still incorporating many of its solutions to solve the scalability issue, which means the coin only offers limited capabilities from a corporate standpoint, at the time of this writing. That will change, assuming the solution is as strong as promised. But it's hard to value the coin under this scenario, since much of the transactions remain small and targeted to speculation about what the company could be more than what the company is.

The History and Fundamentals of NEO

China's notorious for being an unkind environment for the proliferation of cryptocurrencies. In the years that bitcoin grew to become a stable name in the space, China did much to try and dampen the excitement around the fad, at least within its own nation's boundaries. That's why it's strange that a Shanghai-based cryptocurrency has become one of the more prominent speculative plays within the crypto market. That's because NEO could accomplish something that very few cryptos have a chance to do: it could become the crypto of China.

The Onchain Link

Da Hongfei, a Chinese entrepreneur, founded NEO. He also founded Onchain, a company which works to provide businesses and governments access to blockchains, whether they be private or public. While NEO uses rules developed by Onchain, users aren't required to use the coin on Onchain's blockchains. In fact, the two are considered completely separate entities. NEO, however, does benefit from increased use and adoption of Onchain, since it improves the notoriety of the crypto.

What's unique about Onchain—and NEO—is that the company was designed with developing blockchain technology with regulation in mind. While many early blockchain adopters embraced cryptos as a way to circumvent governments and regulation, Da took a different angle, believing that regulators would still need to oversee the coins and the technology. That's why Onchain has become a growing tool within the blockchain universe, since companies see value in a chain that can work with their compliance and governance efforts. It's a particularly attractive scenario in China, since it's a heavily regulated market. It's why Onchain has received investment from the large Chinese investor Fosun International.

One reason people clamor for NEO is because of Onchain's success within the Chinese economy. China, for all its anti-crypto actions, has actually touted the potential of the blockchain. Da's company could be well positioned if China chooses specific blockchain firms to proliferate the technology throughout the country.

ESSENTIAL

This is where early crypto investors may split with someone like yourself who is interested in the potential, but not necessarily concerned with destroying regulated markets. Onchain is an example of a company that's trying to adapt the concept of cryptos with the realities of regulation in mind. It may gain, simply because it provides easier access to this regulation.

A Rebranding

Even though NEO and Onchain first launched in 2014, you won't find much information about the coin until 2017. That's because it used to go by the name Antshares. In 2017, as the Onchain technology grew in significance, and bitcoin's price began to rise, Antshares was rebranded as NEO. Since that moment, it has gone from less than a few cents a coin to a height of over $150.

You're Betting on the Future

There's not much you can look at in terms of fundamentals to show that NEO will suddenly take off. Instead, it's a play on what Onchain can become. As of 2018, Onchain and NEO aren't dependent on the other, meaning you won't necessarily use NEO on an Onchain-developed blockchain. But the company wants to reportedly change that, where NEO is traceable for a company or regulatory purpose, on Onchain. It's an important wrinkle for the development of NEO, since Onchain has attracted interest from huge companies, including Alibaba and Microsoft. If those companies use NEO, it makes the crypto much more attractive as the demand for the coin increases.

The History and Fundamentals of NEM

Similar to Cardano, NEM offers a change in how transactions are processed and new coins harvested. While bitcoin uses the proof-of-work concept in its blockchain, providing a way for miners to process transactions, and Cardano uses the proof-of-stake, which rewards those who hold more coins to dictate which nodes process transactions, NEM introduced proof of importance. It's this tweak that has turned NEM into a growing altcoin among enthusiasts. It's also becoming an increasingly popular blockchain in Japan.

The Proof of Importance

The downside to the proof-of-stake strategy used by Cardano to encourage users to host the blockchain and approve transactions is that it rewards those who have the highest number of coins. This means those hoarding the coins can dictate some of the rules within the system. NEM has tried to tweak the process by providing scores to those that own the coins. If you own more than 10,000 NEM coins, you become eligible to harvest tokens and approve transactions. But in doing so, you also receive a score based on how many transactions you make with the coin (and not just to yourself). This encourages the use of the coin. Those who have a higher score will harvest more blocks and obtain more coins. It spreads the harvester's weight based around usage, instead of just general ownership.

What Value Does Proof of Importance Bring to NEM?

Since the ability to harvest is based on this score, it's not a requirement to have large servers and constantly running computers in order to harvest more coins. In fact, since these harvesters connect to a supernode within the NEM system, there's no need to even download software. This keeps the overall energy requirements to harvest new coins lower, which helps NEM scale, if it becomes more popular. It also makes it easy for enterprises to join the system, since they don't have to worry about the issue of software compatibility.

Keeps Fees Low

Since there's little lift for harvesters to approve transactions, the fees are kept much lower than bitcoin. Every transaction is subject to a .01 percent fee, which doesn't change, whether you're purchasing something worth $100 or $1,000 or more. It's a small fraction of the amount that you might find with bitcoin, which increases in price. A flat transaction fee encourages greater use.

This also speeds up transactions. Within seconds of buying the coin, it will show up in your account. The same goes when selling, assuming there's a demand for the coin.

ALERT

At launch, NEM issued 9 billion coins, which were distributed to 1,500 different trusted partners. In order for these coins to move, these partners had to be willing to part with their coins. Otherwise, the available supply of coins would remain small, hurting adoption rates.

Transactions Are Public...Sometimes

NEM's purpose is to provide blockchain capabilities to enterprises, and it has a public and private blockchain that it uses to conduct this service. Companies have shown a greater affinity for the private chain, with hundreds of companies reportedly using the service. Since there isn't the software component, companies can design different use cases that are then easily added to the system.

But NEM, Cardano, litecoin, lumens, and NEO all exist because their founders and users see a purpose in the design. That's not the case for all of the coins that come to market, which is why you need to know how to sleuth out scam coins. Doing so will protect you from the next great heist.

CHAPTER 11

Sleuthing Out Scams

More than 1,600 different cryptocurrencies are on the market. The number of ICOs happening each year is reaching the multiple hundreds. By and large, this is a good thing. More players in the field breeds more innovation, options, and eventually breakthroughs. But it also has allowed in a group of much-unneeded players: scam artists. Many fake or illegal ICO offerings have tried to accumulate initial funding and then walk away with the gains, with no intention of supporting the coin or business they claim to be creating. Other criminals target crypto investors, looking to steal coins out of the owners' digital wallets. It's these scams you must watch for if you find yourself interested in an ICO or cryptocurrency investment. This chapter will discuss how to root out such scams, detail how past victims fell prey, and offer ways to protect yourself from harm.

The Dark Side of the Crypto Market

As you grow more comfortable with the idea of investing in cryptocurrencies, there's an urge to test your crypto-picking abilities, and start looking at the new ventures—pre-ICO—to try and find one that could lead to riches one day. While this isn't a winning strategy, since you have to be incredibly lucky to pick the right one, it's a tactic that you might toss a few dollars at if you can afford to bet on dart throws. If you do so, remember that the world you're entering is filled with scams, and, therefore, there's a good chance your money will disappear without a trace.

Even opening a crypto account, you will be making yourself a target. Since the information on and credibility of most crypto investment tools is slim, a number of bad players have jumped into the fray, trying to swindle those new to the space.

Most ICOs Are Scams

This isn't hyperbole. In fact, it's the vast majority. Eighty-one percent of ICOs that took place prior to March 2018 expressed a goal to create an initial coin offering but had no intention of actually fulfilling the goals stated by the ICO, according to an analysis conducted by the ICO advisor Statis Group. The research firm only looked at ICOs that sought to raise funds for a coin the providers claimed would be above $50 million in market capitalization. Of the ICOs that weren't scams, 11 percent either had failed as an ICO or succeeded but have gone dead from listing on exchanges. This indicates they failed post-ICO. Only 8 percent would move on to trade through an exchange, and just a handful become prominent enough to discuss beyond the fringes of crypto message boards. This also highlights how tricky ICO investing can be as an overall strategy.

FACT

From time to time, you'll notice that law enforcement agencies will crack down on these efforts. In May 2018, the North American Securities Administrators Association (NASAS) announced an initiative involving forty different jurisdictions across Canada and the US to investigate potential fraudulent ICOs. It led to the opening of 200 investigations and forty-six different situations where regulatory enforcement was needed.

There're a Lot of Different Types

The scams don't just show up during the ICO. Instead, because of the lack of knowledge about the crypto space, the high amount of enthusiasm, and the limited traceability of stolen coins, they've become the targets of scammers looking for quick bucks just as much as those looking for the huge payday. These scams vary widely, both in style and the size of expected returns, but they typically take one of these forms:

- **Email scams:** If it's from a Nigerian prince needing your bitcoins, delete the email. It's an old trick, but one that still somehow works.
- **Fake exchanges:** It's exactly as it sounds. A site pretends to be an exchange offering low fees and great opportunities, then steals your cryptos as soon as you commit.
- **Hacks:** Every once in a while, a hacker will target unsafe coins or exchanges, walking away with millions of value in coins.
- **Malware:** Hackers use holes in the code to steal your cryptos.
- **Ponzi schemes:** A promise of riches using a crypto structure, only to disappear as soon as the money forked over runs out.
- **Ransomware:** You click the wrong link, and there's someone threatening to release information about you, unless you send bitcoins.

While it may seem easy not to fall for these types of tricks, there's a reason that hackers and scammers keep going back to the same tactics: they work. It's why once you have a crypto exposure it's time to protect it from the bad players.

FACT

The advocacy group Crypto Aware found that from 2011 to 2018, crypto investors lost $1.7 billion worth of cryptocurrencies to hacks or scams. It's a particularly striking number, if you consider that the value of lost cryptocurrencies didn't dramatically rise until 2017. The value lost would have been even greater if the coins had been held through that year.

You Don't Know Your Other Buyers

It's also important to keep in mind, if you go the ICO route, you don't know who else will be purchasing the available coins. It could be other speculators like you. It could also be people with darker motives. When bitcoin first came onto the scene, the Dark Web welcomed it, as criminals used the coins as a way to conduct illegal transactions, believing it was anonymous. As bitcoin's popularity grew, so did law enforcement's ability to track the transactions. As well, as prices rose, transaction fees and the influx of price changes turned more criminals away from bitcoin and into altcoins. Recorded Future found in early 2018 that the favorites among criminals had become litecoin, dash, and Monero. If other coins' ICO show they have low transaction costs, fast speed rates for conducting the transactions, and limited visibility to third parties, then they're going to appeal to a bad player in the crypto game just as much as it may appeal to a mainstream investor.

FACT

When the Feds shutdown criminal online wonderland, the Silk Road, they seized more than 144,000 bitcoins. They then sold those bitcoins in an auction in 2014 and 2015, before bitcoin's dramatic climb. It wasn't until October 2017 that the legal obstacles to collect on the auction sales could move forward, allowing the FBI to collect $48 million, pricing the average coin sale at $334.

The Feds Are Warning People

You know once the government has begun to issue warnings on scams that they've had to investigate then it has reached a fever-pitch level. It also means that these complaints of fraud are real. In August 2017, the Securities and Exchange Commission issued its warning about ICOs. One warning sign it gave at the time was that if the ICO says it's "SEC compliant" but then doesn't explain how it's compliant with the oversight agency, it's probably a scam. Those offering the ICO are trying to sell you on safety when in fact it's the exact opposite of that.

The FBI has also issued warnings about ransomware using bitcoin, and the scams can get even stranger from there. In March 2018, Austrian authorities called on Interpol to help with an investigation that involved the scamming of 10,000 bitcoin owners, leading to losses that could have reached as high as 12,000 bitcoins or $110 million at the time of the loss. According to the authorities, a group called Optiment said that it could promise returns of 4 percent a week if you invested the bitcoins. On top of that, they hosted in-person, live events that had hundreds of people in attendance, all networking and discussing their outsized returns. If you attracted more investors to the fund, you could gain higher rewards. This strategy brought investors in from other countries as well, such as Poland and Romania.

ALERT

Sometimes scammers use social media tools to improve their own investments, as opposed to stealing yours. They will use accounts that look like famous crypto investors, tweet that a certain unknown crypto is due for a rise, and then wait for money to flood in. If it does, they sell, leaving them with a profit for the fake post.

In the end, the group disappeared overnight leaving the investors with very little to show for their trust.

As you can see, scams have a wide range of possibilities and vary from very small to very large. You have to watch out for both because by buying into this market, you will become a target.

What Does a Scam Look Like?

While you must protect your coins from hacks as much as you possibly can through the use of the crypto wallets, scams are different because they typically involve tricking you into handing over the coins. This means that part of the effort is to ensure that you don't fall for the common tricks that will convince you to do this. Since there's plenty of excitement in the crypto space, these scams typically involve playing on people's enthusiasm and lack of knowledge in what exactly cryptocurrencies are and the expectations around their returns.

Promise Outsize Returns

No matter what you invest in—whether it's stocks, mutual funds, or cryptocurrencies—there doesn't exist a person in this world who can accurately predict how the market will move. Traders can use statistical analysis and strategies to give them hope of predicting where the market will move next, but there's a fatal flaw in this strategy: past returns don't predict future gains. If you read an announcement that guarantees 4 percent returns every month, or 10 percent gains, yearly, it's an impossible rate to predict. And these guarantees can get more outlandish, trying to say that returns will reach 25 percent to 100 percent of your invested dollars.

These people are at the whim of the market, just like everyone else and don't have the funds to make these claims. Instead, more likely, they're funding your returns with other people's investments. It's fine for a while, but like any Ponzi scheme that has grown to a sizeable level, it will eventually fail. That will leave you without much money in the account, and talking to lawyers and the Feds about seeking repayment that will likely be cents on the dollar.

ALERT

If you need further proof of this lack of true understanding about the market's movements, take a look at the S&P 500. This index of large stocks had gained, historically, about 7 percent per year after accounting for inflation. However, year-by-year, the S&P 500's movements range from a 50 percent rise to a 35 percent fall, and anything in between. This is the most studied group of investments on earth. If investors can't accurately predict this set of investments, how can anyone be expected to do so in a new vehicle, like cryptocurrencies?

Target the Lack of Knowledge in the Technology

When Prince Harry and Meghan Markle set to wed in May 2018, there was the typical excitement, grandiosity, and extravagance we expect in a royal wedding. There was also an ICO effort to sell coins called the Royal Coin. These funds were gifted to the couple, and distributed to their favorite charities. While this effort sounds like it could be a scam, it wasn't. You know this because it was linked to the British Monarchist Society and Foundation, a credible group within England. While it certainly didn't offer much in the terms of investment, using the excitement to raise funds for the British wedding, it did have a genuine reason to exist.

If this hadn't had the backing of a legitimate organization, it would very well look like a scam. It's using the idea that you can buy something called Royal Coin to somehow participate in the royal wedding, and selling the notion that it's the blockchain that's making it all happen. But again, the blockchain plays very little role in this effort other than serving as the tool to develop the token. Once the ICO ends, and the royal wedding vows are taken, there's not much use for these digital coins, other than as online souvenirs.

This ICO would have been a bad investment, but it's not a scam.

ESSENTIAL

It's not as if a coin such as the Royal Coin is unique in the gold and silver world. You only have to turn on the TV during a weekday to catch one of a handful of commercials trying to pitch the idea of a commemorative coin. This Royal Coin did the same, except instead of a gold-plated quarter you're left with an encryption key. In the end, neither will likely be a good investment.

Yet, the line between a scam and the Royal Coin is very thin. Scams will heighten the benefit of the blockchain technology in their efforts, but then if you break it down, there's really no need for the blockchain innovation. Or, more likely, when you read the fine print, it has nothing to do with the blockchain at all. So be wary of cryptos selling the idea of participating in a big event or allowing access to something the blockchain can't really provide access to. More often than not, it's a scam.

They're Asking for Personal Information

One big red flag to look for is if the ICO sponsors are seeking your personal information, your encryption-key information, or your log-in information for your exchange. Unless you're planning on handing over your cryptos to these people, then you must ask yourself if there's any legitimate reason for them or their website to need your personal information. If not, then it's likely a scam. Even if you think there's a legitimate reason that they might need your personal information, if you give it to them, you'll need to assume that the cryptos are no longer in your control. There are very few reasons, other than working through an exchange to buy or sell more cryptos, that you would need to do this (unless you've fallen for some promising sales pitch, in which case you should run from the conversation immediately before giving over the information).

ALERT

When handing over your personal information, if for some reason you thought that was a good idea, make sure it's through a credible website and not by email. Most websites use third parties to process and secure this transfer of information. Since they're not worried about stealing your data, they would prefer another group takes the onus of securing that information. If you're passing your data to someone or a company via email, then it's not likely legit.

Phishing Scams

It's a trick as old as email: some stranger asks for your information to help him with a dire situation. Or a hacker uses a friend's email to try and get you to click on some weird link. These phishing scams are being manipulated to also steal bitcoins and other cryptocurrencies. How do hackers find you, you might ask? It's remarkable how many crypto investors like to share on social media that they've bought into a specific coin. It probably has to do with the enthusiasm behind the investment, but social media has become ripe with this type of information. And once it's public, there's little you can do to take it back. Scammers know to mine these mentions for potential targets.

Since cryptos remain a nascent market and completely digital—which makes it harder to trace if it disappears—the protections you have in your other investments don't exist with cryptos. By discussing your specific investment publicly, you're putting yourself at risk. It's important to keep in mind, even if you want to discuss your efforts with your social community. Do so, but try to limit the specifics.

The Dark Money Flowing Through Cryptocurrencies

The dirty truth of investing in cryptocurrencies is that you're also potentially investing in a coin that has a dark underbelly. Criminals like cryptos because they're far more anonymous, easier to launder, and can move across borders with little trace. Plus, cryptos open up entirely new markets—through the digital world—if the criminals are able to sell their illegal wares online. Illegal trade in cryptos remains, however, a small portion of the crypto market. According to studies, from 2013 to 2016 less than 1 percent of bitcoins converting to a currency were linked to illicit activity. Of course, that number requires an exchange for currency and you can imagine many of these bad players storing bitcoin in order to pay for other services as well. This limits our understanding of the full magnitude of illegal activity within the crypto space, but it also indicates that it's not driving the entire crypto marketplace.

New Cryptos Become Popular

As bitcoin's popularity grew, so did the fees to make the transactions. This moved many crypto users away from the coin because it got so expensive. There are other issues with bitcoin, such as the slow transaction speed and the fact the FBI has gotten better at tracking transactions. This has encouraged the dark money to move to other cryptos that have more anonymous capabilities and lower fees. Expect this sort of migration to continue. It's a concern if you're investing in a young crypto, because you can't possibly know what coins offer this potential to the criminal element.

WeissRatings.com evaluates some for the most stable cryptocurrencies to determine the level of safety and legitimacy in the cryptocurrency tools that investors have shown interest in. It's sort of like how Moody's rates companies on the stability of the firm. But Weiss will downgrade cryptos that have too much illegal element potential. Their ratings can serve as an initial look if you have suspicions about your investment.

Real-Life Crypto Scams

It's sometimes easier to understand how rampant these scams are by first viewing some real-life examples. Luckily, the following scams were discovered before they became too large. But they still left plenty of investors with empty pockets.

BitConnect

BitConnect attracted investors by the promise of outsized returns. You could go to them, loan them your bitcoins, and receive up to 40 percent monthly returns, which included daily bonuses. The problem? It was all funded by the promise that others would provide their bitcoins and the dream that the crypto would continuously climb.

Prominent crypto names, such as Ethereum founder Vitalik Buterin, called BitConnect a fraud. In December 2017, law enforcement agencies began to agree, as both Texas and North Carolina regulators warned the platform about its strategy. A month later, it shut down, making the coin it used, BitConnect Coin, worthless. A class-action lawsuit was filed against the company, arguing it owed the complainants $700,000.

Pincoin and Ifan

In April 2018, these two coins ICOed to much fanfare, producing nearly $660 million in funding for the company that developed the cryptos. Investors thought one company was run out of Singapore while the other out of Dubai. It turned out both coins were developed by a Vietnamese firm, which went by the name of Modern Tech. Since many of the coins were sold in Vietnam, investors demonstrated outside the Modern Tech offices, claiming that the executives were frauds. However, Modern Tech had liquidated a month before the outraged bubbled over, while the leaders went into hiding.

GainBitcoin

Operating in India, GainBitcoin promised massive returns and bonuses if investors brought on new investors. Amit Bhardwaj founded the company, which involved some heavy-hitters in the country, including Raj Kundra, a British investor and husband of Bollywood actress Shilpa Shetty. GainBitcoin shut down in June 2018 after authorities began to question the legitimacy of the organization. At its height, a reported 100,000 investors had joined the platform, providing over $300 million worth of funds.

The Five-Step Security Checklist

It's good to have a strategy for when opportunities arise in which you might have some interest. You should make sure you're looking at the opportunity with clear eyes, to prevent a scammer from preying on your optimism. The following checklist will serve as a barrier to any potential scams.

- ❑ **Does the opportunity make sense?** Does this sales pitch have a purpose beyond just taking your money? If it claims to be a blockchain effort, make sure that there's an actual need and purpose to this blockchain "innovation."
- ❑ **What are they promising?** If they're promising the sun and the stars, then it's an opportunity you want to miss out on.
- ❑ **What do they need?** Scams require you to submit something to them, or else they have nothing. If they need your coins or personal information, then there's probably no reason to give it to them.
- ❑ **Could they really know more than you?** Scammers like to take advantage of the fear you have that others know more than you or that you're somehow missing out on an opportunity you didn't know about. Whether or not it's true, you can make one guarantee: they don't know the future either. If that's what they're claiming, then ignore them.
- ❑ **What happens if you do nothing?** If they're using pressure tactics, like you only have twenty-four hours to take advantage of the opportunity, then it's not an actual opportunity.

Asking these five questions isn't an absolute guarantee of safety from scammers, but it will stop the overwhelming majority of them dead in their tracks.

Protection from Hackers

There's another danger lurking in your crypto investment and it rears its head far too often for comfort. Every few months, it seems, another cryptocurrency exchange suffers a hack. Mt. Gox, at one time the largest bitcoin exchange, was stripped of over $400 million worth of the coins in 2014, leading to its demise. In 2018, Japan's Coincheck saw hackers walk away with over $500 million of NEM coins, becoming the largest such breach on record. Besides those high-profile attacks, there are a number of much smaller infiltrations that have taken place over the years, stripping owners of millions of dollars in coins.

What can you do about it? Not much, if you're storing your coins on an exchange. By leaving the coins on the exchange, you've chosen a hot storage tactic, which means you're susceptible to a hack while the coins sit online. And since you've chosen a hot wallet on an exchange, your crypto fortunes are entirely tied to the security of the exchange itself. If that exchange gets hacked, then you will have little recourse other than hoping the company pays back some of the lost coins.

Make sure that any exchange you use has the most up-to-date security protocols in place. This isn't easy for most users to figure out, but some signs that your coins are safer is if the exchange uses two-factor notification (meaning you will have a log-in then a code that you will enter, sent to you via email or text message) and encrypted communications. You'll also want to see that the exchange stores most of the coins it handles in cold storage, leaving the majority of its funds offline. This guarantees a high percentage of its vault sits free from the prying eyes of hackers.

For US exchanges, the SEC has become more involved in regulation, but this oversight continues to adapt. You can't yet simply rely on the SEC coming to your aid if something happens.

FACT

Coinbase began the proceedings to officially register as a brokerage with the SEC in April 2018. If it receives the SEC's backing, then it would not only allow Coinbase to offer more products on its platform, but it would require similar security measures that companies such as Fidelity and E*TRADE Financial use.

The only real way to completely protect your coins from a hack infiltrated at the exchange level is to hold them in cold storage—outside the exchange—via wallets that live offline. Whether it's a paper wallet or a hardware wallet, these storage methods are recommended for the majority of your crypto portfolio, even if you leave some of your coins in hot storage within the exchange.

Who Can You Turn to If You're Fleeced?

As of now, there's very little you can do when your cryptocurrencies are hacked or stolen. It's partly because the regulators and authorities don't view cryptocurrencies as having enough legitimacy yet, so they don't make recovering coins a priority. It's also due to the difficulties in finding the stolen coins.

If you're hacked, then you can report it to the FBI's Cyber Division or to your local authorities. You want a trail of reports, in case your hack is related to a larger scheme, which forces the authorities to respond. There's also the possibility of suing the operator. Neither of these options will guarantee you will gain back what was stolen from you, nor will it happen quickly, but they're the ones available today.

As cryptos become more legitimate, more layers of protection will build, providing a greater level of protection and reimbursement. Until then, be sure to keep your coins close.

Why It's Getting Better

The good news about the rise in popularity of the crypto market is it has forced law enforcement agencies to take notice of those selling wares in the space. This ray of sunshine has provided protections for the investor if something goes awry, as well as put criminals on notice that there are eyes lurking. It will help clean up some of this dark side activity within the crypto market. While it will never go away, new scrutiny and regulation will ensure it remains just a minor corner of the investment community.

Now that you know about how to avoid scams, it's time to start talking with your money. Your options are different, if you have a lot of funds to play with.

CHAPTER 12

Okay, You Have a Lot of Money to Play With

With more money at your disposal, it's not surprising that you'll have more options open to you, especially if you prefer to avoid investing in cryptocurrencies directly. Regulations limit (as of this writing) many of the typical avenues you might find when investing in the stock market, like index funds. But with enough dough on hand, you can access certain vehicles, more geared to institutional investors. These come with some benefits, like the outsourcing of your security concerns. One thing that won't be any different than investing in cryptos directly: these tools remain risky and have significant downsides to consider. This chapter will discuss some of the options you have when there's a little more dough at your disposal.

The Budding Crypto Markets

As money flooded into the popular cryptos that have become (almost) household names, like bitcoin and ether, naturally businesses and investing groups looked for ways to offer different strategies to appeal to a wider net of investors. On the one hand, it's important for tools like this to crop up, because it provides more mainstream ways to invest in cryptocurrencies, shifting the investment from the staunch libertarians, paranoids, or technology enthusiasts who were cryptos' earliest adopters. However, it doesn't then follow that every new investing tool comes with a guarantee or seal of approval from financial advisors. Instead, because of the current regulations preventing index funds and other cheaper options to trade, it has relegated many of these tactics to the very wealthy.

They Still Come with Problems

Since only a few different types of tools can come to market under the current restrictions in the US, the alternative ways to invest, which include placing cryptos in investment trusts or accessing the futures market, come with significant fees. There are only a few different companies providing these strategies, which allow them to sport these higher fee rates. It's also because they're really targeting institutions with their offerings. It means, since you (let's assume) don't have tens of millions to play with, that the fee will remain at its current mark, which often runs 2 percent or more a year. That will cut into your potential profits, and limits the returns you can expect, even if bitcoin sees a significant increase in price. These fees do provide some benefits, including security.

This is also a highly undiversified strategy. Since bitcoin and ethereum have shown the strongest push forward as well as some semblance of stability (for cryptocurrencies), those two coins receive the vast amount of attention, exposure, and tools in this alternative offering space. Maybe that's not important to you. But if you're someone who wants more access to other altcoins besides Ethereum, then you're more limited in the ways you can access the different coins, other than by investing in them directly. The number of offerings is expanding to allow more access to altcoins.

Finally, from a more macro standpoint, particularly in the case of futures, there's potential for even more market manipulation than what you'll find in the regular crypto exchanges. This means that manipulation and speculation could drive the prices higher, until the bottom falls out, leaving you with a futures contract that has busted.

They Offer Hope

Despite the concerns that these new markets provide, they're still positive steps in legitimizing the crypto market. They offer a way for institutions to have more preferred methods to invest, creating some calm in the futures market, which is counter to what you'll find in the regular exchanges.

ALERT

Even though futures have become an option, it hasn't been followed by a whole bunch of enthusiasm. After an initial day of trading, the CME Group and CBOE saw about $50 million traded in futures. Meanwhile, on December 10, 2017, various exchanges across the world traded about $18 billion worth of bitcoins. This gap declines as trading volume in the exchanges is reduced, but futures volume rarely surpasses 10 percent.

Accessing Cryptos Without the Security Concerns

The biggest benefit from using these tools is that you're accessing cryptos with a much greater security. Instead of making sure you have your password, encryption key, and digital wallets secured from hackers while still easily accessible (by you only), through these alternative methods, you don't own any cryptocurrencies yourself. You can't somehow spend these investments. Instead, you're paying for access to the cryptos owned by a third party. In the futures market, you're betting on whether the price of bitcoin will rise or fall, but it's settled in cash, so you never actually hold the bitcoins that are transacted. This reduces your exposure to the risk of an unsecured crypto investment.

ESSENTIAL

In order to provide strong security measures, the Bitcoin Investment Trust uses a third-party security provider. It's an effort to ensure that there's not one way to hack and steal all of the bitcoins. There's value in that, but would you rather trust yourself to keep your investment secure or trust a third party?

You Can't Spend Them

Since you don't actually hold any of the cryptos that you have purchased via a trust or futures contract, you can't spend the bitcoins or ethereum that you have invested in. This differs significantly from when you buy cryptos through the exchange, since in those cases you're buying the actual coins or tokens. There's nothing stopping you from using that purchase to then turn around and buy a video game. If you're concerned about your short-term purchases with the coins, the trusts provide a tool to prevent the unplanned splurges.

The Bitcoin Investment Trust

Started by Grayscale Investments, the Bitcoin Investment Trust (ticker: GBTC) became the first investment tool that investors could buy into, gaining access to bitcoin, providing an ETF-like purchasing experience. That means you buy GBTC through shares, as you might if purchasing a stock or ETF on an exchange.

Unlike ETFs that have bitcoin exposure, the Bitcoin Investment Trust is directly purchasing bitcoins, which the investors then gain as the price of bitcoin moves. Now, because this is like an ETF, when it comes to returns it's not exactly the same as buying bitcoin directly. You have other market influences playing into the supply and demand of GBTC shares. The demand for the share could increase the price, even if bitcoin's price remains unchanged.

Where It Comes From

GBTC was launched in 2013 by Grayscale, which is owned by Barry Silbert's Digital Currency Group. Silbert, a former banker, invested early in the crypto craze, then turned his riches into a blockchain seed fund, providing early financing to a number of names, including the exchange Coinbase, Ripple Labs, and crypto wallet and trading platform Circle. Grayscale Investments was the arm that would help ETFs and other Wall Street vehicles earn access into the bitcoin craze, since many would prefer not to hold the physical assets. That makes the investment more difficult from a liquidity standpoint; since instead of selling the share in the trust, they would have to sell the physical coin.

What You're Buying

While it seems that by buying the Bitcoin Investment Trust, you're purchasing bitcoins through a trust at the price of the share (remember it isn't an ETF even if many compare it to one) this amount isn't just based on the price of bitcoins. Instead, it's also influenced by the supply of shares available and the demand of investors wanting in. The more investors who want in, the more expensive those shares become, regardless of bitcoin's price.

When you own one share of GBTC, then you actually gain access to less than 0.001 bitcoin. But the price of the share will fluctuate based on whether or not investors want to buy more shares, and not just due to fluctuations from bitcoin. When bitcoin is expensive, then expect the difference between bitcoin's price and the net asset value of a GBTC share to be greater, since the demand for shares will further influence price, above and beyond the impact from bitcoin's price increase.

ALERT

Although GBTC trades based on its per-share price, it doesn't reduce the volatility of the investment. You saw this following the 2018 stock split, which took place in January. In the five months that followed, both GBTC and bitcoin fell the precise same amount: 37 percent. The experience won't drastically change just because you're paying to avoid holding the crypto directly.

For instance, in order to appeal to a broader group, in 2018 Grayscale split the GBTC fund by providing investors with 91 extra shares for each one they owned at the time of the split. This spread the number of shares out further, reducing the price of a single share. The split increased the number of shares available to investors from 1.9 million pre-split to 174 million post-split. It, in essence, reduces the amount of bitcoin a GBTC investor invests in when she buys a share.

You're Not Buying an ETF

Remember, despite many saying what you're buying is essentially an exchange-traded fund, that's not the case. The Bitcoin Investment Trust doesn't go through the same regulatory controls as an ETF. It doesn't have to register with the SEC, for example, and it doesn't trade over an exchange. Instead it moves through the over-the-counter market. This reduces the protections you have as an investor if something goes awry.

How Do You Buy In?

There are a number of restrictions on gaining access to the trust. First, it's only available to accredited investors, which typically means advisors or portfolio managers. You can also qualify if you made at least $200,000 in income over the past two years or have a net worth of more than $1 million, which can't include your primary residence. Also, if you manage to pass that very high bar, then you'll have to invest a minimum of $50,000 in order to gain access. If these high marks don't scare you, then you purchase the shares via your broker, financial advisor, or individual brokerage account.

Fees, Fees, and Fees

Beyond the lack of actual bitcoins that you own by buying shares in GBTC, the fees may be the most important drawback. Since it's one of the few options on the market, its fees are 2 percent annually. That's a significant hurdle to overcome, since, if bitcoin is rising, you're buying shares that come at a premium price to the regular currency, due to the requirement to buy an individual GBTC share, and then be forced to pay at least $1,000 in fees for access, if you invested the minimum amount ($50,000) and the price didn't move at all during that first year.

But you're getting something with the fees: the security. Since the trust owns about $800 million worth of bitcoins, some of the fees cover the security measures that it has taken to secure the coins from hackers.

Expanding Into Other Cryptos

Clearly the trust has managed to succeed. In March 2018, it expanded into more altcoins with the addition of an Ethereum Trust, Ripple Trust, Litecoin Trust, and Bitcoin Cash Trust.

The Coinbase Index Fund

For a number of years, Bitcoin Investment Trust was the only game in town when it came to investing in outlets outside of the currency itself. Then, in early 2018, the crypto exchange Coinbase decided to enter the asset management business when it launched the Coinbase Index Fund. It offered something that Bitcoin Investment Trust didn't: a minimal level of diversification. It came with a caveat as there's not a ton of diversification that you can achieve within the crypto space, since so many of the coins move with bitcoin. But if bitcoin were to crumble, this type of fund would have provided some security from that scenario (assuming bitcoin wouldn't bring the entire crypto market to the brink of destruction as well). But investors never took to the tool, and Coinbase announced it was closing the index in October 2018, four months after launch. Still, it's worth looking at the structure of the index fund, since it's something that could be copied down the line.

Coinbase Index Fund's Structure

Unlike GBTC, the Coinbase Index Fund had stakes in seven currencies. It tracked the Coinbase Index, which measured the currencies that are listed on Coinbase's exchange. The assets included were:

- Basic Attention Token
- Bitcoin
- Bitcoin Cash
- Ethereum
- Ethereum Classic
- Litecoin
- 0x

The weighting of each currency depends on the overall market capitalization, which is measured by the price of the currency multiplied by the number of coins in existence. The market capitalization measures how much value the currency has. If bitcoin's price surges, which means its market capitalization increases, then the weighting of bitcoin in the index increased.

ALERT

Don't be fooled by the use of "index" fund within the Coinbase fund name or another similar product that comes to market in the future. It wasn't the traditional index fund that you likely have some of your retirement accounts in. Instead, it was called an index because it tracked the Coinbase index, so it's not actively managed. But it didn't offer the advantages that typical index funds provide, such as low fees or a wide-range of access to the players within a market.

What Did This Provide?

By using a mix of cryptocurrencies, what Coinbase wanted to provide was a level of diversification. It was based on the concept that you don't know what currency will increase, or when it will increase, you just believe it will. This index provided some sense that you've gained some level of access to a variety of coins, even if it included only a handful of names.

Don't Overplay This Diversification

In the stock market, studies have found that you need at least sixty stocks to capture 86 percent of the diversification in the US public companies. Even still, those sixty names wouldn't capture many parts of the market that are left out of that selection.

When you say you've captured a diverse set of cryptocurrencies, with seven names in an index, it only accounted for about two-thirds of the crypto market. Since the names in cryptos remain more unknown than most of the names in the stock market, the fact that 33 percent remained unaccounted for raised the possibility of missing the next big gainer in the space. Don't think you're diversified because you have seven names under your belt or if another such index fund becomes viable, especially being that cryptos often move together.

You're Still Overweight in Bitcoin

Since bitcoin remains by far the largest cryptocurrency, by buying into a similarly designed index fund, more than 50 percent of your investment will sit in bitcoin. It's something you should remember when you're evaluating your entire cryptocurrency portfolio. If you have some of your funds directly in bitcoin, you'll need to take into account the fact you also have more than 50 percent of the funds invested in the index fund sitting in bitcoins as well. If you don't account for that, you could find yourself overweighting toward one coin.

Watch Out for the Expenses

Similar to the Bitcoin Investment Trust, the only people who could have taken advantage of Coinbase's index were the very wealthy, which may be one reason why it couldn't gain more interest. You had to have at least $200,000 in annual income, or a net worth of over $1 million in order to have had the opportunity to place the funds into the index. Again, like GBTC, the fund came with a 2 percent annual fee. But, unlike the GBTC, Coinbase's Index Fund had a minimum investment of $10,000, which opened it up to a slightly larger investment pool of wealthy investors looking to dip their toes into the water of cryptos. In ending the index fund, Coinbase instead launched a tool on its site that would allow any investor access to few currencies with a minimum investment of $25. But unlike an index fund, they won't rebalance automatically as prices move. And you'll own the cryptocurrencies directly, instead of through a fund.

Calculating the Fee Impact

Now, it's obvious that the fee impact by using an investment vehicle, like the Bitcoin Investment Trust, is huge. When looking at a 2 percent fee, it's something worth asking yourself: "What does that mean?" Essentially, the better your investments do, over time, you could lose much of your gains strictly from fees.

Take a look at an initial investment of $50,000, as we discussed previously, versus $50,000 invested directly into a cryptocurrency. Let's say the first year, the price of the cryptos ends up flat, leaving you with $50,000 at the end of the year. In the Trust scenario, you actually only have $49,000 because of the fees. Now, say the investment jumped 10 percent in 2020. In the cryptocurrency, you now have $55,000 worth of coins. In the Trust, you now have $53,900 and an annual fee of 2 percent, which leaves you at $52,822.

In the third year, this time the investment drops by 5 percent. Now the Trust investment, after the fee, has $50,234, netting you just $234 over three years. The crypto investment has $52,250. While these aren't the most flattering return scenarios, they remain very possible outcomes. It's important to see the fee impact from the losses and gains.

Finally, the fourth year, you see the gains that you've been waiting for, with a 25 percent improvement in your crypto investment. That leaves you in the Trust with $61,537 while the crypto investment comes in at $65,313, leaving a difference of $3,776. These differences will only grow larger the more years you invest, no matter whether the investment falls or gains.

ALERT

There are two ways you can view this fee impact. If bitcoin rises 15 percent, then your real returns for that year will be 2 percent lower, meaning they're actually coming in at 13 percent. That's nice, but doesn't show the long-term effect of these large fees. To understand this, look at a brokerage account that you've added $500 over thirty years and saw an average annual return of 7 percent. The financial site NerdWallet looked at exactly that and found over the period, with fees of 0.25 percent, you would have lost about $26,500. At 2 percent, that number rises to $179,000.

That Shouldn't Rule Out the Trust Options

While going the individual route certainly saves you plenty of money, there are reasons why you might still prefer the trust over directly buying your preferred crypto, and that's due to security. If you lose your password or the drive in which you keep the coins, then that guarantees you have lost all of the money you have invested. It's a scenario that's more than common in the crypto space.

Another possibility is that scams could bleed you of your stake. Even Steve Wozniak, the cofounder of Apple, reportedly fell for a scam that led to the loss of seven bitcoins. While as a billionaire he can take such a loss without much thought, most investors won't feel the same.

The trust or index options do provide a sense of security, since they've invested heavily in protecting their assets. Also, if something were to happen to their vault, then you would likely receive at least a portion of the investment back.

Alternative Ways to Play

While the fund tactic serves as the most mainstream tool, if you can call it that, to access coins indirectly, there are a couple other strategies that more experienced investors might use. As the complexity of the tactic grows, so do the expenses and the potential for losses.

Investing in Crypto Hedge Funds

As bitcoin fever took hold, one of the first third-party institutions to rise up, offering a similar experience to traditional investing has been the crypto hedge funds. Like regular hedge funds, these crypto-focused ones have little regulation or oversight, allowing them to invest in anything that they see would work, based on their specific mandate. Crypto hedge funds' mandates lead them into cryptos.

As the name suggests, hedge funds typically look to provide a hedge against downside. They will short and go long on stocks (meaning they bet that the stocks will fall or improve) to try and manufacture a rate of return. They can also invest in other areas of the market, whether it's mutual funds, real estate, or another area that the mandate dictates. But in the crypto space, this means that many of the hedge funds are betting long on different cryptos, since there are not a whole lot of other options within cryptocurrencies. Some crypto hedge funds also provide venture capital in blockchain startups, offering another outlet beyond the coins directly.

Watch Out for Fees

Like all hedge funds, it's fees that eat up a lot of returns. Most hedge funds—including crypto ones—charge the standard two and twenty. This means that your fee total will be 2 percent as a management fee, then 20 percent of any profits gained.

FACT

The high fees and a lack of long-term performance have led to a backlash against hedge funds. In 2007, famed investor Warren Buffett bet hedge fund leaders $1 million that his index fund of large US companies would outperform the selected funds picked by the hedge fund over a ten-year period. It wasn't even close: Buffett saw 7.1 percent returns, annually, while the hedge fund saw 2.2 percent returns. And that was before fees.

You'll Need a Large Amount to Invest

Hedge funds aren't for the small investor. Pantera Capital has one of the larger crypto hedge funds in the space, and it requires a minimum investment of $100,000. You also need to be an accredited investor, which comes with some more caveats. Again, this isn't for most, and that's probably a good thing.

Investing in the Futures Market

Instead of investing in bitcoin directly, or even a fund that invests in the coins, you also have the option of trading contracts that offer the ability to bet on the future increases of the coins, based on your belief of how the coin will move. This isn't a recommended strategy, as it adds significantly more risk to your investment, especially if you're borrowing—called trading on margin—in order to fund the contract, which is common in the futures markets (remember it's often institutions using these as a way to hedge bets).

Still, it's one tool available, if you would like to explore the strategy. However, it's only for highly advanced investors, since the ability to use margin when trading can quickly leave someone in debt.

ESSENTIAL

If you're looking to play the futures market, the easiest way is to open a brokerage account via E*TRADE or TD Ameritrade. The other option is to work with your own broker. While few specialize in crypto investing, it's a strategy that more brokers are starting to refine, as demand grows.

Where to Find More Information on Future Investing

The intricacies of investing in the crypto futures market are outside the domain of a beginner, and therefore you should find more information about it before getting started. In order to learn exactly what you're doing when investing in futures, you can turn to Howtotoken.com's guide to trading bitcoin futures. It's a good introduction to this risky investment strategy.

Yet, wealthy or not, most of your crypto investment will probably come in the form of buying individual coins. How you go about doing this depends on the goals you have when you invest.

CHAPTER 13

Okay, So You're Like Most Investors

Most investors taking a stake in cryptocurrencies only put a small portion of their portfolio into one or two names. If you're like the majority of people reading this book, you probably don't have millions to play around with and that's more than fine. The market hasn't progressed and matured in a way that gives the wealthy advantages that the less wealthy miss out on, other than the basic ability to purchase more coins with little fear of losing it all. This leaves you with a few much cheaper and more common options that could still move your crypto portfolio speeding forward, if you get lucky and the coins take off. These tactics are the same ones that many wealthy investors use as well.

Crypto-Picking Remains Best (Among Few Options)

With less money to invest, there's really only one way to develop direct cryptocurrency exposure, and that's through buying coins directly. Since the Securities and Exchange Commission hasn't allowed index funds backed by cryptocurrencies for retail investors, the only way you can access the coins is by purchasing them on an exchange or actually mining them yourself. If you go the exchange route, it doesn't mean you can't have a strategy.

ALERT

You should also note, if you want to only invest in bitcoin or Ethereum, that's a perfectly reasonable decision. Since so much of the market moves based on bitcoin's fluctuations, it's not a terrible strategy to take a stake in the coin that's moving them all. You're just not protecting yourself from another coin replacing bitcoin, if you take this tactic.

Develop a Plan

With so many various names available within the cryptocurrency space, you can't expect to take a stake in each one. Instead, you want to maximize your exposure in the names that you believe have a chance to break out within the blockchain space. To do this, you need to first understand the different options of cryptos that you could be buying into. Here's a way to look at the different types of coins in the space, breaking them out by the blockchain tactics they use to differentiate themselves.

Decentralized Currency

In this type of blockchain, which you'll find from names like bitcoin or litecoin, there's only one purpose for its existence: to act as a currency. These coins need to find adoption from more mainstream outlets, since they require mass use in order to grow. The ultimate goals of decentralized currencies are to replace the dollars that we spend in fiat currencies with the digital option.

ESSENTIAL

It's important to remember that all cryptocurrencies, for the most part, are decentralized. There are layers of decentralization within the space, since some argue that XRP isn't a decentralized currency, since it's heavily shaped by the company, Ripple, which runs it. But even then, there's no government running the coin.

Mainstream Blockchain Company

Some cryptocurrencies were developed with a specific purpose—to improve cross-border transactions, fix the way businesses track supply chains, and hundreds of other uses. Behind the coin sits a for-profit firm that isn't much different from a regular startup that you would find in Silicon Valley. But some of these coins have become prominent players within their own rights, attracting cash from regular investors as more mainstream outlets accept the digital dollars.

Coins like ether fit this mold. They're starting to become name brands, beyond just how they serve the business, Ethereum. This gives them two opportunities for growth: through corporate adoption and mainstream adoption. It will become more difficult, however, for them to receive complete mainstream adoption, since they can't ignore the paying customers.

Up-and-Coming Blockchain Companies

These want to become the Ethereums of the world, as their name brand grows and their use cases expand. As of now, though, they have only attracted testing from name-brand customers, and their mainstream appeal remains limited. How you rank these firms against the more mainstream ones will depend on your individual analysis, but you would expect the up-and-coming companies to have less mainstream acceptance on platforms such as PayPal or even Coinbase.

XRP and lumens fall into this mold. While both coins have a lot going for them, they have not reached mass adoption from customers or retail users, alike. But they could.

Forks

It's smart to keep some attention on the more prominent forks of bitcoin and Ethereum, since you never know if an advantage in the fork could supplant the original coin's code. Something in the code could catch on, leading to a shift in use from the mother coin to the offshoot. Right now, bitcoin cash best fits this description, but keep your eyes out, in case other forks become prominent players in the space.

Initial Coin Offerings

You can also place a few dollars in names that are only now launching to the world in the form of an initial coin offering. The likelihood that you hit on an ICO that will prove profitable remains extremely slim. But for the less risk-averse, it's an option to think about within the blockchain universe.

Pick Your Percentage

From those four buckets (five if you invest in ICOs), you'll want to pick a certain percentage that will account for each section of the blockchain universe. Say you have $500 to buy in, and you don't want to put it all in one name. You could take 40 percent, and buy bitcoin, 30 percent in the mainstream blockchain company, which would mean ether, 20 percent in the up-in-coming blockchain company, and 10 percent in the fork, bitcoin cash. That would give you a little bit of exposure to a wider range of the blockchain world.

If you think that it's more beneficial to have more of that percentage in ether, for example, then you can play with the percentages until it matches a level that you're interested in and comfortable with.

You're Not Diversified

Remember that just because you have four or five names under your portfolio now, it doesn't necessarily diversify you across all 1,600 names. First, most of these names you've bought into will still move as a direct reflection of bitcoin's path, whether it jumps or falls. This doesn't leave you secure from that exposure. Second, there are still plenty of cryptos that you have never heard of, one or two of which could suddenly skyrocket in price, due to some unforeseen opportunity or benefit. This won't protect you from that scenario, and without a true index fund, you're always going to have this particular risk. Finally, it also doesn't protect you if a new innovation or technology comes along, making cryptos obsolete. The most likely scenario would be if the government decided to develop a cryptocurrency with the US dollar supporting it. There's a chance this could make other cryptos obsolete, and you can't protect against this threat by holding a whole bunch of names.

Bitcoin Remains a Key Coin

Due to bitcoin's price tag, and the fact that other coins move on bitcoin's changes, there may be an urge to ignore the coin as an investment. It's a difficult proposition, since it's the largest name in the space. If the coin does double in price, that's a significant size improvement. Becoming a $20,000 coin from $10,000, as opposed to a $2 coin from $1 would result in the same percentage of gains, but you would likely enjoy the real value of the bitcoin return more than the other coin.

Most importantly, though, by not having some direct exposure to bitcoin, you're betting against the crypto market, since it's bitcoin that holds the most value and has the highest adoption rate. While other coins move with bitcoin, they still aren't bitcoin. If there's one token that could replace more fiat transactions, bitcoin remains the best bet simply due to its name recognition.

FACT

During the run-up of bitcoin in 2017, estimates determined just 1,000 users owned about 40 percent of the coin. This became an issue when the coin reached its extraordinary height in December, since users wanted to sell. Since this ownership base wanted to capture gains, it played a role in the reduction of value within the coin in the year that followed since so much of the supply became available.

You Can Go the ETF Route

While the option to invest in an ETF that only follows cryptocurrencies remains unavailable to the common investor, it doesn't mean you can't find ETFs with crypto exposure. In 2017, ARK Innovation ETF (ARKK) earned the title of the best-performing ETF for the year, improving 83 percent over the past twelve months. What caused the forward momentum? It took a 6 percent exposure to bitcoin at the time the coin began to make its ascent.

The 6 percent exposure in bitcoin came through ARKK via the Bitcoin Investment Trust and not through a direct investment in the coin. Such an ETF, which takes significant stakes in technology stocks, like Tesla, Amazon, or Twitter, was willing to put a portion of the ETF in bitcoin. Most ETFs won't, at this point in time. That doesn't mean they won't start, but bitcoin hasn't gone that mainstream yet.

The Bitcoin Investment Trust

You'll notice that the ARKK bought into the trust and not bitcoin directly. Many ETFs will go this route even if the SEC were to allow them to purchase coins for their funds because it allows the ETF to own the name without having to invest in security to protect the coins. It outsources the security and liability of the coins, so if the SEC suddenly allows crypto-ETFs to function, you will still see a number of names using investment trusts and other third-parties to actually purchase the exposure. Plus, it's easier to unwind if the funds decide to divest.

Here Today, Gone Tomorrow

The portfolio of an ETF changes as often as the managers want (if it's actively managed) or as much as the index it tracks changes (if it's an index fund). If you place your money in such an ETF, there's no guarantee that they will continue investing in bitcoin. In 2018, after the remarkable year for bitcoin, ARKK reduced its exposure to the Bitcoin Investment Trust to less than 1 percent of the portfolio. To regain your exposure via ETFs, then you'll have to move your funds to another name that has taken a stake. Doing so could create a fee, so you'll have to calculate the cost before making a shift. Since funds only need to update their holdings quarterly, you may not even realize you've exited for a few months.

ALERT

Divesting from such a fund will also likely create a taxable event, and you'll have to declare capital gains. Capital gain taxes range from 0 to 20 percent, depending on your income. Unless you're investing within an IRA or 401(k), then moving the funds from one ETF to another will likely require you to declare any gains.

It Remains a Small Portion of the Portfolio

Again, when things were going well, ARKK only invested 6 percent of its portfolio in the trust. That leaves this investment with a 94 percent exposure to other names within the technology space. When you're calculating your crypto portfolio, in this case, then you only have to count 6 percent of your ETF investment as a crypto investment. If you place $1,000 within the ETF, as you calculate your own portfolio, you don't have $1,000 exposed to bitcoin. You have 6 percent of $1,000 invested in bitcoin (even if the entire $1,000 could drop due to a significant fall in the price of the coin).

Finding Complementary Investments

What you'll have to ensure you avoid, since you have to put together your crypto exposure on your own, is accidentally doubling up on one investment. Say you take $500 and invest $200 in an ETF, $200 in bitcoin, and $100 in other cryptos, then how much bitcoin exposure have you created? You would then have two-fifths of your portfolio directly in bitcoin. But you also have to calculate the percentage that the ETF is exposed to bitcoin. Say it's 6 percent of the ETF, that's $12 of the $200 with direct exposure, which then goes to $212 of your total exposure to bitcoin, or 42 percent of the $500.

While the 2-percentage point change might not impact your decision, it highlights what could happen if you place a greater percentage of the investment in the ETF. Instead, if you split evenly the entire $500 between a bitcoin and an ETF, hoping that you've diversified your crypto investment, think again. First of all, only $265 has exposure to cryptos, assuming the same 6 percent ETF portfolio exposure to bitcoin. The remaining $235 is invested in other stocks the ETF has chosen. Of the $265 in cryptos, it's 100 percent invested in bitcoin. You haven't diversified within cryptos at all, other than as a way to protect a very small portion of your portfolio from a hack.

If You're Going to Diversify, Diversify

Again, work under the assumption that once you invest this money, it's gone. Since you've already lost it by placing the dough into the blockchain sphere, why not just go for the names that could prove the most valuable to you? This would mean ignoring the ETF option—unless the SEC changes its rules or you genuinely like the ETF for other parts of your portfolio. Instead, take a bet, since that's what you've decided to do, and throw your investment at specific names. This will provide you with as much diversification as possible when investing in the crypto space, and it commits your money to names that could rise significantly. It may remain a small possibility, but you won't see large gains from the ETF, unless all of its investments perform reasonably well.

The Build-Your-Own Index Guide

If you've decided to place a few bets into names that would give you exposure to different types of opportunities, coins, and blockchain companies, then you can build your own index, moving the exposure as the fluctuations of the market move down and up. You can do so by matching your investment portfolio to what you can expect to see within the crypto market.

Let's pretend you have $1,000 to use for this process. You've decided that you want a broad range of names, somewhere between five and seven coins. Use the market capitalization of the coins to determine what percentage of your portfolio should go in each coin. It's how many index funds would calculate the coin exposure, if a crypto-index fund existed.

Since bitcoin fluctuates around 50 percent of the total crypto market capitalization, you have $500 in bitcoin. It's prudent to listen to the crowd sometimes in investing, and the crowd supports the idea of ether right now, which accounts for 10 percent of the market cap, so $100 will go into Ethereum. You've now also got 50 percent in a decentralized currency and 10 percent in a mainstream startup.

Next find some non-mainstream names to also place a few dollars in. Say you're a fan of XRP, Stellar, and Cardano. Those names combined, have about 15 percent of the market cap, so you can split them along their percentages, with $100 going to XRP and $25 going to both Cardano and Stellar, respectively.

You probably want some exposure to decentralized currency platforms not named bitcoin. This could lead you to coins such as litecoin, Monero, and IOTA, which would account for about 5 percent of the portfolio.

Now you can look at bitcoin cash in order to hit the forks, by placing $50 in the coin, which accounts for about 5 percent of the total market cap.

ALERT

These market capitalizations change often. For instance, as cryptocurrency prices rose, bitcoin accounted for closer to 40 percent of the market and ethereum accounted for 20 percent. But as prices tumbled, the altcoins saw downgrades, leading to a significant drop in their market capitalization percentages.

That leaves you with 15 percent to move out to different names within the space, as well as the opportunity to place $100 or so into ICOs directly (if you want to take that risk). With the biggest names, you've accounted for about 85 percent of the top 100 market caps in the crypto space. The extra 15 percent can be used for various other targets. You can also use the 15 percent to invest more in bitcoin or ethereum or another name you particularly like. Just know that by doing so you're investing more into the name than the value of the coin, compared to the market. You're overinvested in that name. It's fine to do this, especially in a nascent market like cryptos, but by doing so, you're making a claim that you believe that name will rise more than others.

What This Portfolio Looks Like

Once you've done the research, and figured out what names to invest in, then this is what it will look like if you have $1,000 to invest:

- Bitcoin = $500
- Ether = $100
- XRP = $100
- Bitcoin cash = $50
- Litecoin = $30
- Cardano = $25
- Stellar = $25
- IOTA = $10
- Monero = $10
- Various other names and ICOs = $150

This strategy gives you exposure to nine different names, along with whatever coins you choose to invest in with the extra $150.

ESSENTIAL

Coinbase has made the ability to do something similar to this a little easier by providing a bundle option when you purchase coins. By selecting the bundle, you will gain access to a few different coins—bitcoin, ether, bitcoin cash, and others—broken down by a percentage of the amount you're spending, based on the market cap of the coins you're buying. You will, however, need to rebalance your portfolio yourself.

Prices Will Fluctuate

Prices will move the size of this portfolio up and down, depending on whether certain names perform well and others perform poorly. This, over weeks and months, will drastically change the percentage of your portfolio in each name.

For instance, if bitcoin falls by 60 percent and ether rises by a similar amount, your portfolio could now be almost equally balanced between bitcoin and ethereum. You'll want to keep an eye on these percentages, and every month or quarter, rebalance these coins by purchasing those that have fallen and selling some of the coins that have gained.

You can reinvest the gains back into the coins that have fallen, which will also give you more coins of the ones that drop in price. This is beneficial if the coins rise, since it will create a compounding effect where you're no longer just gaining on, say, five coins (the original purchase), but now profiting on ten coins (the amount you rebought plus your original purchase, in order to rebalance the portfolio).

You're Not Diversified

Remember that this doesn't create a diversified investment portfolio. It creates as much of a diversified crypto portfolio that you can gain within the crypto space. Since most of the coins are inherently linked to the movements of bitcoin, the space doesn't offer diversification. It does, however, provide you with exposure to various areas within the space.

Remember Fees

The urge when developing such a wide range of coin exposure will be to keep updating your account, buying and selling different coins based on daily fluctuations of the market. Going this route can hurt any gains due to the fees involved. You'll be charged by your exchange each time you buy or sell, so you have to keep those calculations in mind as you adjust the portfolio. It's also why in the hypothetical portfolio just presented, many people would cut the total number of coins to four or five, since it reduces the amount you're buying and selling individual coins—paying fees each time.

It's another reason to stick to specific time frames in which to adjust the portfolio, whether it's quarterly or more. This could cause your portfolio to spend some time out of whack with your plan, but it also ensures you're not eating your gains by trading too much.

ESSENTIAL

You could also choose to adjust your portfolio by percentage increases instead of time. For instance, you could adjust your portfolio every time a coin increases 50 percent or drops 30 percent. This will require much closer tracking of your investment on a day-to-day basis. You could also get stuck readjusting more often, if there are a lot of price changes in certain coins.

What to Do If Your Cryptocurrency Folds

When a public company goes bankrupt, securities law protects investors. While they may never recover the full value of their investment, there's a possibility they will regain some of that initial purchase. The same guarantee doesn't exist when investing in cryptocurrencies. What's strange, in this weird new world of the blockchain, is that it also doesn't mean that the crypto will immediately fall to zero.

Most Go Away

Since most ICOs never take off, due to the community realizing it's a fraud or because the project just can't get off the ground, there's the overwhelming possibility that the ICO investment will fall to zero if it fails. It's not because you can't trade the coin, but because there's no market to trade it. Without anyone willing to buy the coin, it falls to $0. If there are no servers (or nodes) willing to support the code in which the blockchain runs, it will also disappear.

Some Stick Around

While once the company disappears there's less incentive for the coin to stay, every once in a while, there's a coin that hangs on and eventually appreciates. Since the code the blockchain runs on is open-sourced, if there's a community willing to keep the blockchain alive, it can continue to function. If the functioning currency finds a market, there's no reason it can't continue to appreciate in price. It's rare, but a possibility.

FACT

There's a group of crypto enthusiasts who have gotten together to create CoinJanitor. This tool sweeps up dead coins, providing the owners with CoinJanitor tokens in exchange for the dumped crypto. It's an effort to clean the space and create a network effect around another coin. For those holding a dead coin, it provides a way to retain some value.

The projects that have a chance to survive are typically those that have good code behind them, but something has gone wrong with the management of the company. If the community of crypto enthusiasts recognizes that situation, then they may keep the coin alive, even if the founders didn't have the skills to build a business.

This chapter discussed how to plan your first purchases, but you'll also have to ensure you're keeping that plan in mind as you watch your investments rise or fall.

CHAPTER 14

Remember Your Purpose

By the time you've had a few dollars in cryptocurrencies for a few months, your interest will likely turn one of two different ways. Possibly you'll find that you're not at all interested in the investment and ignore the dollars you placed into coins. Or you'll become consumed by the excitement and intrigue that the investment brings. In both cases, you should take a step back and return to the reason you invested in the first place in order to provide you with a strategy to move forward. This chapter will provide some things to think about once you've had the chance to take a stake in cryptos.

Remember Why You're Investing in Cryptocurrencies

There's a reason you decided to research cryptocurrencies, weigh their downsides, and place a few dollars on specific names, whether they were names you had never heard of before your crypto dive began or were industry staples, like bitcoin. It's now time to return to these reasons, since depending on when you invested, your original commitment could look a lot different than it does now.

When Things Start to Perform Poorly

The biggest fear new crypto investors have is that as soon as they put their money in, they will only see dramatic falls, confirming their dread that they bought at the height of the hysteria. While there's no way to avoid the price fluctuations (if you've invested), there are tactics you can turn to so you're not trapped by this fear. If you do happen to buy during a heightened sense of exuberance in the market, and you only bought in because of the rising valuations, then you won't likely stick around for long. If you believe in the technology, however, then the ability to remain committed will be much easier, even as prices see a short-term tumble. Hopefully you bought in because you believe in the innovation.

FACT

While only 8 percent of investors have taken a stake in cryptocurrencies, those that do follow a process. In a survey conducted by personal finance website Finder.com, 54 percent of those that do invest pick their currencies based on the independent research, concluding the coin was the best. But nearly two out of five surveyed picked coins because their peers made money off of it or because the news covered it the most.

It's also why you should only invest the amount you can afford to lose. Some think they can lose $500, until that money starts to disappear. If you see your money shrink, and immediately begin to stress about the commitment, then you probably invested too much. Right size the amount you've invested to make sure it's only the amount you can afford to see disappear—and not lose sleep over it—in a blink of an eye.

While limiting your exposure protects your finances, it also provides you security from the urge to pull out too early. Since markets fluctuate (especially crypto markets), you will experience moments where your investment falls. The goal isn't to time every movement. That's impossible. Instead, over an extended period, you should expect a gain of some sort. Hopefully, after years, you see a very large profit. If you invested too much, and you stress out as the investment falls, then you're going to exit before you get a chance to see those gains.

When Things Perform Really Well

One could argue this is the more dangerous scenario. If your investment starts to propel upward as soon as you commit your funds, there's an urge to think that it's due to your own intelligence or ability. Let's just get this out of the way: the price appreciation of your investment has practically no connection with your own ability as a crypto coin picker. It's complete luck. Yet, when people fall for this seductive pull, they tend to become overexuberant about the coins, committing far more funds than they can afford to lose, buying into their belief of their inherent skill. Even worse, they may start to spend on the margin, borrowing the funds to buy more coins, putting themselves at the threat of bankruptcy.

That's why it's even more important in these situations to return to the reasons for investing. What did you hope to gain from your investment? What was the best-case scenario? The worst-case? Using that as a guide when you see your investment double in three days will prepare you for an eventual fall and leave you restrained enough to not overcommit.

Don't Forget to Diversify

One of the biggest mistakes an exuberant investor can make is to take the initial rise in the coins as a sign that this will continue forever. What happens in these situations is that the investor will cash out his retirement funds or savings to commit more money at the rising investment. It's not only a mistake that could leave you with very little at the end of the day, it's also a poor understanding of why you diversify your investments.

Since, at any moment in time, you will have some investments gaining while others decline, diversification—where all of your investments are working in tandem with each other to provide protection—will prevent deep declines that could leave you with nothing. The basement-level goal here, with all of your investments working together, is that they will gain a percentage greater than inflation, leaving you with enough at the end of your career to retire with. It's not to capture a runaway investment train.

Those who ignore diversification will commit their funds to cryptos, thinking that they will continue to guess the coins that perform best, leaving them with mammoth victories. Over years, you will end up worse than when you started and, in the process, destroy your safety net.

That Goes for Cryptos As Well

If you started your investment journey by trying to diversify into different parts of the cryptosphere, then stick with that strategy, even if some names suddenly perform remarkably well. It takes some fortitude to do this, but you're not diversifying into different crypto names in order to have exposure to all and then abandon the plan as soon as one name starts to outperform. Diversification is done so you can have exposure to a number of different names, in the case a few start to show that they're lasting options in the space. If you abandon your plan, then a few months later you could find yourself on the wrong end of the momentum stick, while the names you exited surge.

One Caveat

Since this space is so new, you're not diversifying within cryptos because it's a balanced market. Instead, it's because no one knows which names will last or start to outpace the entire space. If you see some names show significant gains in transaction volume, draw commitment from third-party companies, and gain overall acceptance by mainstream outlets, then those names could be becoming much safer plays within the crypto space. This is why it's not always a bad strategy to place your investment in bitcoin, since it has shown the most mainstream acceptance.

If it becomes clear that one name will take over the entire crypto space, potentially replacing bitcoin, then it makes sense to invest significantly in that crypto. The future may have room for many cryptos, it also may have room for very few. You have to adjust if it turns out few will last in the crypto space.

ESSENTIAL

If one crypto began surging, replacing all others, what would that look like? There's no real good example of this, other than what we see in past industries as a new technology or offering overtakes a space. Take Google as an example. When online search was new, many players tried to position themselves as search engines (remember Ask Jeeves?). But Google's technology was far superior, outpacing and making most other players obsolete. There are still other search engines, but they're a fraction of the search traffic compared to Google.

Reinvesting Gains

There are going to come times when you see a coin move forward in value at a significant pace, forcing you to think about selling in order to capture gains. Say you bought $50 of Stellar's lumens at $0.20, and it's now worth $10. So your 500 coins are now worth $5,000. It's perfectly reasonable to want to cash out, and capture the gains since you've participated in a bull-run on the coin. Say you do cash out all but five shares. What should you do with the $4,950?

From a tax perspective, you have cashed out, meaning it's a tax incident requiring a measure of filing. So you can pocket the change and feel good about your decision, using it to pay down debt or splurge on a vacation. You can also spread that cash among your other crypto investments, buying more coins in the other names that could also show improvement over the next few years. If you stick to your portfolio strategy, then you could reinvest in the names that have fallen below your target percentage.

It's a Lot Like Dividends

When investing in the stock market, your investments will often receive periodic payments in the form of dividends. Investors then must decide: do they keep the dividends, providing a small influx of cash, or do they reinvest. All you have to do is look at the S&P 500 to understand the impact. Over ten years, it has returned about 8 percent on an annual basis. Reinvesting the dividends returns a total of 9.5 percent a year during the same period. Why? It's because when you reinvest, you're buying more shares. That allows for greater gains when the market moves up.

FACT

This has a dramatic impact on your savings, as you invest over a life-time. Take someone investing $10,000 in 1988. Thirty years later, if she pulled that money out without adding any other funds, she would have nearly $91,500 if she cashed out the dividends over the years. If she reinvested those dividends? Her total would round to $182,000.

The same can occur in the crypto space. If you have five coins that have doubled in value, you can keep waiting out those coins. Or you can divest from some of those coins—say two—and reinvest that money elsewhere. Since the coins you would be purchasing are likely to be cheaper than the ones you just sold, you can end up with more coins across the crypto universe. If there's forward momentum in one coin, you do well. If there's forward momentum in both coins, you do much better.

What This Looks Like in Practice

Reinvesting gains has significant power when you're rebalancing your portfolio. Let's say you've decided to stick with a portfolio that gives you a stake that equals 40 percent in bitcoin, 20 percent in ether, 10 percent in XRP, 10 percent in lumens, 10 percent in litecoin and 10 percent in various ICOs or other coins.

After a couple months, some of the coins have performed better than others. Now your portfolio looks more like 52 percent bitcoin, 30 percent ether, 10 percent XRP, 5 percent lumens, 2 percent litecoin, and 1 percent the ICOs (remember that this is likely due to the rate of failures in the ICO world).

It's time to rebalance, so you'll sell a portion of your bitcoin and ether stakes to move them in line with the target range of 40 percent for bitcoin and 20 percent for ether. But then what do you do with the extra gains, once you've brought your lumens, litecoin, and ICO percentages back up? That's where you can reinvest equally through all five coins. This gives you more coins in each bucket, without necessarily changing the percentage of your portfolio. When further gains occur, then you'll own more coins which will compound your returns.

ALERT

Make sure to do these calculations prior to selling. If you sell, then calculate the percentages needed, you may find yourself rebalancing part of your bitcoin stake, for example, then rebuying it in order to reach your target percentage. In that case, you're paying an unnecessary fee to repurchase the coins.

Give It the Portfolio Treatment

One reason people who see short-term gains overweight their picking capabilities is that they don't look at their overall portfolio. While some may see gains, there's also a likely chance that others will see falls. But ensuring that when certain names take a dramatic move forward, remaining committed to the portfolio will provide stability to the emotional pull that could lead you into trouble by dumping all your funds into the coins that are surging.

ALERT

Reinvesting gains works in the stock market because owning more US companies, for example, has proven over a century that it's a relatively safe place to put your money. That's not the case in cryptos, so reinvesting gains isn't necessarily going to leave you with an advantage if the market crumbles. Instead, you reinvest gains because you believe the market will continue to mature, which will grow your ownership of the coins. If you're right, then you'll end up with a greater piece of the crypto pie.

Tweak the Portfolio As Needed

Cryptos do have a significant amount of momentum playing into the performance. Sometimes, it's smart to play the momentum by keeping the investment moving in the direction where the momentum is currently going. It won't last forever, but it can provide some short-term improvement. To take advantage of this, use the portfolio to safely play momentum.

Let's say you have decided to take a 10 percent stake in XRP. Suddenly, after a year of investing, XRP starts to show significant gains, jumping 30 percent over ten days. This momentum continues for the next month, as it shows signs of interest from financial firms. What should you do?

If you want to capture more of this momentum, increase the percentage of the portfolio that is dedicated to XRP. Say you increase the percent you want exposed to XRP from 10 percent to 15 percent. That's not going to get you in trouble, since the XRP gains will likely have moved it close to 15 percent anyway. You just don't need to rebalance as quickly as you would otherwise expect. This will allow you to increase your exposure, playing the momentum, without overleveraging to one coin.

Be careful with these decisions. You don't want to go from 10 percent to, say, 75 percent of your portfolio in XRP, just because of a few good months. You're still trying to time the market, but by going this route, you're doing so within the confines of your portfolio.

Regularly Test Your Investing Assumptions

When you begin to research crypto names and dive into what separates one from the other, you will undoubtedly begin to form opinions and assumptions about each one. Some you will begin to embrace, cheer for, and support. Others you will doubt, turn your back on, or call a fraud. This will form the basis of your earliest investments, and it's a sign of a growing understanding of the crypto space.

Remember, though, that you'll have to reevaluate these assumptions as time goes on. You may, in the beginning, believe financial institutions will never use XRP in everyday transactions. But after six months, if more firms are signing up, then you'll need to reevaluate that assumption. You may believe that ether will overtake bitcoin as a currency of choice among mainstream crypto users. But if a year later, ether has lost track with bitcoin, you'll need to return to that original hypothesis and determine if you still stand by the opinion or have changed your mind. As you do, you can change your portfolio structure to reflect your views.

Again, since this isn't money you're relying on, it's best to have intellectual intrigue, and embrace the research and findings. It's the only way you'll feel as if you have a stake in the game, besides putting a few dollars down to try and take advantage of the trend.

Remember though, when you rebalance, you're selling coins. At that point, it becomes a taxable moment. Read on to learn more about what that means for your finances come April.

CHAPTER 15

The Tax Man Cometh

Some of cryptocurrencies' earliest advocates came from those seeking a libertarian dream of escaping the systems that control monetary policy in the United States: the Federal Reserve, the Internal Revenue Service (IRS), and others. Since cryptocurrency is decentralized, that also means you can escape taxes, right? Well, not so fast. If your investment performs like you hope it does, then you certainly should expect the IRS to collect. In this chapter we will discuss what you need to know about paying taxes on your cryptocurrency investments, so you can limit your liability when the IRS cracks down.

The Tax Conundrum

When cryptocurrencies first entered the general consciousness of mainstream users, the IRS didn't have any way to treat the coins. How could they, really? Cryptos are a brand-new asset class, which requires even government agencies to learn how they're bought, sold, and transacted. Are they currency? Or should they be treated differently? How the government views it significantly changes how you track and sell your cryptos.

The Fall of Mt. Gox

The lack of guidance from the IRS became an issue in 2013, when bitcoin's popularity first began to pick up steam. With the increased exposure from news outlets and a growing exuberance among investors, it was only a matter of time before the IRS weighed in. Then, in February 2014, Mt. Gox, the world's largest cryptocurrency exchange filed for bankruptcy after a reported hack led to the loss of nearly $500 million worth of bitcoins.

FACT

At its height, Mt. Gox was estimated to conduct about 80 percent of all bitcoin transactions. Its demise provided the impetus for agencies to crack down on the exchanges used to trade cryptos. Now any crypto exchange that operates in the US has to register with the SEC. In order to do so, they have to comply with federal securities law, including having proper protections in place to protect investors. The net result of this regulation? It's safer to use the exchanges, although they still aren't fail-proof.

The fall of Mt. Gox still reverberates through the crypto market today, serving as a warning to just how unsecured this investment vehicle can be. But it also brought to light other suspected concerns, like the fact that money launderers use the cryptos to achieve insidious goals. The IRS has a reason to care for that loss of revenue, while other federal authorities look to stamp out the criminal activity.

The IRS Enters

Money laundering, the fall of Mt. Gox, and bitcoin's rising valuation forced the IRS to draw a line in the sand and explain how it views cryptos. It did so in early 2014, issuing guidance, declaring that spending cryptos was a taxable event and that it viewed them as property instead of currency. This vastly different view from the term "currency" means that you're susceptible to capital gains tax when you sell your cryptocurrencies. But since cryptos are spent on a regular basis, this property designation adds a significant complication to how you buy, sell, and store your coins.

It's on You to Track

This designation adds a unique wrinkle if you spend your cryptos on a regular basis. Since it's property, every time you spend or sell a cryptocurrency that has appreciated in value, you have to report it to the IRS. Whether you're buying a sandwich, purchasing a video game, or buying a car with the cryptos, that transaction goes on your tax form. It's calculated by the amount you've gained on the investment, just like if you sold some stock. How much of a percentage you will lose from taxes depends on how long you've held the crypto and how much it has appreciated.

The IRS Cracks Down

Despite the issuance from the IRS in 2014, very little changed in how often people reported their cryptocurrency gains. It appeared, from the outside, that the IRS had little incentive or concern to police cryptos, despite their designation. That changed when the price of bitcoin reached unprecedented levels in 2017.

FACT

Just how few people followed through with the cryptocurrency reporting on their tax forms? Only 802 filers reported bitcoin profits in 2015. It's not as drastic of a misfiling since the crypto gains were minimal that year. But tax year 2017 numbers will tell how the IRS really feels about collecting on the gains, since nearly anyone that entered the market (unless you bought in mid-December) likely saw profits.

The IRS Finds Owners

The IRS has long sought more information about those buying and selling bitcoins, beyond what they can find in the blockchain. In early 2018, the exchange Coinbase complied with an IRS request for user data on about 13,000 of its customers. Uncle Sam sought social security numbers and transactional records for anyone owning more than $20,000 worth of cryptos on the exchange between 2013 and 2015.

Coinbase fought the subpoena, but the judge overseeing the dispute said that the IRS could request such data. Judge Jacqueline Scott Corley wrote in her ruling that the fact "only 800 to 900 taxpayers reported gains related to Bitcoin in each of the relevant years and that more than 14,000 Coinbase users have either bought, sold, sent or received at least $20,000 worth of bitcoin in a given year suggests that many Coinbase users may not be reporting their bitcoin gains."

This gives the IRS the ammo to target other exchanges as well.

The Data Is There

You also might want to consider, if you're thinking of avoiding the tax implications, that since these transactions live on the blockchain, there's a historical, public record that the IRS can tap whenever it feels like further cracking down on cryptos for tax purposes. They don't need to subpoena exchanges in order to get the information they require for bitcoin transactions, if someone cashes into a bank. It's probably easier, but not necessary. As the technology matures, the IRS will develop further methods to more easily track these past transactions. It's why, eventually, you'll likely have to pay the piper on taxes. As painful as that may be, it isn't as painful as an IRS audit.

Short-Term Investors

Because the IRS views cryptos as property, this changes how you treat cryptos on a tax form based on how long you have held the investment. Short-term investors, in this case, would indicate they had held the cryptos for less than a year. If you hold the crypto for less than a year, it's considered short-term capital gains, and you're taxed at the regular income tax levels.

For short-term investors, the rate you owe will depend on your income level. The current income rates for unmarried, filing individually are as followed:

- **10 percent:** $0–$9,700
- **12 percent:** $9,701–$39,475
- **22 percent:** $39,476–$84,200
- **24 percent:** $84,201–$160,725
- **32 percent:** $160,726–$204,100
- **35 percent:** $204,101–$510,300
- **37 percent:** $510,301 and up

Look at Your Income Rate

Unlike long-term investors, who will have a set rate to their gains, short-term investors will be subject to taxes on their income. Say you bought $10,000 worth of cryptos that you held for less than a year before selling them at $20,000. You've made $10,000, which is fantastic, but you now will have to add that $10,000 to your yearly income. If you make $100,000 and you're filing individually, then that $10,000 would be taxed at a 24 percent rate, which means you'll owe approximately $2,400 from the divestment alone. That's not exactly the windfall you might have hoped for.

Spending Can Be Worse

The same would happen if you bought the $10,000 worth of cryptos, and began spending them for regular, everyday items. Each time you transact with the coins, you'll have to report the appreciated value. So if the cryptos doubled in price, you'll report the transaction and pay taxes on the appreciation.

ESSENTIAL

In a declining market, however, this can be a way to reduce your tax exposure since by purchasing items with the coins, you're locking in a small loss in the investment (assuming you bought at the peak). These losses can be used to reduce the tax exposure from other cryptos that gain. It's a tactic called tax-loss harvesting, and one that you can consider, as your crypto portfolio grows.

On top of that, you'll likely pay sales taxes on whatever you buy, which means you're taxed twice on one purchase. It's not the most frugal way to spend your money, which also speaks to holding your crypto investments for at least a year, since they will come with a reduced tax rate.

Impact on Transactions

There's little evidence, yet, that the lack of transactions in the crypto space has been partially caused by the tax treatment from the IRS. That's, however, because the IRS has yet to fully crack down on reporting your transactions. If they were to ever take the extra steps of seeking back taxes from major crypto users in a significant way, this could cool the use of cryptos from a transaction standpoint. It hurts the perceived value of cryptos since it reduces the ease with which to use them. It's something to watch for, as you analyze the space.

Long-Term Investors

For those holding onto cryptocurrencies for longer than a year, the tax impact will look a lot like when you sell a stock or bond. In this case, you're subject to a capital gains tax rate, which typically is lower than the full income rate, as you can see from the following benchmarks:

2019 Capital Gains Tax Rates	
0 percent	$0–$39,350
15 percent	$39,501–$434,500
20 percent	$434,501 and up

Let's refer back to the $10,000 investment in cryptos that doubled to $20,000. If you held back from doing anything with the investment over the past year, then sold it on day 366, you won't owe a single cent on the amount gained—$10,000—if that's your only capital gains for the year.

Remember that the capital gains rate is based on your total amount of capital gains earned throughout the year. If you earned $10,000 in capital gains from cryptos and $30,000 from other investments, then a portion of your gains will be subject to the 15 percent bracket, since you must combine the total amount before calculating your tax.

For bigger spenders, say you invested $50,000 in cryptos, then the amount you owe if the investment doubles after more than a year of waiting will be taxed at the 15 percent level. That comes out to $7,500 (assuming it's all taxed at the 15 percent level). That would significantly beat the $12,000 you would owe if you had an income tax rate of 24 percent and didn't hold the investment for a year.

What Constitutes Selling?

When you roll over a 401(k) into an IRA, you can just adjust the funds into the new account without ever touching them and avoid any tax penalty for doing so. The same perk does not exist in the crypto space. As soon as you sell your stake, then the tax penalty will go into place, whether you cash out of the exchange or not. Since it's when you sell that constitutes a tax event, you can't invest in cryptos, see the market double in two months, then pull out by dumping the coins and avoid paying income taxes by simply holding the funds in the exchange. Even if you immediately reinvest those funds in a different crypto, you'll still have to pay the taxes on the sell. It's another reason the tax treatment of cryptos can hold back the spending of the coins.

Most people are holding on to the coins, instead of transacting them. In a survey of crypto investors and users, Bitcoin Exchange Guide found that 56 percent never spend the cryptos to purchase something of value and just 11 percent of users spend them at least once a month. Those heavy users that spend daily only account for 5 percent of the survey's respondents.

Tools to Track Taxes

Since this tax treatment can be overly burdensome, it's best for you to keep very clear records, especially if you're buying, selling, trading, or transacting cryptos often. You could potentially have hundreds of transactions to print out by the end of the year.

While the services aimed at crypto investors and spenders, like the crypto market in general, are nascent, there are a few tools worth looking at to help with this tax predicament.

Google or Excel Spreadsheets

There's not much to this tactic, but new investors often use it. While it's a popular option, it's the one that requires the most hands-on work by you. You'll have to track every transaction or trade you make, including the date you bought, the date you sold, and the gain or loss. You can then send this information to your accountant when it's time to accumulate your total tax hit.

Anything Crypto Coin Tracker

This is a free option for lighter traders. You can sync your exchanges to the Coin Tracker, which will provide you with a rundown of where your current assets sit. Then within the exchange and wallets dashboard, view transaction history. You will still have to transport it yourself into a form that will comply with the IRS.

CoinTracker

This tracking tool is one of the more robust offerings in the crypto space, but you will have to pay for most of the services. It tracks your transactions across all of the exchanges you use, which gives the added bonus of showing you how your crypto portfolio is performing as one unit. The free version will track your transactions. But for about $50 a year (for lighter traders) the software will actually transmit the transactions into the tax Form 8949, which you can export to TurboTax or send to your accountant.

CoinTracking

For very active traders, this platform provides very robust features, since you can pull in data from nearly any exchange you would use and develop various reports about the movements of the currencies you're tracking. For the tax reports, you'll have to pay for it.

ALERT

If you spend your cryptos often, then make sure to find a coin tracker that allows for higher transaction levels. Typically, this strategy will force you to pay for the service, which will also bleed into your yearly returns. It's an expense you must consider. But if you're an active spender of cryptos, it's going to be one of the few ways to ensure you keep strong records.

Don't Get Caught in the Wrong Tax Strategy

This treatment of cryptos as property adds another layer of complexity to this tax equation, since you probably will own multiple cryptos. That means you're also buying multiple cryptos at different points in time, which complicates when you sell. You have to track if you waited a year on the specific cryptos you sold. Each individual cryptocurrency you own has its own time stamp, and when it's sold, that stamp will determine if you're taking out capital gains or income taxes. When you do sell the coins, you will need to determine if it's best to use a first-in-first-out cost basis or a last-in-first-out basis. The difference is dramatic.

FACT

There's a third option called specific identification. In this method, you would identify the specific coins you want to sell. While you will tell the IRS only the amount you sold and for what price, you'll need to keep clear personal records, with the individual coins identified, in case you're audited.

First-In-First-Out

It's a rather straightforward concept, but one that takes on immense complexity as you build out your cryptocurrency portfolio. First-In-First-Out

(FIFO) cost basis dictates that when you sell your cryptos, you will sell the cryptos you bought first. This has some benefit if you're a long-term investor since it will ensure that you're not selling the cryptos you've bought in the current year (assuming you're holding your oldest cryptos for longer than a year).

It's also beneficial in a declining market, if your investment in your first coins has resulted in a loss. With a large loss, you can use it toward your overall capital gains exposure, cutting out part of the potential tax. This comes in handy, protecting you from future capital gains, if the market turns back upward.

ESSENTIAL

If you're a buy-and-hold investor with only a few coins under your belt, then the concerns of FIFO versus LIFO are minimized, since you're likely to be holding all of your coins for longer than a year and you don't have many to worry about. You will still want to do the math, though, when you're ready to sell, since your buy-and-hold strategy has hopefully created a larger chunk of price appreciation.

Last-In-First-Out

When the market is rising, however, you may want to consider a last-in-first-out (LIFO) strategy. This provides the chance to sell your most recent purchases first, which can reduce the tax exposure if the market hasn't climbed too high. It's particularly useful if you have held all of your crypto assets for more than a year.

If you haven't, which is more likely the case, then you will need to determine the cost of selling your older cryptos first with the cost of unloading the newer ones, which will come at a higher tax rate.

Take the $50,000 crypto portfolio that doubled to $100,000. Let's break that down, and say you bought your first bitcoin at about $900 in early 2017. Your last bitcoin you bought was in mid-2018 at $7,000. Now the price of bitcoin has risen to $10,000 and it's less than a year since you purchased the last bitcoin but you want to cash out some of your holdings. Does it make sense to sell your last crypto or first crypto? For this we will assume you have a 24 percent income tax rate.

The $900 crypto, if cashed out, would have a gain of $9,100. At the 15 percent capital gains tax (assuming with your other capital gains, you reach the 15 percent mark) then you will face a tax of $1,365. For the last crypto you bought, the tax burden is $720. In this case, it's much more advantageous to use the LIFO method. However, the FIFO method would be more advantageous if that was the only investment you sold during the year, since you then would not face a tax burden on the sale.

ALERT

When filing your taxes, the IRS will assume you're using the FIFO method, unless you provide clear documentation that you're using LIFO or another tactic. It's why it's important to track these transactions, especially as you trade more often. It's sort of like tracking each dollar you make, when you made it, and when you spent it.

You Might Want to Consider a Tax Advisor

It's no surprise that the tax implications of cryptos remain a jumbled mess, since the IRS has only recently really begun to hone in on collecting taxes on them. It also means that the rules and implications of your buying and selling could change drastically and very quickly if the IRS (Congress or the courts) decides to change the requirements around crypto taxes.

It's strongly advised that you use a tax advisor when filing your crypto taxes. More and more tax professionals are dealing with cryptocurrency issues on a tax form, creating a greater pool of experts to tap. It's worthwhile, since the difference in doing it right versus doing it wrong could be thousands to hundreds of thousands of dollars, depending on how much you invest.

These are rules only for US taxpayers. But, unlike many of your other investments, how your cryptocurrencies perform will depend on the movements of governments, worldwide. Next, we will take a look at other laws impacting your cryptocurrency portfolio.

CHAPTER 16

The Laws Are A-Changin'

With cryptos becoming a world currency, bought and sold in various countries across the globe, unique scenarios are evolving where any government decision in any country can lead to a fall or rise in crypto prices. This adds a wrinkle to investing in cryptocurrencies, since the laws of various nations will have a dramatic impact on the price of coins, depending on whether countries encourage greater use or discourage the technology altogether. In this chapter we will discuss the views of those countries that have the largest impact on crypto prices.

The World's Outlook

Governments' opinions on cryptocurrencies have varied widely. In some countries, such as Canada, cryptos have been embraced, while the government seeks ways to ensure scams don't run unheeded. In other countries, such as China, they're viewed as a threat and the laws dealing with crypto trading reflect that perception.

ALERT

Even in countries that embrace cryptocurrencies, there are dissenters who can provide a voice to the anti-bitcoin crowd. Take Canada, for example. In March 2018, the Quebec regional council in Brome-Missisquoi passed a three-month ban on new mining operations within its borders. "At this moment, the council doesn't see positive social, economic, or environmental benefits from that kind of business," said Robert Desmarais, executive director of the municipalité régionale de comté (MRC), at the time of the ban, according to the Canadian Broadcasting Corporation (CBC).

Banning Bitcoins

In many cases, countries have supported outright bans of crypto trading. You see this more often in smaller, tightly controlled economies, where the threat of an alternative currency could lead to a dramatic fall in the local currency. In some, their financial system isn't robust enough to support the unknown entrant. They're not the only cases you find, though. Here are a few countries that have cracked down on buying, selling, trading, mining, or accepting virtual dollars:

- Bolivia
- China
- Ecuador
- Kyrgyzstan
- Morocco
- Nepal
- Russia
- Venezuela

FACT

Not every crypto play works, and that's true even when it's supported by a government. Venezuela has banned cryptos except for its own state-backed coin, Petro, which it propped up as the Bolivar (Venezuela's fiat currency) succumbed to hyperinflation in 2018. Venezuelans didn't seek out Petro as the answer and instead turned to bartering.

From an investing perspective, when countries install these bans, it sends shockwaves through the market since it reduces the total potential demand for the coins. If fewer people can access the coins, it reduces the number of potential buyers, which hurts the price. But when certain countries cut off access, it hurts more than others, like when China stepped up efforts to crack down on crypto providers. That's a painful cut, since China's population has been shown to have a large crypto appetite. How a country's decision will alter the crypto market depends on the size of the population and how much the crypto universe relied on the country to conduct business.

FACT

Prior to China's ban, estimates suggested about 85 percent of bitcoin trades took place in the Chinese yuan. The Japanese yen took much of that supply, becoming the most common currency to trade bitcoins. But the volume doesn't match one to one, as the yen accounts for just 51 percent of the market.

The Major Players

While there's pain whenever any country reduces the ability to conduct crypto transactions, the countries you need to keep a close eye on are:

- China
- Russia
- South Korea
- Japan
- The United States

The Japanese yen, US dollar, and South Korean won account for more than 70 percent of the currency used to exchange bitcoins. These are the countries that are open and free to trade and transact cryptos, with as minimal oversight as can be expected at this point in crypto's history. It's also why any news that comes from these countries that indicated further restrictions can send tremors through the market.

ESSENTIAL

While Canada has become a prominent player in the cryptocurrency mining market, it remains a sliver of the overall trading volume. The Canadian dollar isn't embraced among the community of crypto traders, as the US dollar dominates the North American trading scene. Cryptocurrency trading within the country remains small as well.

China and Russia used to have a large stake in the bitcoin craze as well—and they continue to tangentially—but their markets remain restricted to bitcoin and other cryptos. It's still worth understanding how the countries view the electric coin, since if rules were to change then it could boost crypto prices across the globe.

China's View

China's 2017 crackdown on the cryptocurrency market has led to the largest shift in the cryptocurrency space and threatened to derail bitcoin when it had begun to ascend to all-time highs. That's because the country was quick to jump at the idea of mining the currency. Even with the crackdown, China holds the largest crypto mining organization—Bitmain—and has more servers searching for cryptos than any nation. It's not an easy accomplishment, considering where China's government stands on virtual coins.

China Cracks Down

Beijing has taken three major steps to reduce the access of Chinese citizens to bitcoin. First, in September 2017, they placed a ban on initial coin offerings, which removed the possibility of homegrown blockchain companies from raising funds through crypto enthusiasts. Then, later that month, the government ordered all local crypto exchanges to cease operations. This hit the BTCC exchange particularly deep, since at the time it was one of the world's largest exchanges. Then, in January 2018, the government essentially stopped mining operations within the state by reducing the electricity available to the companies running servers that mine deep within bitcoin's and other cryptos' code. Estimates suggested that China's miners accounted for 75 percent of the bitcoins discovered.

ALERT

While China has taken a hard stance on cryptocurrencies, it isn't blind to the potential of the blockchain. President Xi Jinping called blockchain a "breakthrough" technology, according to a translation of a speech in May 2018. China has remained at the forefront of developing blockchain-based tools, as startups work with the local government to find new uses for the concept.

The Impact in the Market

When these pronouncements and rule changes are made, it sends reverberations through the market, which can be felt for days. For instance, when the mining ban occurred, bitcoin fell by 40 percent over the next month.

Yet, even China's crackdown on the currency hasn't killed the bitcoin trend. Many of the exchanges and miners moved to nearby countries that would allow them to function as a business. Hong Kong, which escaped many of the restrictions, attracted a number of transplants, while Japan became the biggest beneficiary of the migration.

Russia's View

In Russia, it's never a good thing to land on Vladimir Putin's bad side, and that's where cryptocurrencies ended up in October 2017 when the Russian president said crypto "carries serious risks." It wasn't the first time he had taken this stance, but this time around his legislature quickly moved to reduce the ability Russians had to access cryptos.

Russians Restricted

Within a couple months of Putin's comments, Russia took the step to limit access to exchanges from operating within the country while legislators work out rules that would govern cryptos. What has resulted, due to the delays in passing such rules, is that companies are hesitant to operate without first understanding where the state lands on cryptocurrency trading. Meanwhile, citizens can trade, but without exchanges, do so through unregulated markets. Until Russia passes legislation—which it hopes to do so by the end of 2018—it's difficult for companies and investors to operate freely.

A Different Purpose

One reason Russia has taken steps to limit and define the cryptocurrencies markets at least, in some way, has to do with Putin's other plans for cryptos. He's long hinted that Russia should develop its own cryptocurrency, cryptoruble, supported by the national currency. It could be a way to move past sanctions that the US or United Nations has placed on certain countries; restrictions Russia doesn't recognize or agree with. While cryptoruble doesn't exist yet, it could soon.

South Korea's View

The South Korean government's public views on cryptocurrency have wavered dramatically over the past two years. In January 2018, Justice Minister Park Sang-ki said that the government was preparing to ban cryptocurrencies. Hours later, South Korea's Blue House announced that statements on such a ban were premature.

The "Kimchi Premium"

To get a sense of just how important South Korea is to the crypto market, it houses three of the world's five largest ethereum exchanges. The frenzy over cryptos had grown so large by early 2018, that purchasing bitcoins and other cryptos on South Korean exchanges would come with what has been dubbed with the unfortunate nickname, the "kimchi premium" because prices would surge sometimes up to 25 percent higher than on other exchanges. While the holes in these market inefficiencies have dwindled, there's opportunity to turn a profit from time to time, if you're a quick arbitrager.

ALERT

How did this premium play out in the real market? You could actually buy a bitcoin on a US exchange for $10,000 and immediately sell it on a South Korean exchange for $12,500, assuming the height of the premium of 25 percent. As with most arbitrages, these opportunities didn't last long.

Exchanges have caught on to the difference in prices and have tried to discourage this inefficiency. Due to this premium, CoinDesk chose to remove South Korean exchanges from its listings, which reduced prices on a number of cryptos overnight.

Where South Korea Stands Now

Amidst the local hysteria around cryptos, South Korea did take steps to reduce the amount of fraud and scams that were circulating through local banks and ICOs. They've banned the use of anonymous crypto trading and heightened antilaundering procedures. But the government didn't go as far to ban exchanges or the ability to purchase and trade cryptos.

Japan's View

When China effectively banned the ability to exchange and buy cryptocurrencies within its border, Japan became the country that attracted most of the traders and exchanges looking for a new home. This has made Japan the epicenter of global crypto exchanges.

Coincheck Hack Changes Things

While Japan has embraced its role as the leader in cryptocurrency, its regulators found a reason to clamp down on exchanges when in January 2018, the Japanese exchange Coincheck was ransacked. Hackers walked away with $500 million worth of NEM coins. While NEMs aren't a widely traded coin, it still brought into focus just how quickly hackers can destroy confidence in the cryptosphere. In Coincheck's case, they did provide refunds for the lost coins, paying back $0.83 on the dollar for each stolen NEM token. But this set up a scenario that forced Japan's regulators to move in and provide some rules to reduce the potential for another such hack to occur.

FACT

There's no better way for a crypto exchange to go bankrupt than to suffer a hack. But in Coincheck's case, it sought a reprieve by selling itself to the online brokerage firm Monex Group for $33 million. It's a significant drop in value, since in the ten-month period prior to the hack, Coincheck took in $490 million.

Japan Reacts

Unlike some other countries' response to crypto scandal, Japan chose not to take out the mistake of Coincheck on the entire crypto market. It didn't look to ban cryptocurrencies, prevent all exchanges from operating, or even greatly reduce ways in which people can access exchanges. Instead, it improved security measures that the exchanges must live up to in order to operate. These measures included not storing currencies on computers connected to the Internet, improving the password practices, and strengthening money-laundering preventions with regards to large transfers.

ESSENTIAL

Since cryptos started under the eyes of libertarian ideals, regulation has long been discouraged. But many crypto investors have embraced some safety measures, in order to protect the market and encourage further growth. "When [regulators] come out with regulation, it's going to open the floodgates for new money to come into crypto," crypto trader Ran Neu-Ner, an early bitcoin investor, told CNBC in 2018.

This makes the crypto market more secure and safe, improving the experience for traders and at-home investors. You'll notice, when reasonable restrictions go into place, there isn't a large selloff in the space. There wasn't a significant one when Japan's rules became public in May 2018.

The US's Evolving View

Similar to Japan, there's really no concern that cryptocurrencies will be outright banned anytime soon in the US. But that doesn't mean regulators won't step in and tighten restrictions on how investors trade and sell. It's something a multitude of regulators have signaled at least initial warnings about, especially as more institutional groups enter the crypto space.

Heed Our Words

US agencies have come out and vocally warned investors that more oversight of bitcoin and the general crypto market will soon come. In December 2017, the Securities and Exchange Commission Chairman Jay Clayton warned the community that the SEC would watch the market closely, saying, "A number of concerns have been raised regarding the cryptocurrency and ICO markets, including that, as they are currently operating, there is substantially less investor protection than in our traditional securities markets, with correspondingly greater opportunities for fraud and manipulation."

He argued that even though cryptos aren't a security, the SEC had the right to provide oversight, similarly to how it monitors other currencies like the US dollar or euro, to ensure the currency's not interrupting the securities market.

These comments came with the support of the Commodities Futures and Exchange Commission, which already approves futures contracts that are listed on the Chicago Board Options Exchange (CBOE).

Denying Certain Investment Tools

As of now, the biggest way (beyond taxes) that the US has prevented the growth of cryptos is in the denial of index funds and ETFs that target regular retail investors. The SEC was skeptical in allowing such index funds to move forward. The appeal of these types of funds is that they provide an indirect way to own the currency. This means there's less chance of having the money stolen or lost. It also allows investors to buy a package of cryptos; for instance, such an offering could provide a 20 percent exposure in bitcoin, and 80 percent in a mix of other cryptos. Since the world doesn't know which crypto will rise, it's a better bet in gaining access to a whole plethora of names. But without that ability, it's a practice in guessing.

Moving Ahead

While regulators—probably for the best—will remain cautious on allowing certain opportunities in this space, as more institutional investors enter, the more opportunities this group will help support. It can lead to tools, like index funds, since the SEC would find some comfort in the fact larger institutions also see a viable future in the currencies. The more money flowing in, the more difficult it would be to manipulate the market. Goldman Sachs, for instance, plans to open a bitcoin-trading desk. Having trusted institutions (at least from the government's standpoint) behind the currencies provides a stronger case to move forward with some of the instruments that are currently missing from the market.

Regulation's Doubled-Edged Result

The original investors of bitcoin shunned the idea of regulation, assuming it would destroy any uniqueness in what cryptos offer. But as the number of cryptos grows, the ways to invest spread, and institutions entering some regulation can actually provide the stepping-stones to further push bitcoin and other tokens forward. It legitimizes them in ways that fanboys can't. It provides structures that make it more likely that larger institutions will utilize the uniqueness that cryptos provide. This could bring in more money into the market, increase transactions, and, as a result, grow the young tokens.

Of course, too much, and it threatens to cut off the entrepreneurship and attractiveness that cryptos can bring. It's a fine line, but regulations shouldn't be discouraged on their face, just because this is supposed to be a decentralized market. It still is decentralized, but these rules and laws help it become safe. That's helpful for investors and spenders, alike, as these laws help shape the future of the coins.

CHAPTER 17

Cryptocurrencies 2.0: What's Next?

Where will cryptocurrencies go from here? It's the eternal question within this space. Due to a lack of a clear answer, it's also why investing in cryptos brings such risk and volatility. While prognosticators see countless numbers of different scenarios that could play out, the only real known is that cryptocurrency is reliant on the blockchain. It's not just reliant on the blockchain's growth, but on its continued need to incorporate specialized cryptos to offer its service. Yet, there's a world where the need for specialized cryptos doesn't exist. That world could rear its head in fifty years, or five, or never. There's no way to tell. In this chapter we will discuss some of the issues that cryptos face moving forward, which will shape how they grow.

The Evolution to Come

Many have compared the blockchain's current state to that of the dot-com boom in the 1990s. That may be a little premature considering where the current state of the blockchain currently resides. In terms of use and viable businesses, it's closer to the garage state of development than the Silicon Valley level of acceptance. Yet, the blockchain has been referred to as a "foundational technology," meaning it's not just disruptive to the Internet but will actually create new platforms and develop new uses that the world hasn't yet imagined.

What does that mean for cryptocurrencies? It depends on how closely linked cryptos remain to the blockchain. You have to remember that cryptocurrencies rely on the blockchain, but the blockchain does not have to have cryptocurrencies—or its own cryptocurrency—to function. Where cryptocurrencies go beyond this initial phase, where the coins serve as the primary entry point for investors and enthusiasts, depends on their continued growth as the ongoing currency within the blockchain. The worst-case scenario for those placing funds within cryptocurrencies would be for a government to develop a crypto that becomes the standard for the space, since it implies that the bet on blockchain, while correct, didn't actually lead to crypto riches.

It also remains a less likely scenario today, since blockchain founders seem intrigued by the cryptocurrency funding model, which allows them to raise funds without ceding control of the company to a venture capital firm.

Testing It Out

At this point, businesses and governments are mostly just testing the waters of the blockchain world. You see financial institutions trying out blockchain technology to test cross-border transactions. Countries such as Estonia are evaluating the use of the blockchain to securely store information for different government agencies, where it serves as the digital storage file that's hacker-proof and available all day, every day. Hospitals have looked at the blockchain as a tool to safely hold medical records. Theoretically, this could be adapted so each person has her own living health record on a blockchain, which doctors can access, giving them the patient's entire medical history in one location. These uses cases show much promise, but they do not provide definite successes yet. And they certainly haven't developed viable businesses to date.

In the future, look for clear winners and losers to break out from of all of this testing, similar to how Apple and Microsoft separated from all the companies building computers back in the day, or how Google became the search engine of choice or Facebook the predominant social media firm. Whether or not these breakouts use a cryptocurrency will depend on the business model, technology, and specific use case.

Blockchain Is Everywhere

There are some similarities between the blockchain's early adoption and cloud computing. When cloud computing became a more powerful tool to store large blocks of data, companies wanted to market their use, but most people didn't understand what exactly a company said when it indicated it would store your information "in the cloud." It became more of a buzzword, adding a lot of distractions to cloud computing and some companies were just marketing services as a form of quasi-cloud storage, even if it had very little to do with storing the information on independent servers.

Don't be surprised to see more firms marketing the idea of the blockchain, when in fact the technology or use case has very little to do with the blockchain at all. With the popularity of cryptocurrencies, the idea of the blockchain has become a mainstream phenomenon, even if the understanding of the blockchain remains very niche. While people will hopefully become comfortable with this type of platform, don't be fooled that increased mentions of the blockchain will lead to a greater valuation of your coin, since many of these mentions could very well be superficial.

Eventually, just like the cloud, consumers will come around to understand when they're using true blockchain technology. A few companies will probably step into the mainstream as the primary providers, similar to Amazon and Google within the consumer cloud space.

Expect a Bubble to Burst

As the technology evolves, and companies form that gain traction in the general market, valuations will rise among this early group of creators. If this technology has the legs that some believe, many of these companies will become unicorns—or startups with at least $1 billion valuation. Some will have initial public offerings, others will be sold to much larger firms for millions to billions. At some point, the belief in the technology will reach peaks seen in the cryptocurrency market, moving the price of blockchain companies to untenable levels. Once the enthusiasm reaches these heights, the market will fall back, similar to the way the tech bubble burst in the late 1990s and early 2000s.

ESSENTIAL

The crypto market has been led by exuberance since its step into the mainstream, but that's to be expected. Rarely, if ever, is there such an easy way to invest in a new tool and technology. But for it to reach the heights to which many people think it can grow, it will require far more exuberance. That will have to eventually lead to a pullback, but that's natural within a growing sector.

This won't spell the end for the blockchain. Instead, it will separate the legitimate businesses from the weaker firms. As with the promulgation of a vast number of cryptocurrencies, a culling of the fat isn't necessarily a bad thing. It will lead to short-term pain, but the blockchain universe will be better for it. Hopefully, it will also create stability in the crypto markets as well.

How Technologies Must Improve

In order for cryptocurrencies to have a place at the table as the blockchain moves steadily forward, there are a few issues that companies are working to solve. These attributes will be absolutely imperative for cryptos' future. While solutions have already come to the forefront, it's going to require multiple rounds of fixes to these issues before they're set in stone, if individual cryptocurrencies will continue to serve as the primary tools for transacting on the blockchain.

Scaling Cryptos

There's a major problem with scale, which refers to the ability for the crypto to become larger without sacrificing speed of transactions or liquidity. The most popular cryptos, bitcoin and ether, only transact a handful of transactions per second. It creates a glaring problem for cryptos, since to become more mainstream you have to compete with the mainstream processors. Visa is capable of processing over 55,000 transactions per second, but processes closer to 2,000 transactions, on average. PayPal transacts around 200 per second, even if it can go much higher. If cryptocurrencies are going to compete in these waters for the type of clients that Visa, Mastercard, PayPal, and others cater to, they will need to solve this problem in a big way.

QUESTION

What will happen if cryptos don't provide large enough scale for mainstream businesses to use the technology?
It will cap the long-term potential of the coins, since the transaction rates couldn't grow to the levels required to produce significant investment returns.

Some have. You see this with some processors such as Ripple, which can process nearly 1,500 transactions per second. But it's a more tightly controlled network. Cardano also makes similar claims. The potential is there, but it needs to be implemented within cryptos that are more mainstream to help clear this hurdle on a wider scale.

Privacy of Using the Coins

Bitcoin's transactional history sits on its blockchain, waiting to be downloaded by anyone who chooses to look at it. There's nothing that prevents someone from tracking a coin through the history of its spending (even if it would be incredibly difficult to do). It's why businesses are hesitant—among other reasons—to use the coin on a wider scale. Instead, if companies accept bitcoins, they usually then immediately cash out the coins. This locks in a determined price, but it also prevents them from using bitcoin to make other transactions, like buying supplies for the business. Why wouldn't they want to use bitcoin for that purpose? Most companies don't want a public ledger of all of their transactions, even if it takes time for someone to actually determine the person or entity making the purchase. The larger the organization, with a greater number of competitors, investors, followers, critics, and journalists, then the more the company will want to keep nearly all of its purchases as secret as possible. They won't want to buy and sell on the public blockchain.

Ethereum has taken steps to make transactions private, which will encourage greater use among their business clients. Other cryptos have also instituted more private settings as well. But what these coins will need to fight, with these private options, is the acceptance of the currencies for more sinister means—for instance, on the black market. The more private these coins become, the more likely a criminal subgroup will adopt them. The goal: to create safe privacy.

They Must Surpass Governmental Threats

Cryptocurrencies captured the interest of those in the antigovernment crowd because they provided another refuge from fiat currency, controlled by a central bank. For the mainstream, however, there's an appeal to having the dollar serve as the primary tool for conducting business or making transactions. It's simple; it's good to know the currency is stable, viable, and not threatened with obsolescence.

For all of these various cryptocurrencies to survive, they must continue to provide a benefit that can't be captured by the fiat currency. Right now, that benefit is the use of the currency within the digital world. Yet, if a major fiat currency, like the US dollar, decided to develop a cryptocurrency version of itself, there's no reason that wouldn't become the most accepted form of cryptocurrency on the market. Companies would ask blockchain firms to develop solutions to accept the dollar cryptocurrency. And if there were enough support for the dollar crypto, it would likely become the most accepted form of crypto fairly quickly.

It's not likely something blockchain companies would accept right now, since the crypto is how they've made the majority of their gains in the business, up to this point. That, however, could change, if blockchain companies grow into billion-dollar businesses. Then the value of the business will look as attractive—and probably more so—than the specific crypto. Would they bend to these requests? It's entirely possible, which is why these cryptos will have to continue to evolve, adapt, and grow beyond what a fiat crypto can offer. Part of that is mainstream acceptance. The other part has to do with technology.

One caveat to this potential is would people and businesses want to use a government-issued crypto if the government tracks every purchase made with the coin? That would certainly create doubt in the privacy of the coin, leaving some preferring the cryptos being developed by third parties.

Legal Clarity Will Help

Trading the news isn't a winning option in the crypto space, but in many ways, it makes sense as to why investors are jumpy when another government has come down strongly against cryptocurrencies. With such a new market, there's no proof this tool will last, which leaves an investor nervous if another government determines it's not a solution that will be allowed to flourish within the confines of the country's borders. Development of laws around cryptocurrencies—with a clear definition of what is and isn't legal—will certainly produce a greater ability to trust the tools from a mainstream perspective.

If, instead, the laws continue to fluctuate on the whims of individual leaders, then cryptocurrencies will struggle to take off in full force, since another restrictive law would crush any forward momentum. These rules are still being formed, and there's none set in stone, yet. Hopefully, some clarity will shine through soon.

Rethinking the US's Viewpoint

One of the spending problems with cryptocurrencies in the US is that it's treated as property, requiring crypto investors and spenders to track every transaction. This stifles spending, makes it much more complicated to use on a regular basis, and reduces the ease of the currency (which is one of its main selling points).

If cryptocurrency investing and spending continues to become more mainstream, the IRS will likely have to adjust how it views cryptos. Theoretically, if the spending continues to climb, and users continue to track each transaction, you could imagine a point where the IRS becomes overwhelmed with crypto transactions, making their status untenable. The world hasn't reached that point yet. It could one day, but either way, treating cryptos more as currencies, instead of property will encourage greater use of the coins.

ESSENTIAL

If cryptocurrencies reached this size, then it's possible they would earn their own status as not quite currency, and not quite property. It would allow a middle-ground approach that would reduce the restriction on users while ensuring it's still taxed properly.

Smart Protections

Ideally, as a believer in cryptos and an investor in the coins, what you will want to see from a legal standpoint are measures that make the trading and transacting of the coins much safer. Restrictions to encourage greater security from exchanges and developers, will allow understanding, research, and implementation of the coins. It's why you don't want to discourage legal restrictions on the coins. You just want the restrictions to deal with securing your investment, as oppose to restricting it altogether.

Options for All

Right now, cryptocurrencies land in very niche verticals. For mainstream users, it's about spending bitcoin. For companies, depending on the purpose of the company, it's Ethereum, Ripple, Stellar, or another up-and-coming altcoin. Ripple, for now, attracts banks, while Ethereum looks like the option for development. Yet there hasn't been a cryptocurrency to traverse all these purposes. It's also why there's not one cryptocurrency that stands above all the rest in both valuation and technology. (Remember, from a technology standpoint, bitcoin stands behind many of the altcoins that were developed to improve upon the original design.)

Whether or not, one day, there will be one cryptocurrency to stand above the rest will depend on whether or not this cryptocurrency is adaptable to different situations, technologies (i.e., blockchains), and purposes.

What Happens If Such a Currency Arises?

Let's say that one crypto becomes the only name in the space. Dubbed ultimatecoin, this becomes the accepted coin for all blockchain companies, mainstream users, and businesses. It's the only one to survive. While this scenario seems farfetched right now, it's a possibility.

If this were to occur, then expect ultimatecoin to trade like other fiat currencies, where its use and value eventually plateaus, leading to small changes over time, impacted by inflation or demand, depending on whether the coin has an upper limit to the number of coins available. If you're an early investor in this type of crypto, then you will be rewarded handsomely, since it would have to gain significant value before it reaches this plateau. Outside of that, it won't be a particularly exciting investment, since it won't move much once it reaches a level of consistency.

What Happens If No Such Currency Arises?

You could argue, while looking at the current market, this seems like the most likely scenario. Instead, crypto coins will become more like stocks, where they're solid coins, with a long track record and proven consistency. Meanwhile, other coins will arise, offering legitimate purposes and use-cases, solving problems that the current market can't fix. In this scenario, these coins will continue to produce volatile returns, since they will be dependent on a high-level of acceptance. Even with the acceptance, the market will be split, which will include daily fluctuations that will scare some investors. But you could imagine a few coins showing consistency in this situation, which means they will be the stalwarts in the portfolio, while some prefer betting on newer names.

The good news, as the market progresses in this fashion, is that the use of fake ICOs will slow. The market won't be as easily fooled by weak coins or technology, especially as best practices are developed, while organizations adapt to funnel out bad players before they can gain any traction.

The Hope of Indexing

Index funds and exchange-traded funds (ETFs) have become a point of contention between the crypto universe and the Securities and Exchange

Commission (SEC). A number of organizations have filed to provide such funds with the SEC, which has yet to allow a single one to move forward with government approval. In July 2018, the agency rejected for the second time a proposal brought forward by the Winklevoss twins to launch a bitcoin ETF. Their concerns relate to the safety of bitcoin serving as the underlying asset, arguing that the Winklevoss twins couldn't prove that bitcoin was secure enough and not at risk of manipulation. It's very similar to their initial rejection of the ETF.

FACT

Not everyone agrees with the potential ETFs bring. Vitalik Buterin, the founder of Ethereum, has argued that too much attention has been given toward trying to establish crypto ETFs. He believes more attention should go toward ways to encourage adoption and use of the coins, like through easier purchase methods at popular outlets.

Since the SEC doesn't allow such funds, it's difficult for regular investors to gain access to the crypto market without simply buying individual currencies. It's why the idea of an index fund or ETF sounds appealing to many, since it could give investors access to many different coins and they wouldn't have to worry about protecting the security of the coins; that would fall on the ETF provider.

It's similar to how most people gain stock exposure. Since few people buy stocks directly, they gain exposure through ETFs and mutual funds, as they give a wider breadth of the market. It's advantageous since stock picking itself has been found to be a poor way to choose your investments. Instead, ETFs and index funds give you an area of the market, allowing diversification. Since even more unknowns lie within the crypto world, you can see why there's an appeal for such funds.

If Funds Were Approved

It's not as if, were funds approved, you would immediately want to jump into the market. First you would want to see a few specifics of the funds, to make sure they're worth the money. These would include:

- **The fees:** You don't want all your gains cut out from unnecessarily high fees.
- **The cryptos:** What's the ETF or index fund investing in? You want a wide swath of the crypto market.
- **Active management:** Who is deciding where the money goes? A better bet is to go with an index fund tied to the size of the crypto space.

It's important to remember that just because you have access to such a fund, you're not diversified. Since so many coins move with bitcoin, there's little proof diversification exists within the crypto space. Instead you've gained a larger exposure to a greater number of names within the crypto world, capturing any that might start to rise or break out of the bitcoin ceiling.

If the crypto market popularity grows, then there's a good chance the SEC will eventually have to approve these funds. It helps that more traditional investment firms have started to show interest, but when the government begins to take the market seriously remains anyone's guess.

The Long-Term Hope

Determining where cryptocurrencies move from here is why you place your extra investment funds in the space. The opportunities remain wide open. Could they become a universal currency, used to traverse the financial markets across the globe? Will they be relegated to the corners of the digital marketplace, remaining a niche tool for buying? The greatest likelihood likely falls somewhere in between.

What you want to see, though, are those transaction rates rising. Seeing companies actually use the tools to conduct significant sized business will provide the greatest comfort—and eventual stability—in the marketplace, which would reduce the volatility of your investment. It will also lead to rises that aren't disparate or bubble-like, and instead show a long-term value in the purpose and technology that reflect the evolving digital age.

And what if it does become the universal currency for the world? Well, you will certainly be happy you got in when you did.

Crypto Publications to Know

Like the tools themselves, the places you can go for credible information about the day-to-day machinations of cryptocurrencies and the blockchain remain in their infancy. But out of these early tools, there's some high-quality reporting, analysis, and writing done about these investments. You just want to return to your investing process before acting on anything you see in print. Here are some of those publications you can follow for credible content.

Bitcoin.com

Created by crypto evangelist Roger Ver, the news vertical at Bitcoin.com has become an incredibly valuable resource for global information about cryptos. When you see a site started by such a supporter of the trend as Ver is, you have to worry about the editorial's independence. But Bitcoin.com has shown an ability to be true to its mission of covering what has "taken place, not promises on what will happen in the future."
https://news.bitcoin.com/

Bitcoinist.com

Much of Bitcoinist.com reads as if it's a newswire service, pumping out breaking news based on what leaders or investment strategists say about different coins or the landscape itself. It's refreshing, since the writing is very concise, to the point, and not filled with hyperbole. The content itself provides insight into how the world at large is currently viewing the coins.
https://bitcoinist.com/

Bitcoin Magazine

Founded by investor Mihai Alisie and future Ethereum creator, Vitalik Buterin, the first print magazine for the bitcoin world remains a valued and detailed source on cryptos. Over the years, as bitcoin bred thousands of others, the coverage has expanded to blockchain and the crypto industry, but it's a valued source of information, particularly about those driving change in the space.
https://bitcoinmagazine.com/

Blockchain at Berkeley Blog

Want to keep abreast of how the young and innovative minds view where blockchain has gone, and where it's going? This comes from the students at University of California, Berkeley, and provides some fantastic insight in how they see the blockchain shaping in the years to come. It's important to know, since it will impact how cryptocurrencies move as well.
https://blockchainatberkeley.blog/

CCN.com

It's a smaller site, compared to Bitcoin.com, but after a relaunch in late 2017, CCN.com has started to provide some quality analysis and news that's worth your attention. It's very heavy into the crypto investing world, and most of the stories touch on information that someone invested in the coin might need to know.
www.ccn.com

CNBC.com

The problem with mainstream outlets is that they cover cryptocurrencies only when something big happens or when there's a run on the market (like in 2017). It's a numbers game for them, and when markets are climbing it becomes a popular story. CNBC has shown a greater commitment to the crypto space than most other mainstream outlets, providing daily updates on bitcoin or other very large cryptocurrencies.
www.cnbc.com

CoinDesk.com

CoinDesk.com is one of the top news sites within the crypto space. Founded in 2013, it has become a powerful voice of crypto, building an audience of 10 million unique users. It's also one of the best places to find breaking news about comings and goings of trends and laws within the crypto space, since they're often one of the first to post on any change, across the world. They don't talk about every coin, but they still cover a wide swath.
www.coindesk.com

Cointelegraph.com

This site may be more known for the unique images it uses within its stories, which look more like what you would see in a comic book than a news site. But don't let that fool you. This publication, which launched in 2013, has become an important spot for wide-ranging news on the crypto industry and specific coins. They will also discuss more obscure issues within the crypto space, which other sites might avoid, so it's a particularly important tool for your altcoins.
https://cointelegraph.com/

Fortune's *The Ledger*

This is a dedicated newsletter to the blockchain and cryptocurrency universe developed by *Fortune*. It tracks the leaders of the blockchain space, as they seek to build a sustainable, viable, and highly profitable market. While it won't provide as many specifics about investing, it does give you a sense of what the managers who guide your coins are doing.
http://fortune.com/section/ledger/

Unchained & Unconfirmed Podcasts

Laura Shin, a former *Forbes* writer who created the first crypto "Rich List," hosts these two podcasts. She's as plugged into the crypto space as anyone you will find, and it's unbiased since she's a "nocoiner," meaning she doesn't invest. Do you want to keep up-to-date on how the most powerful people in the space are viewing the latest movements within cryptos or the blockchain? Then these two podcasts are worth listening to.

http://unchainedpodcast.co/

http://unconfirmed.libsyn.com/

Wired.com

It's not surprising the magazine and website focused on technology wouldn't also have a place in this new sector. It's certainly more focused on the blockchain, but it's a valuable resource to find pieces that touch on the potential—and those who are on the forefront of it—of the blockchain. There isn't a dedicated vertical, but you will find some valuable information if you follow it regularly.

www.wired.com

Links

As you grow your cryptocurrency understanding, you're going to need further resources as you prepare to invest or to monitor your growing portfolio. Here are a few places to get started, although once you do, you will find that there are far more places to turn to beyond this simple list.

Exchanges

These are the places you will go once you're ready to drop a few dollars and invest in specific coins.

Bitstamp
www.bitstamp.net

Coinbase
www.coinbase.com

Coinmama
www.coinmama.com

Gemini
https://gemini.com/

Kraken
www.kraken.com

Market Research Resources

These resources will help you track prices, and provide detailed information on the movements and size of the various coins.

Bitcoin Fees
https://statoshi.info/dashboard/db/fee-estimates

Blockchain (Transaction Rates)
www.blockchain.com/en/charts/transactions-per-second

CoinDesk
www.coindesk.com

CoinMarketCap
https://coinmarketcap.com/

CoinMetrics.io
https://coinmetrics.io/

TradingView
www.tradingview.com

WorldCoinIndex
www.worldcoinindex.com

Crypto Wallets

When you've purchased coins, these are where you will store them, assuming you want to protect your investment from hackers.

Bitcoin
https://bitcoin.org/en/choose-your-wallet

Bitcoin Wallet
https://wallet.bitcoin.com/

Cryptocurrency Wallet Guide by Blockgeeks
https://blockgeeks.com/guides/cryptocurrency-wallet-guide/

MyEtherWallet
www.myetherwallet.com

Paper Wallet Tutorial
www.coindesk.com/information/paper-wallet-tutorial/

Other Resources

These tools can be used for research, gauging community interest, or as resources for help.

Reddit Blockchain Forum
www.reddit.com/r/BlockChain/

Reddit Cryptocurrency Forum
www.reddit.com/r/CryptoCurrency/

GitHub's Cryptocurrency Discussions
https://github.com/topics/cryptocurrency

Khan Academy Course
www.khanacademy.org/economics-finance-domain/core-finance/
money-and-banking/bitcoin/v/bitcoin-what-is-it

Medium's Blockchain Vertical
https://medium.com/tag/blockchain

MIT's Digital Currency Initiative
https://dci.mit.edu/

Princeton University's Online Course on Bitcoin
www.youtube.com/channel/UCNcSSleedtfyDuhBvOQzFzQ/videos

Vitalik Buterin's Website
https://vitalik.ca/

Whitepaper Database
http://whitepaperdatabase.com/

A List of Extra Resources
https://lopp.net/bitcoin.html

Glossary of Terms

Here are a few terms you saw throughout this book and can be used for future reference or as you read along, serving as a reminder of what they mean.

altcoin

This term arose to refer to any coin in the digital currency space that wasn't bitcoin. After bitcoin's development, a number of other digital coins cropped up, trying to improve on the functionality bitcoin provided. Altcoins was the term the community gave these coins, which some have become sizeable as well.

block

It's how the blockchain verifies transactions on the ledger. Many have described it like a page in a physical ledger. It records a set amount of information for the blockchain; then a new block is needed to record the next amount. No transaction moves forward without first checking all previous blocks, to ensure it's a valid purchase.

blockchain

It's the digital ledger that provides the platform in which cryptocurrencies exist. It's decentralized and verified by a community, so it becomes impossible to alter, without the support of the network. It keeps the record intact through sets of code, called blocks, which records every movement, addition, or spending of a cryptocurrency that ever took place on the blockchain.

coin

Most of the time, when you're referring to a cryptocurrency, you're referring to the coin. It operates as a currency on a specific blockchain, and only that blockchain. Bitcoin, ethers, XRP, and most cryptos you can think of are coins.

cold storage

This is a form of storing cryptocurrencies in which the coins remain offline when you're not exchanging them. Used in wallets, such as paper and hardware wallets, cold storage is the preferred method of storing coins when saving them for an extended period of time. It safeguards them from hackers by remaining offline.

cryptocurrency

A digital coin developed via code, where encryption tools provide the basis for development, confirmation of ownership, and verification of spending. The coins do not need a central repository, like a central bank, to monitor their use or produce more currency. Bitcoin, ether, XRP, lumens, bitcoin cash, and ADA are all examples of cryptocurrencies.

Crypto Exchanges

These work similar to a regular brokerage exchange that you might use to buy or sell stock. Crypto exchanges, however, operate specifically for the purpose to provide access to different cryptocurrencies. Here you can buy, sell, and store your portfolio of cryptos.

cryptography

A tactic to secure information by storing data using algorithms and decentralized tools, producing unintelligible information, which can only be put back in order by the owner of the data. For cryptocurrency purposes, it's the type of security used to provide the coins, secure the transactions, verify the information, and support the blockchain ecosystem.

crypto wallet

Crypto wallets serve two purposes: they're used to store cryptocurrencies in a safer environment, ideally separating the coins from hackers, and they also are used to spend the coins. Since cryptos are simply a piece of code on a ledger, they're susceptible from hacks. It's why wallets exist, and there are many different versions of such wallets on the market.

digital contracts

Surmised by Nick Szabo and put into the wild by Vitalik Buterin, digital contracts are a form of agreement developed on the blockchain. These contracts utilize the blockchain to confirm an agreement between two parties without the need for an independent third party to verify the work and transactions. Instead, it's the blockchain that provides that verification.

exchange-traded fund (ETF)

This is a form of investment, in which a basket of securities, which tracks an index, like the Standard & Poor's 500 largest companies in the US, yet trades like a stock on an exchange. When demand increases, the costs of ETFs also rise. In the cryptocurrency world, there's an effort to encourage regulators to support a cryptocurrency ETF for retail customers.

fork

When a blockchain community votes to make a change in the code, then it forks. Imagine when your mobile phone updates its software. This is essentially what a fork is. Except in the crypto world, some community members might not agree with the fork, which creates a hard fork producing another cryptocurrency. Most forks, however, are soft forks, providing the software upgrade without producing a new coin.

hard fork

A hard fork occurs when a cryptocurrency community agrees to a fork, but a large minority of the community disagrees with the change. The hard fork can often create a new cryptocurrency, typically for those community members disagreeing with the fork. Bitcoin cash and ethereum classic came into existence through hard forks.

hardware wallet

This form of crypto wallet stores your currency on a piece of device, similar to a USB drive. When the drive is inserted into a computer that's online, then it's in hot storage. Otherwise, it remains offline, in cold storage, providing a safe tool to protect coins. Hardware wallets can also be formed via computer desktops that primarily remain offline, except for when exchanging coins.

hot storage

This is a form of storing cryptocurrencies in which the coins are connected to the Internet at all times. While this form of storage comes with some risk, since if the coins are connected to the Internet, there's a chance they could be hacked, it does provide easier access to spend the currency. That's why it's the preferred method of storing coins for short time periods.

index fund

These are mutual funds that simply track an investing index, like the Standard & Poor's 500 largest companies in the US. The goal with these funds isn't to beat the market, but instead to simply track it. There's no such index fund available for retail investors in the crypto space.

initial coin offering (ICO)

It's a tactic by blockchain companies to raise funds, offering the cryptocurrency that runs on its network to the public. Similar to an initial public offering of stock, the company provides a set amount of currency that the general public can purchase. Unlike IPOs, however, ICOs aren't regulated and you do not gain ownership of the blockchain company by purchasing a coin.

mining

This is the process in which new coins are uncovered and released to the market within many cryptocurrencies, particularly bitcoin. It's a vital process, in which miners verify blocks of the ledger and then are rewarded via a mining fee and a new coin. In the bitcoin blockchain, the miner must solve a puzzle in order to gain the right to place the next block on the blockchain and earn the next mined bitcoin.

mobile wallet

This form of crypto wallet is best used when you want to spend coins periodically, for everyday purchases. Mobile crypto wallets are always connected to the Internet, so they're a form of hot storage.

node

Computers that connect to the bitcoin code are referred to as nodes. Bitcoin is a decentralized, peer-to-peer network, which means it doesn't live on one server. Instead, communities of users access the bitcoin code, while also keeping it alive in the process, by running the code. A computer or electronic device that stores the entire set of bitcoin rules goes by the term *full node*.

online wallet

This form of wallet uses an online tool, like an exchange or coin-specific wallet, to store the coins. It's not considered among the safest forms of storage, since it ensures your coins remain connected to the Internet—and therefore hackers—at all times.

paper wallet

A form of crypto wallet where you transfer your cryptocurrency key onto a sheet of paper. This key can be in the form of a series of numbers and letters, or incorporated into a QR code. It's among the safest ways to store your coins from hackers, although if you lose the paper, you lose the coin.

private key

When you purchase a cryptocurrency, you're given two keys, one public and one private. The private key is similar to your personal signature, and only you will know the key of the coins when they're sent to you. When you sell your coins, it's the use of this private key that informs the blockchain that these coins can be sold. If you lose this private key, then you lose your coins. The private key is typically a long set of letters and numbers.

public key

The public key is the identifier that the blockchain uses for the coin. Your private key derives this code, and it informs the blockchain community that you own the coin and have the right to sell or spend it. The public key is simply a long set of numbers and letters, randomized, which is then compressed as the identifier of your coin on the blockchain.

soft fork

A soft fork occurs when a blockchain community agrees to a change in the software, and it's not contested. The coin will then work within the parameters of the software upgrade, and it's "backward compatible," meaning that all past transactions and code adapts to the fork.

tokens

The term *tokens* are often used interchangeably with the term *coin*. In reality, there's a difference. Tokens represent a value or an asset. These representations can vary widely, from representing a unit of gold, to customer loyalty points, or a set amount of free car washes. The token doesn't operate on its own blockchain; instead it exists via a third-party blockchain, like when a developer creates a token on the Ethereum chain.

unit

When you purchase a bitcoin, you don't have to buy a full coin. Instead, you can purchase a sliver of a coin. These slivers are referred to as units. The smallest unit that bitcoin blockchain tracks is referred to as a satoshi, and it's one hundred millionth of a single coin. Units vary in size from a full coin to a tiny fraction of a coin.

Index

About the Author

Ryan Derousseau first began researching bitcoin in 2013 when people thought it was just a weird currency used by hackers. There wasn't much to invest in then, but Ryan was sold on the concept and continued to follow bitcoin and other cryptocurrencies as they grew to become the hot investment of our time. Ryan has over a decade of experience writing about investing, and his work has been read widely in *Fortune*, *Money*, CNBC, BBC, *Fast Company*, and *US News & World Report*, among many other national publications and websites.